Contents

Chapter 6

Long-Term Assets

LEARNING OBJECTIVES

1. Identify how the acquisition cost of a long-term asset is determined.
2. Understand the problems encountered when measuring intangible assets.
3. Account for wasting assets from acquisition to disposal using depreciation, depletion, and amortization.
4. Interpret changes in reported long-term asset amounts and changes in accounting estimates.
5. Appreciate the limitations of GAAP as they apply to the measurement and reporting of long-term productive assets.

ECONOMIC BACKDROP FOR LONG-TERM ASSETS

Not all businesses are significantly dependent on long-term assets. For example, the so called "dot-com" industry does not rely on large investments in long-term assets to be profitable. However, nearly all product-oriented companies and many service industries require significant investments in long-term assets for their operations. For these businesses to be successful, they must invest in an *efficient quantity* of long-term assets, and combine these with an appropriate mix of human resources. The resulting combination must give the business a *comparative advantage* relative to its competition in order for profits to result from its business activities. The productive long-term assets must generate enough profit to cover the cost of carrying dead-weight assets such as cash, receivables and inventory. They must also generate enough profit to pay for the cost of debt (interest expense) and income taxes and still have enough left to pay the shareholders an attractive return. It is not uncommon for product-oriented companies to earn operating profit of 25% of sales to be considered profitable. It is important that we understand how to evaluate whether companies have made efficient investments in long-term assets.

In today's business world, people talk about *old-economy companies* and *new-economy companies*. What do they mean by these labels? During the 20th century most U.S. companies (other than financial institutions) made large investments in tangible, durable long-term assets such as buildings, machinery, and equipment. The human capital needed to make these assets profitable relied primarily on unskilled and semiskilled labor to run assembly lines to manufacture mass-produced goods.

This old-economy approach to making money was the mainstay of the developed nations, but by the late 20th century the ability of old-economy companies in Europe and North America to create profits became more and more difficult. Rapid, low-cost international transportation and communication created a world marketplace. For old-economy businesses that now faced foreign competitors from Asia, South and Central America with much less costly unskilled and semiskilled labor, this meant decline. At the end of the century, a semiskilled worker in the U.S. earned as much in one day as a semiskilled worker in China earned in a year.

Today, new economy companies are finding ways to apply technology with ever increasing sophistication in the production of goods and services, resulting in a resurgence of manufacturing in Europe and North America. Social, political and economic problems in Asia and South and Central America, along with rapid increases in employee compensation, have contributed to this resurgence. The workforce of the 21st century has a different skill set requirement for successful manufacturers. By bringing technology to bear, the efficiency and effectiveness of US manufacturing has once again become competitive in important segments of the international marketplace for durable goods such as farm equipment.

As with prior generations, the formula for success remains one of efficiently and effectively combining the best mix of skilled and unskilled labor and the best quantity and technology of long-term assets. Management's job is to have a deep understanding of their business and its competition in order to make optimal decisions regarding labor and capital. Analysts and other outside investors, with the aid of financial accounting information, must decide how well management has achieved these objectives.

This chapter focuses on the accounting methods and issues pertaining to long-term **productive assets**. These assets include long-term **tangible assets**, such as machinery and buildings, and **natural resources**, such as coal and timber. They also include long-term **intangible assets**, such as patents and copyrights. Accounting for long-term productive assets will be seen to contain serious limitations concerning the relevance of the accounting measurements and the information reported in GAAP financial statements. Hence, our objective in this chapter is twofold: 1) to first explain how companies account for the acquisition and use of long-term assets under the rules of GAAP; and 2) to understand the limitations of financial statement data as it applies to the measurement and reporting of long-term productive assets.

LONG-TERM TANGIBLE ASSETS

The **acquisition cost** of any asset is determined by the concept that was introduced in our discussion of inventory: *the recorded cost should include any cost that is necessary and reasonable to place the asset into its intended useful state.* Only in certain special cases will GAAP provide more specific guidance as to what should or should not be included in the cost of an asset.

Application of the cost concept often requires some professional judgment. Some costs incurred in obtaining a new asset are likely to seem as if they might or might not fit the guiding concept. For example, assume that $1,000 is spent to clean, paint, and organize a site for a new machine on the floor of a factory. Is this a part of the cost of the machine? Accounting provides no specific rule to resolve such questions. However, there are two aspects of cost measurement that mitigate this concern: (1) the ambiguous costs tend to be relatively small in amount; and (2) each company will develop its own policies for dealing with such costs and they will be consistently applied to all similar costs in all future periods. These two facts render the cost measurement process to be of little or no concern to financial statement users.

However, from time to time, the differences in how companies have determined the cost of particular assets have become so significant that accounting rules were required to increase the uniformity of the measurement and reporting. One such difference was in the way companies treated interest costs on funds borrowed to construct an asset. For example, if a company borrowed $300,000 to finance the construction of a new warehouse, and during the construction period they paid $30,000 in interest costs, is the interest a part of the cost of this warehouse or not? Companies argued that the answer was both yes and no, based strictly on the general guidance of "necessary and reasonable." Because the difference in the cost of self-constructed assets like buildings was significant depending upon the approach taken, an accounting rule was established to require that interest costs during the construction period be included in the cost of self-constructed assets. Once the asset is put into use, any further interest cost is expensed.[1]

Stretching the Cost Concept

There have been several high profile accounting scandals in recent years based on companies stretching the cost concept to the limit. One such scandal involved WASTE MANAGEMENT, INC. An important part of WASTE MANAGEMENT's business was obtaining landfill sites. The reported cost of obtaining these sites (asset) included many costs that WASTE MANAGEMENT said were "necessary and reasonable" to obtain the landfill sites. However, it was later determined that these costs were normal expenses of operating the landfills. The company had overstated the asset value of their landfill sites and at the same time understated their operating expenses. As a result, the business looked much more profitable than it really was. GAAP requires companies to annually review their long-term assets for "impairment," which effectively requires that they identify any overvalued assets and write them down to their fair value. This requirement eventually resulted in the detection of the illegal practices of WASTE MANAGEMENT.

Property, Plant, and Equipment (PP&E)

Long-term tangible assets in the balance sheet generally consist of *property* (= land), *plant* (= buildings and their improvements), and *equipment* (= machinery, vehicles, etc.). All long-term tangible assets, except land, become less useful as they are used or as they age. To account for this decline in future benefits, the cost of all tangible assets except land, less expected **salvage value** (sometimes called *residual value*), if any, is expensed over the expected **useful life** of the asset. The amount of the asset's original cost to be expensed over its life is the **depreciable base**; and the amount charged to

---

[1] The formula for measuring the cost of interest during construction and other details of this requirement are beyond the scope of this text. It is sufficient to note here that interest is a required part of the cost of all self-constructed assets of a business that has debt, even when the debt was not specifically borrowed to finance the construction of the asset.

the income statement in each period is called **depreciation expense**. The estimated useful life and the estimated salvage value are two important *estimates* that can have an impact on the measurement of total assets and net income.

In the first three chapters, when we illustrated how companies record the use of a long-term asset, we debited depreciation expense and directly reduced (credited) the asset. We did this to avoid introducing the concept of contra accounts at a time when you were just learning the basics. Now that you understand the use of contra accounts from Chapters 4 and 5, we illustrate how companies actually record depreciation expense using the contra asset account **Accumulated Depreciation**. The use of a contra asset account preserves the original cost of the asset in a separate account. For example, assume the annual depreciation expense on a machine is $3,000 per year. The following contrasts the earlier illustration with the more detailed entry that we will use from now on.

Journal

Date	Accounts	Debit	Credit
	Earlier illustration:		
December 31	Depreciation Expense	3,000	
	Machinery		3,000
	More detailed illustration:		
December 31	Depreciation Expense	3,000	
	Accumulated Depreciation		3,000

In this way, the financial statements can reveal both the original cost and the total accumulated depreciation to date for each asset. Later in this chapter we will illustrate the usefulness of this information in financial statement analysis.

Straight-line Depreciation

The goal of **depreciation** *is to assign the original cost of the asset to the periods of use in a pattern that approximates how the usefulness of the asset is consumed.* Different depreciation methods have been devised to match the different patterns of use. For example, assume you acquired a machine on January 1, 2013, for $16,000 that has an estimated salvage value of $1,000 and an estimated useful life of 5 years. If the machine is expected to be equally useful over its life, the **straight-line method**, a method that assigns an equal amount to each period of use, would be an appropriate method to use. Straight-line depreciation expense for the machine would be $3,000 per year, computed as follows:

Straight-line Depreciation	=	Depreciable base ÷ useful life in years
	=	[Cost – salvage value] ÷ useful life in years
	=	[$16,000 – $1,000] ÷ 5 years
	=	$15,000 ÷ 5 years = $3,000 per year

Straight-line depreciation is the most common method used in practice. Ninety-five percent of companies use the straight-line method for some or all of their assets, and only about 12% of companies use some method other than straight-line for some or all of their assets.[2] Accountants sometimes compute straight-line depreciation by using a *straight-line rate* and multiplying this rate by the depreciable base. For example, if the useful life of an asset is 5 years, then the straight-line rate per year is 20% (1 year ÷ 5 total years = 20% per year). This rate of 20% (.20) times the amount to be depreciated of $15,000 equals $3,000 depreciation expense per year.

Accelerated Depreciation

In addition to the straight-line method, there are methods that expense the depreciable base more rapidly at the beginning of the asset's life. These are referred to as **accelerated depreciation methods**. These methods depreciate the same total dollar amount as the straight-line method ($15,000 in our example). However, the accelerated methods result in larger depreciation expense in the early years and smaller depreciation expense in the later years. These methods are appropriate when the usefulness of an asset is greater in the years immediately after acquisition than near the end of the asset's life. The two most popular accelerated methods are: sum-of-the-years'-digits and double-declining balance.

Sum-of-the-Years'-Digits (SYD)   This method takes the years of useful life remaining at the start of the year for which depreciation is to be computed and divides by the sum of the years of its life. This fraction is then multiplied times the asset's depreciable base.

Double-Declining Balance (DDB)   This method takes double the straight-line rate and multiplies this rate times the undepreciated balance in the asset account. The mechanics of this method are quite different from the straight-line and sum-of-the-years'-digits methods in that (1) *the salvage value is not taken into account until the end of the asset's life* and (2) the depreciation rate *is applied to the undepreciated asset amount (book value) and not the amount to be depreciated.*

SYD and DDB Illustration   To illustrate sum-of-the-years' digits and double-declining balance depreciation methods, we show the depreciation expense calculations for the $16,000 machine that was introduced on the previous page.

The double-declining balance (DDB) method generally will not automatically depreciate an asset to its salvage value. In this example, we see DDB depreciates 40% (2 times the 20% straight-line rate) of the **book value** (= cost minus accumulated depreciation) each year, so in the last year of the asset's life 60% the book value at the beginning of the final year of the asset's life will remain and this is not likely to be the salvage value. To overcome this limitation, companies that use the double-declining balance method force the final year's depreciation amount to equal an amount that brings the book value down to the asset's salvage value, as is done in Exhibit 6-1.

---

[2] Companies may use different depreciation methods for different classes of assets. These figures are from *Accounting Trends and Techniques* (AICPA, New York, NY, 2011).

Exhibit 6-1 Depreciation Expense for Accelerated Methods

	Sum-of-the-Years'-Digits[3] Sum of years = 15 [5 + 4 + 3 + 2 + 1 = 15]	**Double-Declining Balance** 200% times straight-line rate = 2 x .20 = .40 (40%)
Amount to be depreciated	$15,000	$15,000
Depreciation Schedule:		
Expense for Year 1	5/15 x $15,000 = $5,000	40% x $16,000 = $6,400
Expense for Year 2	4/15 x $15,000 = $4,000	40% x $9,600 = $3,840
Expense for Year 3	3/15 x $15,000 = $3,000	40% x $5,760 = $2,304
Expense for Year 4	2/15 x $15,000 = $2,000	40% x $3,456 = $1,382
Expense for Year 5	1/15 x $15,000 = $1,000	Forced = $1,074*
Total depreciation expense	$15,000	$15,000

* $15,000 – $6,400 – $3,840 – $2,304 – $1,382 = $1,074 to bring book value down to $1,000.

Exhibit 6-2 summarizes the straight-line, sum-of-the-years'-digits, and double-declining balance methods and their balance sheet and income statement effects over the five-year life of the machine. Note that the total amount of depreciation expense is $15,000 in all three cases and any difference in depreciation expense in one year is offset in another year.

Exhibit 6-2 Numerical Comparison of Depreciation Methods

End Of	**Straight-line Method** Book Value*	Depreciation Expense**	**Sum-of-Years'-Digits Method** Book Value	Depreciation Expense	**Double-Declining Balance Method** Book Value	Depreciation Expense
	$16,000		$16,000		$16,000	
Year 1	$13,000	$3,000	$11,000	$5,000	$ 9,600	$ 6,400
Year 2	$10,000	$3,000	$ 7,000	$4,000	$ 5,760	$ 3,840
Year 3	$ 7,000	$3,000	$ 4,000	$3,000	$ 3,456	$ 2,304
Year 4	$ 4,000	$3,000	$ 2,000	$2,000	$ 2,074	$ 1,382
Year 5	$ 1,000	$3,000	$ 1,000	$1,000	$ 1,000	$ 1,074

* Book value is the cost of $16,000 minus the accumulated depreciation shown on the balance sheet at the end of each year. This example assumes the salvage value of the asset is $1,000.
** Depreciation expense is the amount shown on the income statement for the year.

---

[3] The formula for computing the sum of a series of numbers is: if "N" is the number (years of useful life in this application), then the sum from N to 0 is: [N (N + 1)] ÷ 2. For example, N=10, [10(11)] ÷ 2 = 55, the sum of 10 + 9 + 8 + 7 + 6 + 5 + 4 + 3 + 2 + 1.

Exhibit 6-3 provides a graphic illustration of the machine's annual depreciation expense under the three different methods.

Partial-Year Depreciation

Nearly all depreciation methods are based on the passage of time. But how is depreciation determined when an asset is acquired or disposed of during the year? A **partial year of depreciation** must be computed. This may be done using: (1) the actual days of use; (2) by rounding to the nearest whole month; or (3) using what is called the half-year convention where, no matter when during the year an asset is acquired or sold, a half-year of depreciation is recognized in both the year of acquisition and disposal. For example, assume the above machine was acquired on May 11 and straight-line rounded to the nearest whole month is used for depreciation. Partial year depreciation is computed as follows:

Step 1:   Compute an entire year's depreciation for the first year—for this machine this is *$3,000* [($16,000 – $1,000) ÷ 5 years = $3,000].

Exhibit 6-3   Graphic Comparison of Depreciation Methods

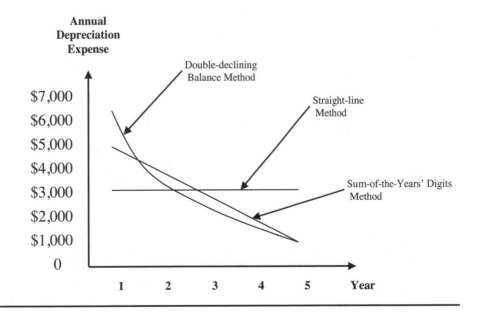

Step 2: Round the acquisition date to May 1 and record eight months' (May through December) of depreciation expense. This results in *$2,000* of depreciation for the first year ($3,000 x 8/12 = $2,000).

Units-of-Production Depreciation

A non-time-based depreciation method is the **units-of-production method**. This method assigns the cost of a long-term asset to expense based on the units of the asset (i.e., units of time, units of distance, units produced, etc.) that are used during the year. For example, assume the useful life of the machine in our example is estimated at 10,000 hours of running time. The depreciation rate for the machine would be $1.50 per hour computed as follows:

Units Depreciation Rate	=	Depreciable base ÷ useful life in units
	=	[Cost – salvage value] ÷ useful life in units
	=	[$16,000 – $1,000] ÷ 10,000 hours
	=	$15,000 ÷ 10,000 hours = $1.50 per hour

If the machine is used for 1,800 hours during the current year, depreciation of *$2,700* ($1.50 x 1,800) would be reported. The units-of-production method is appropriate when the usefulness of the asset is consumed by its physical use.

Like inventory accounting, GAAP allows companies to use different methods of depreciation for different types of assets. However, in the U.S., most companies use straight-line depreciation for all of their depreciable assets. Consider the following excerpts from the policy footnote of a recent annual report of GOOGLE:

From 2014 GOOGLE Inc. Annual Report

Property and Equipment

We account for property and equipment at cost less accumulated depreciation and amortization. We compute depreciation using the straight-line method over the estimated useful lives of the assets generally two to five years. We depreciate buildings over periods up to 25 years. We amortize leasehold improvements over the shorter of the remaining lease term or the estimated useful lives of the assets. Construction in progress is related to the construction or development of property (including land) and equipment that have not yet been placed in service for our intended use. Depreciation for equipment commences once it is placed in service and depreciation for buildings and leasehold improvements commences once they are ready for our intended use. Land is not depreciated.

Important Limitation of PP&E Measurement under GAAP

It is important to remember that depreciation is a way to assign the cost of an asset to the periods of use, *not a way to value the asset*. Depreciation methods are not intended to result in a **net book value** equal to the market value of a depreciable asset. However, if the market value or **recoverable value** of an asset declines below the depreciated historical cost, GAAP "impairment" tests require that the asset be written down to its recoverable value. On the other hand, GAAP does not permit the write-up of assets if their **fair market value** is determined to be higher than depreciated historical cost. As a consequence, the GAAP-based historical cost measures of depreciable assets reported in the balance sheet are, in nearly all cases, significantly lower than the current **replacement cost** of these assets (e.g., the cost to acquire these same assets with a similar amount of wear and tear).

If GAAP rules are followed, long-term assets should never be reported at more than their recoverable value (their fair market value or their value in use). Accounting standards provide guidelines to determine when long-term depreciable assets reported at their net depreciated cost are overstated.[4] These write-downs are the result of what is known as asset **impairments**, and they have become common in recent years. *As a result, the amount reported in the financial statements for any long-term asset is essentially the lower amount of its net book value or its fair market value.* To illustrate how companies implement the impairment tests and report them in the financial statements, consider the following 2014 excerpt from NIKE's annual report:

From 2014 NIKE Annual Report

Impairment of Long-Lived Assets

The Company reviews the carrying value of long-lived assets or asset groups to be used in operations whenever events or changes in circumstances indicate that the carrying amount of the assets might not be recoverable. Factors that would necessitate an impairment assessment include a significant adverse change in the extent or manner in which an asset is used, a significant adverse change in legal factors or the business climate that could affect the value of the asset, or a significant decline in the observable market value of an asset, among others. If such facts indicate a potential impairment, the Company would assess the recoverability of an asset group by determining if the carrying value of the asset group exceeds the sum of the projected undiscounted cash flows expected to result from the use and eventual disposition of the assets over the remaining economic life of the primary asset in the asset group. If the recoverability test indicates that the carrying value of the asset group is not recoverable, the Company will estimate the fair value of the asset group using appropriate valuation methodologies, which would typically include an estimate of discounted cash flows. Any impairment would be measured as the difference between the asset group's carrying amount and its estimated fair value.

While current accounting rules in the U.S. do not provide for reporting long-term assets at their fair value, fair value is usually considered to be the most relevant measure for decision-making purposes. Why doesn't accounting require long-term assets to be reported at their fair value? Current thought among accounting policymakers is that fair value measurements are too unreliable to be reported in the formal financial statements. So, while fair value measurements are acceptable for testing the impairment of long-term assets, the *reliability* of historical cost information has dominated the *relevance* of fair value information for financial statement purposes. For external users of financial statements, this is an *important limitation,* and many analysts and other sophisticated users have found ways to approximate the fair value of productive assets for various decision-making purposes.

---

[4] Accounting rules provides guidance for determining whether the net asset value is recoverable by the company through its future use, and what conditions create asset impairment.

Costs Subsequent to Acquisition

When costs are incurred that relate to an existing asset, the company must decide if the cost is a capital expenditure (= asset) or an expense. **Capital expenditures** are added to the cost of the original asset when they are expected to provide future benefits by improving the usefulness or extending the life of the asset. Capital expenditures are depreciated along with the remaining original cost (= book value) of the asset over the remaining life of that asset. Expenditures related to an existing asset that do not meet the criteria of a capital expenditure should be charged to expense in the period incurred.

The guidelines for determining whether a cost is a capital expenditure or expense are ambiguous (much like the guidelines for determining what to include in the cost of acquiring an asset). While there are few clear guidelines for classifying costs subsequent to acquisition, the summary in Exhibit 6-4 should help you understand the concepts involved.

In Exhibit 6-4, we use common terms such as *maintenance and repairs*, *additions*, and *improvements*. However, you should understand that in practice there are no uniformly accepted definitions of these terms. For example, while everyone will agree that installing a heating system in a storage facility is an improvement that will increase its usefulness, there will be less agreement on whether adding a weatherproof door to the facility is an improvement, and less agreement still on whether a coat of weatherproof sealant applied to the interior walls of the facility is an improvement. We could reasonably argue that the door and sealant provide future benefits and should be recorded as capital expenditures. Yet it could also be argued that they are routine expenses needed to maintain the facility. As suggested in Exhibit 6-4, the combination of the amount of the expenditure and the length of the expected future benefit will determine how a subsequent cost will be reported.

Exhibit 6-4 How to Treat Costs Incurred Subsequent to Acquisition

Amount of the Cost Subsequent to Acquisition

		Relatively Small	Relatively Large
Expected Benefit Period	Short	A. Decision is usually to expense: • Maintenance & repairs • Expected replacements	B. Decision is unclear but leans to capitalizing due to the large amount of the expenditure
	Long	C. Decision is unclear but leans to expensing due to the small amount of the expenditure	D. Decision is usually to capitalize as an asset: • Additions • Improvements • Unexpected replacements

Many companies provide information in the notes to their financial statements to explain to external users how costs subsequent to acquisition are treated. The following excerpt from the 2014 annual report of U.S. STEEL provides such an example:

From 2014 U.S. Steel Annual Report

Major maintenance activities

U.S. Steel incurs maintenance costs on all of its major equipment. Costs that extend the life of the asset, materially add to it value, or adapt the asset to a new or different use are separately capitalized in property, plant and equipment and are depreciated over its estimated useful life. All other repair and maintenance costs are expensed as incurred.

Disposal of Long-Term Assets

When a long-term asset is sold or retired, the journal entry to record the disposal will eliminate both the asset and the contra asset amounts from the company's records. If the company receives anything from the sale of the asset (e.g., cash), it is recorded at the same time; and the journal entry to record the sale will then force the amount of any gain or loss on the sale. Whether a gain or loss occurs depends on the difference between the book value of the asset and the selling price. A gain will be recorded when the asset is sold for more than the book value and a loss will be recorded when it is sold for less than the book value.[5]

To illustrate the disposal of a productive asset, assume a company disposed of used equipment that had originally cost $35,000 and had accumulated depreciation *adjusted up to the date of disposal* of $20,000. If the company sold the used equipment for $22,000 cash, the journal entry to record the sale would be as follows:

Journal

Date	Accounts (*Explanation*)	Debit	Credit
XXXX	Cash	22,000	
	Accumulated Depreciation	20,000	
	Equipment		35,000
	Gain on Sale of Equipment		7,000
	(*To record the sale of used equipment.*)		

This disposal entry would eliminate both the asset and contra asset amounts pertaining to the equipment, record the cash received from the sale, and force the amount of the gain that would be shown in the income statement. This gain would be reported as a non-operating item in the income statement under a heading such as "other gains and losses."

---

[5] Because of the accounting rules on asset impairment, requiring that the reported amount of an asset be reduced when the book value is not recoverable from future use, we expect to see relatively few losses on the sales of long-term assets, and any reported losses should be relatively small. While the recoverability measure in GAAP is not the same as selling price, the concepts are related.

In the example above, the book value of the equipment was $15,000 at the time of the sale ($35,000 original cost minus $20,000 accumulated depreciation). Since the cash from the sale ($22,000) was greater than the book value ($15,000), a gain resulted. If $10,000 in cash had been received instead, there would have been a $5,000 loss on the sale ($10,000 cash − $15,000 book value = − $5,000).

Asset Exchanges

Accounting for asset exchanges, where one asset is traded in for another asset, is very much like accounting for the disposal of an asset. When one asset is exchanged for another, the asset that is given up is completely eliminated from the accounting records and the new asset is recorded in the accounts. For example, assume a company traded in a four-year old truck plus cash for a new truck. The old truck originally cost $40,000 and accumulated depreciation on the truck after four years was $25,000. The book value of the truck was $15,000 ($40,000 cost minus the $25,000 accumulated depreciation). The new truck had a cost of $50,000. The truck dealer agreed to give the company a trade-in allowance of $12,000 in exchange for the old truck, making the net cost of the new truck only $38,000 in cash ($50,000 cost minus $12,000 trade-in allowance). The company would record this exchange transaction as follows:

Journal

Date	Accounts (*Explanation*)	Debit	Credit
xxxx	Truck (new)	50,000	
	Accumulated Depreciation – Truck (old)	25,000	
	Loss on trade in of old truck	3,000	
	Truck (old)		40,000
	Cash		38,000
	(*To record the acquisition of a new truck in exchange for cash and an old truck.*)		

The company would recognize a loss of $3,000 on the trade-in of the old truck, since the trade-in value of the truck was $12,000 and the book value of the truck was $15,000. This entry is based on the assumption that the fair value of the new truck is $50,000, and that the cost of the new truck without the trade-in allowance would have been $50,000.

An exchange transaction such as this is more challenging to record than the outright sale and disposal of an asset because it is possible to become confused about the fair value of the new and used assets, particularly when they are somewhat unique. However, GAAP requires that the new asset be recorded at its fair value, and any difference between the book value and the implicit fair value of the old asset should be recorded as a gain or a loss on trade-in.

Natural Resources

Natural resources are tangible "wasting" assets such as coal, iron ore, natural gas, and timber. Unlike productive assets such as buildings, natural resources are usually obtained through discovery (e.g., locating an oil field) or development (e.g., growing timber) or both (e.g., locating and extracting natural gas). As a result, the cost of the natural resources at the time they are discovered or developed is usually much lower than their fair market value. When a company buys a building, for example, it will initially report the building at its fair market value, although over time the book value will depart from the fair market value. But when a company discovers a natural resource, the reported cost of the discovery will normally be much lower than the fair market value of the resource.[6]

For example, assume a company spends $100,000 searching for natural gas. As a result of their search efforts, they discover natural gas with an estimated fair market value of $1,000,000. The asset, Natural Gas, will be reported on the balance sheet at its *discovery cost* of $100,000, not its fair market value of $1,000,000. As the natural gas is extracted and sold, the $100,000 cost will be expensed through a charge called **depletion expense**, a charge similar to depreciation expense.

Depletion expense is computed in a manner similar to depreciation expense using the units-of-production method. If the geologists estimate that the discovery contains 10 million cubic feet of natural gas, then the **depletion** rate will be $0.01 per cubic foot calculated as follows:

Cost per unit	=	Cost of asset ÷ estimated total number of units available
Cost per cubic foot	=	$100,000 ÷ 10,000,000 cubic feet = $0.01 per cubic foot.

Example   Assume that in January 2013, HAMMER MILL PAPER COMPANY (HMP) acquired land that was heavily forested for $1,000,000. HMP estimated that the land would be worth $250,000 after the trees are harvested, and, therefore, assigned a cost of $750,000 to the trees ($1,000,000 minus $250,000), designated as Timber Lot #87. In March 2013, HMP spent another $150,000 to build roads through the forest to permit the harvesting and extraction of the trees and a building for the site manager, cutters, and haulers to use while at the location. It was estimated that the roads and building would add no value to the land once the trees were removed, and that both would be abandoned, so these costs were added to the natural resource account, Trees.[7]   The forest is expected to yield 30 million board feet of lumber. This results in an expected depletion rate of $0.03 per board foot ([$750,000 + $150,000] ÷ 30,000,000 board feet = $0.03 per board foot). Between May and December 2013, HMP harvested 10 million board feet of timber from this site. The summary journal entries that would have been recorded by HMP during 2013 are:

---

[6] That is, with natural resources, the book value does not equal the fair market value of these assets even when they are initially recorded.

[7] The roads and building, of course, could have been depreciated separately, perhaps using the straight-line or units-of-production method. But, since these assets will have no value beyond the life of the natural resource, it is appropriate to include their costs in the cost of the natural resource.

Journal

Date (2013)	Accounts (*Explanation*)	Debit	Credit
January xx	Land	250,000	
	Natural Resources – Timber Lot #87	750,000	
	Cash		1,000,000
	(To record purchase of land and timber lot #87.)		
March xx	Natural Resources – Timber Lot #87	150,000	
	Cash		150,000
	(To record construction on timber lot #87.)		
December 31	Depletion Expense	300,000	
	Accumulated Depletion – Timber Lot #87		300,000
	(To record harvesting of 10 million board feet.)		

LONG-TERM INTANGIBLE ASSETS

Intangible assets are resources whose value is based on what they represent rather than on their physical form. Most intangibles are legal documents that convey rights to their owners. There are three types of long-term intangible assets reported in financial statements:

1. Identifiable intangibles with indefinite lives;

2. Identifiable intangibles with finite lives; and

3. Goodwill.

Identifiable Intangibles

Identifiable intangible assets are specifically identifiable items that have a cost and have future value to the business. Common examples include:

- Trademarks and brand names;
- Franchises and licenses;
- Patents; and
- Copyrights.

Determining the cost of intangibles is the same as determining the cost of other assets—the cost includes all amounts that are necessary and reasonable to place the asset into its intended useful state. For a **purchased intangible**, the cost that is reported is the price paid to acquire the asset. For an **internally created intangible**, the cost that is reported is generally confined to the legal or filing fees required to obtain the asset. The costs incurred to develop the asset, on the other hand, are not included in the cost of the asset.

Some intangible assets are considered to have an indefinite life, similar to land. **Indefinite life intangibles** include **trademarks** such as the TEXACO "star" and **brand names** such as *Coca-Cola* and *Yahoo!* which are effectively granted forever (although they must be renewed every ten years at a minimal cost to the holder). **Franchise** agreements (such as team franchises granted by professional sports leagues) can convey rights to the franchisee for a limited (finite) period or for an indefinite time, so the terms of these contracts will determine whether they should be classified as indefinite life intangibles or not. **Licenses** or **permits** for the use of public waterways, airways, cable networks, etc. are usually granted for a limited time period. However, the costs of renewals are sometimes very low compared to the initial license or permit fee. In such cases, it may be appropriate to treat the initial cost of obtaining the license or permit as an indefinite life intangible asset and treat the renewal fees as expenses of the current period.

Other intangible assets have a finite life over which they provide value to the business. The process of allocating the cost of **finite life intangibles** to expense over their useful life is called **amortization**. Conceptually, **amortization expense** serves the same purpose as depreciation expense and depletion expense: it is a systematic way to charge the cost of an asset to its periods of use. Straight-line amortization is used for finite life intangibles, unless a convincing argument can be made for using some other pattern of amortization. As with depreciation, you should not expect amortization to result in a net asset value that is representative of the asset's fair market value.

Finite-life intangibles include **patents**, which convey the exclusive right to use a product or process for a period of 20 years. Therefore, patents are amortized over 20 years or their expected useful life, whichever is shorter. Internally-developed patents are usually reported at the cost to file for the patent and the cost of any prototype product or model necessary to define the rights of the patent holder. Internally-generated patents are often the result of long periods of **research and development** (R&D). However, U.S. GAAP does not allow R&D to be included in the cost of a patent.[8] So even though the patent may have been the result of spending millions of dollars of R&D, and may be worth even more if it were sold to another business, it cannot be reported at more than the cost as described above (again, generally only the legal fees to file for the patent).

Copyrights also have a finite life, and they are currently granted to their creator for the life of the creator plus 70 years. Therefore, books, movies, and other artistic or technical endeavors that can be copyrighted have a fairly long life. Like patents, the cost reported as an asset for internally-developed copyrights may be quite small, while the cost of copyrights purchased from others may be much higher. In either case, these assets are considered to have finite lives and straight-line amortization is used to match their costs against revenue.

Amortized Intangibles and Subsequent Costs

For those intangibles that must be amortized, the entries for amortization are similar to those for depreciation. To illustrate, assume that on July 1, 2014, Delta Company (a calendar year-end company) obtained a patent on a new product that has a 20-year life and cost $40,000. At the end of 2014 the patent would be amortized for six months, as follows:

---

[8] Interestingly, even in countries where the reporting standards allow R&D costs to be shown as an asset, it is seldom reported in the financial statements. Deciding how much R&D to capitalize is an ambiguous task, and most managers and accountants prefer the conservative treatment of expensing R&D as incurred rather than report an ambiguous amount that would later be subject to criticism.

Journal

Date (2014)	Accounts (*Explanation*)	Debit	Credit
December 31	Amortization Expense..	1,000	
	Accumulated Amortization...................		1,000
	(To record amortization of a patent;		
	$40,000 \div 20 = $2,000 \times \frac{1}{2}$ year = $1,000)		

The credit to the Accumulated Amortization account might also have been made directly to the asset account, but the use of the contra account is preferred from an information standpoint, as noted earlier. The patent would continue to be amortized at the rate of $2,000 per year from 2015 to 2033 and $1,000 in 2034.

What if this patent was actually a very valuable asset and the related product was a huge success? The patent would still only be reported at its cost less accumulated amortization. Assume, however, that after some years of making excellent profits from this patented product, Delta discovered that a competitor had developed a patent on a substitute product. To protect the market for its product, assume Delta decides to buy the competitor's patent for $500,000 on July 1, 2019, when the Delta patent was five years old. Assume also that Delta will not use the acquired patent to produce the competitor's product, but simply acquired this patent so that there would be less competition for its own product. This is essentially spending $500,000 to provide greater future benefits from the existing patent, and the $500,000 would be added to the book value of the original patent and amortized over the remaining 15-year life of that patent.

Other situations may also increase the cost of an intangible asset. If the intangible asset conveys rights and a legal suit costing $300,000 takes place to successfully defend those rights from being abused by others, then the $300,000 will be added to the cost of the asset, because it is a cost considered necessary to sustain or enhance the future benefits from the asset. The $300,000 would then be amortized over the remaining useful life of the intangible asset.

Whether an intangible asset is considered to have a finite life or an indefinite life, the company must annually test the asset's value for **impairment**, just like the value of tangible assets must be tested. If there is evidence that the book value of an intangible asset is too high, it should be written down to its estimated *fair market value*. Again, if the value of the asset is determined to be higher than the book value, no action is taken. This is a conservative aspect of accounting that is generally referred to as the "lower-of-cost-or-market" concept (similar to the lower-of-cost-or-market test for inventory in Chapter 5). GAAP recognizes all losses or reductions in value as soon as there is evidence to suggest something is overvalued but it does not permit subjective evidence to be used to write up the value of asset.

Goodwill

The largest intangible asset in a balance sheet is often also the only **unidentifiable intangible asset** called goodwill. What is goodwill? In accounting, **goodwill** is *defined* and *measured* as the amount paid for another company in excess of the fair market value (i.e., appraisal value) of the recorded net assets of the acquired company. In essence, goodwill is the previously unidentified (unrecorded) net assets of the acquired company. These unrecorded assets could be the result of the previous R&D or marketing activities of the acquired entity. GAAP requires all R&D and marketing costs to be expensed as incurred but these expenditures may have actually created unrecorded missing assets for the acquired entity that the buyer is now willing to pay for in order to obtain control. Goodwill might also represent synergies that often result from combining two similar companies, permitting the elimination of redundant marketing, distribution, or other costs while maintaining the related revenues from these activities.

To illustrate how goodwill comes about and how it is measured, consider the information provided in Exhibit 6-5 regarding the purchase of COMPAQ COMPUTER by HEWLETT-PACKARD (HP) on May 3, 2002. The book values shown are as of March 31, 2002, the last balance sheet data reported by COMPAQ COMPUTER as a separate company. On May 3, 2002, HP acquired all of the shares of COMPAQ for total consideration of $24.17 billion dollars. To establish the price it was willing to pay for COMPAQ, HP had to examine all of the items in COMPAQ's balance sheet and determine the *fair market value of each asset and liability*.[9] The fair market values determined by HP for each of the various categories of COMPAQ's assets and liabilities are also reported in Exhibit 6-5. These fair market values were provided in the HP annual report following the purchase of COMPAQ, and were (quoting the annual report) "Based on the independent valuation prepared using estimates and assumptions provided by management…"

Because COMPAQ was a company that had significant unrecorded intangible assets (such as its brand name and scientific talent), HP was willing to pay COMPAQ shareholders $14,450 million more than the $9,720 fair value of COMPAQ's *reported* net assets ($23,294 – $13,574). This premium paid by HP to COMPAQ shareholders for the previously unrecorded assets of value to HP was for the brand name and other identifiable assets (e.g., patents) and for the *goodwill* of COMPAQ; the Goodwill was recorded by HP on its books at $14,450 million dollars in this specific transaction, as illustrated in Exhibit 6-5.

While the book values reported for comparison in this example should ideally be as of May 3, 2002, the date of the purchase, these values were not publicly available. So while the March 31, 2002 book values are 33 days too old for an *exact* comparison (for example, we see that cash, whose book value is its fair market value, changed slightly), we realize that the acquired company is essentially as it was on March 31. The important thing to realize from this example is that, because of the purchase of COMPAQ by HP, we are able to actually see measurements of the differences between GAAP values and fair market values for a technology company due to the reporting requirements at the time of an acquisition of another entity. For this example, we can see that the two most significant differences between book value and fair market value stem from the unrecorded assets purchased by HP (= goodwill) and the previously undervalued identifiable intangible assets (book value of $1,588 versus a fair value of $4,939). This evidence supports the claim that GAAP measures of soft assets and assets of technology based companies in general *are not very relevant for decision making*.

---

[9] In other words, HP had to ask what it was willing to pay for these assets and liabilities. Also, COMPAQ's shareholders had to agree it was a fair price to receive for their shares of stock. Companies use appraisers to establish the fair value of the assets of acquired companies.

Exhibit 6-5   Excerpts from the Financial Statements of COMPAQ and HP

Book value before and fair value at date of purchase of COMPAQ by HP:

Balance Sheet Data as of (*in millions*)	Book Value* March 31, 2002	Fair Market Value May 3, 2002
Cash	$ 3,702	$ 3,615
Other current assets	8,963	8,353
Property, plant & equipment	3,171	2,998
Intangible assets	1,588	4,939
Other assets	5,347	3,389
Reported identifiable assets	$22,771	$23,294
Goodwill	**0**	**14,450**
Total assets	$22,771	$37,744
Less liabilities	(11,635)	(13,574)
Net assets acquired	$11,136	$24,170

* The appropriate book value to use is always the book value at the date of the purchase. However, since COMPAQ's balance sheet was not available to the public at May 3, 2002, we show the closest balance sheet instead which was dated March 31, 2002.

If we can observe such significant differences between GAAP and fair market values for the COMPAQ example, we should be able to imagine similar significant differences for most other technology based entities. Sophisticated analysts realize the limitations of GAAP data for such entities and use a variety of estimation techniques, discussed in more advanced courses, to estimate more relevant measurements for long term assets of companies where intangibles are important.

This case also illustrates that goodwill is essentially a forced number. Once HP and COMPAQ agreed on the price of $24.17 billion, and the independent appraisers established the fair value of all of COMPAQ's *identifiable* assets and liabilities, then goodwill was established to be the difference. Note that goodwill, the amount of the unidentifiable assets, is more than the reported book value amount of COMPAQ's entire net assets (= $11,136) just 33 days before the purchase.

Goodwill is an *indefinite life intangible asset that is not amortized but is subject to annual tests for impairment*. In addition, companies may not estimate the amount of their own goodwill and record it in their books. The fact that one company must pay another company for its unrecorded assets in order to report goodwill gives economic relevance to this asset.

Goodwill is a significant asset in the balance sheets of many companies that have acquired other companies. On the other hand, it is common for companies to only have small amounts invested in other intangible assets, and these are often included in "other assets" in the balance sheet. As the U.S. evolves toward more of a technology-based economy, GAAP continues to struggle to find ways to provide relevant and reliable information about intangible assets. Informed users of financial statements must take these limitations into account when using information about intangible assets.

Exhibit 6-6 Key Features of Intangible Assets

	Identifiable Intangibles		Unidentifiable Intangibles
Life?	Finite Life	Indefinite Life	Indefinite Life
Amortize?	Yes	No	No
How created?	Purchased or internally developed	Purchased or internally developed	Must be purchased by acquiring another entity
Write down?	If value is impaired	If value is impaired	If value is impaired
Typical examples?	Patents Copyrights Licenses Franchises	Trademarks Brand names Licenses Franchises	Goodwill

To summarize our discussion of intangible assets, an outline of some of the key features of these resources is provided in Exhibit 6-6.

ACCOUNTING FOR CHANGES IN ESTIMATES

The estimated useful life of productive and intangible assets and the estimated amount of natural resources are accounting estimates that have the potential to make a significant impact on the financial statements. As with any estimate, new information may be revealed to suggest that the estimate should be revised. Accounting deals with **changes in estimates** the same way in every case—the new estimate is applied to the book value of the asset as of the <u>beginning</u> of the year of the change and applied to the year of the change and all remaining future years. Changes in estimates never involve changing prior years' results.

To illustrate changes in accounting estimates, reconsider the HMP example used earlier. Assume that during July of the second year of harvesting (2014), HMP increased its estimate of the total amount of lumber available by 10 million board feet, (from 30 million to 40 million board feet). As a result, after harvesting 10 million board feet in 2013, HMP's new estimate is that 30 million board feet still remained as of January 1, 2014. The new depletion rate would be computed as follows:

$$\text{New depletion rate} \quad = \quad \frac{\text{Book value at the start of the year of change}}{\text{Estimated remaining units}}$$

$$= \quad \frac{\$900,000 - \$300,000 \text{ depletion in 2013} = \$600,000 \text{ book value on 1/1/14}}{30,000,000 \text{ board feet remaining}}$$

$$= \quad \frac{\$600,000}{30,000,000 \text{ board feet}} = \$0.02 \text{ per board foot}$$

The new depletion rate of $0.02 per board foot would be applied from January 1, 2014 forward, even though the estimate was not revised until July 2014. The new estimate is always applied *as of the beginning of the year* in which the estimate is revised allowing the entire year to benefit from the new information.

Changes can also apply to the estimated salvage value of an asset. To illustrate this, assume that HMP purchased a timber-cutting machine on January 1, 2010, for $45,000. At that time, the machine had an estimated useful life of 10 years using straight-line depreciation and zero salvage value. Assume that on December 1, 2014, HMP decided that the salvage value of the machine after 10 years would actually be $6,000. The original depreciation rate, book value of the machine at the beginning of 2014, and revised depreciation rate would be calculated as follows:

- Original depreciation per year = $45,000 ÷ 10 years = $4,500 per year
- Total accumulated depreciation for 2010-2013 = 4 x $4,500 = $18,000
- Book value at January 1, 2014 = $45,000 – $18,000 = $27,000
- New depreciation rate = [$27,000 – $6,000] ÷ 6 years = $3,500 per year

As mentioned, changes in estimates will affect the current and future periods only, never the prior periods. The basic process is always the same: take the book value *at the start of the year of change (the start of the current period)* and apply the new estimate to the current and future periods.

FINANCIAL STATEMENT ANALYSIS

Computing Age and Useful Life

The use of contra asset accounts by reporting companies provides useful information about the long-term assets of the business. Consider the following two versions of balance sheet information that could be made available regarding a machine that had been depreciated for several years.

Partial Balance Sheet Information

Long-term Depreciable Assets	Using a Contra Account		Without a Contra Account	
	2014	**2013**	**2014**	**2013**
Machinery	$4,000	$4,000		
Less: Accumulated depreciation	1,200	800		
Net machinery	$2,800	$3,200	$2,800	$3,200

Notice that the use of the contra account preserves the fact that the original cost of the machinery was $4,000, and that it is 30% used up ($1,200 ÷ $4,000) at the end of 2014. Without a contra account this information is obscured. Also, if the financial statement readers know that depreciation on the machine is $400 per year (from the income statement, for example), they would be able to determine that the machinery was 3 years old at the end of 2014 and has a useful life of 10 years, as follows:

Age = Accumulated Depreciation ÷ Depreciation Expense = $1,200 ÷ $400 = 3 years

Useful Life = Original Cost ÷ Depreciation Expense = $4,000 ÷ $400 = 10 years

Both of these pieces of information could be used to evaluate a company over time to determine whether it is growing or cutting back on its productive capacity and whether or not it is keeping up with its replacement of assets. Because of this increase in information, financial statements provide contra accounts to report the cumulative reductions in long-term assets as a result of depreciation charges.

Analyzing Changes in Long-Term Asset Accounts

In addition to being able to estimate the useful life and age of depreciable assets, financial statement users can extract other information from the data. Consider the typical reasons for changes in the accounts related to machinery: (1) the *Machinery* account increases (debit side) when assets are acquired and decreases (credit side) when assets are disposed of; (2) the *Accumulated Depreciation* account increases (credit side) when the annual depreciation expense is recorded and decreases (debit side) when assets are disposed of (to eliminate the related depreciation taken to date). In general, the expense account, *Depreciation Expense*, will only increase (debit side) when annual depreciation expense is recorded and will not decrease unless an error has been made that requires correcting.

These typical transactions are illustrated in the following set of T-accounts pertaining to the machinery account:

T-accounts Related to Machinery

Machinery (A)		Accumulated Depreciation: Machinery (XA)		Depreciation Expense (E)
Beg. Bal.	*Decreases:* (3) cost of old assets sold or retired	*Decreases:* (3) accumulated depreciation on old assets sold or retired	Beg. Bal. *Increases:* (2) depreciation expense	*Increases:* (2) depreciation expense
Increases: (1) buy assets				
End. Bal.			End. Bal.	

Example   The 2014 financial statements of ATWOOD OCEANICS, INC., a dredging and deep-sea drilling company, included the following information:

<u>ATWOOD OCEANICS, INC.</u>   (*in thousands*)

Financial Statement Data: September 30 year-end	2014	2013
From the Balance Sheets and Footnotes:		
Property and equipment at cost	$ 4,568,153	$ 3,746,005
Accumulated depreciation	(601,125)	(581,281)
From the Statements of Operations:		
Depreciation expense	$ 147,358	$ 117,510
From the Cash Flow Statements – Investing Activities:		
Expenditures for property and equipment	$ 975,731	$ 745,223

Note that the 2014 increase in accumulated depreciation of $19,844 ($601,125 minus $581,281) was less than the depreciation expense for 2014 ($147,358). This indicates that equipment with accumulated depreciation on it was disposed of during 2014. If we put this information into the T-account framework, we can compute some additional information about ATWOOD'S 2014 transactions (remember that the numbers in bold are forced numbers):

Property & Equipment (A)		Accumulated Depreciation: Property & Equipment (XA)		Depreciation Expense (E)	
BB 3,746,005			BB 581,281		
Increases	*Decreases*	*Decreases*	*Increases*	*Increases*	
(1) 975,731	(3)**153,583**	(3) **127,514**	(2) 147,358	(2) 147,358	
EB 4,568,153			EB 601,125		

This analysis suggests that ATWOOD sold equipment with an original cost of $153,583 that had accumulated depreciation of $127,514. This tells us that this equipment was 83% depreciated ($127,514 ÷ $153,583 = 0.83) at the time of disposal. Notice that Atwood invested over $975 million in new PP&E during 2014 while disposing of PP&E that originally cost $153 million which could indicate that the company is growing.

Measuring Total Asset Turnover

The **total asset turnover** ratio is used to evaluate the overall efficiency of a business. It is defined as follows:

$$\text{Total asset turnover} = \frac{\textbf{Revenue}}{\textbf{Average total assets}}$$

This ratio looks at the relationship between revenues and total assets and is based on the premise that more assets should generate more revenue. Greater efficiency in asset utilization can be obtained by either increasing revenue without increasing assets (e.g., greater sales per store) or by decreasing assets without decreasing revenue (e.g., the same sales with fewer stores). Efficiency is also achieved when the percentage increase in revenue is greater than the percentage increase in total assets or when the percentage decrease in revenue is less than the percentage decrease in total assets.

To illustrate the total asset turnover ratio, consider the total asset turnover ratio for UNITED STATES STEEL CORPORATION (U.S. STEEL). The total revenue for U.S. STEEL for 2014 was $17,507 million and the average of their total assets was $12,729 million [($12,314 + $13,143)/2]. The total asset turnover ratio is computed as shown below:

$$\text{Total asset turnover} = \frac{\$17,507}{\$12,729}$$

$$= 1.38$$

Companies like U.S. STEEL require a great deal of investment in productive assets to generate revenue, and the total asset turnover ratio can be very low, with sales not much higher than the average amount of total assets on a regular basis. In other industries, the total asset turnover ratio is much higher. For example, consider THE KROGER CO., a major grocery store chain operating under several different names. For the same fiscal year, KROGER reported sales of $108,465 million and average total assets of only $29,919 million, for a turnover ratio of 3.63 times sales, over 2 1/2 times that of U.S. STEEL. So KROGER generated $3.63 of sales for every $1 invested in assets, U.S. STEEL only had $1.38 in sales for every $1 invested in assets. These ratios tell us a lot about the structure of these companies and their industries and how efficiently their assets are used.

LONG-TERM ASSETS AND DECISION MAKING

This chapter has explained the GAAP measurement and reporting requirements for long-term assets. An overriding limitation of the results of these requirements is that they do not provide users with the most useful information for decision making. The historical cost based measurements are frequently poor approximations of fair values desired by decision makers. However, understanding the nature of the existing measurement methods actually enables sophisticated users to prepare their own independent estimates of the fair value of long-term assets. Estimating the fair values of long-term assets goes beyond the scope of this introductory text. However understanding that there is a limitation is an important step in effectively using accounting information for decision making. Consider the GAAP-based historical cost amounts reported by the following two companies:

	Company A	*Company B*
Plant and equipment	$ 900,000	$ 450,000
Less accumulated depreciation	(90,000)	(360,000)
Net plant and equipment	$ 810,000	$ 90,000

It appears as though Company A has significantly more assets than Company B. But if we understand GAAP measurements we realize that this may not be true! In fact, Company B may have the same or more plant "capacity" than Company A. We can safely assume that Company B purchased its plant and equipment years ago when prices for "capacity" were much less than today. This assumption is consistent with the fact that assets of Company A are only 10% depreciated (i.e., mostly newer), while Company B's assets are 80% depreciated (mostly old)! As with most durable productive assets, we should expect that the newer assets of Company A were more costly than those of Company B. Armed with these simple observations based on our knowledge from this chapter, we should be able to make better decisions related to comparisons between companies. We would expect the depreciation expense per unit of capacity would be more for Company A. If, in fact, the two companies had similar capacity, we might expect this lower depreciation expense for Company B to result in higher profits, all else being equal. Would this actually make Company B better off?

These insights illustrate how simply understanding the limitation of GAAP-based financial statements can help lead to better decision making.

INTERNATIONAL FINANCIAL REPORTING STANDARDS

The reporting requirements and accounting procedures discussed in this chapter would be impacted in the following ways by a change to IFRS:

Tangible Assets   There are two differences in the treatment of property, plant and equipment (PP&E) under IFRS. First, IAS 16, *Property, Plant and Equipment*, allows these assets to be revalued to their current market value on a voluntary basis while GAAP does not allow revaluations of PP&E above their depreciated historical cost. Under IFRS, if revaluations are made, they must be made for *all* assets in the same class (e.g., all machinery or land), and the revaluations must be conducted with sufficient frequency that the reported value at each balance sheet date approximates the fair value of the class of assets that has been revalued. In practice, revaluations are not common, and are seldom, if ever, observed except for land. Note that revaluation of land will increase the reported amount of total assets and shareholders' equity by the difference between original cost and current market value, but it will not impact income measurement since land is not depreciated.

Second, IAS 16 also requires that when the residual (salvage) value of a depreciable asset is a material amount, the **current** residual value of the asset must be estimated at each balance sheet date.[10] If the current residual value is greater than the book value of the depreciable asset(s), no depreciation expense would be recorded on those assets. This requirement of periodically revaluing the residual value of assets could have the effect of changing the amount of depreciation expense on an asset or class of assets each year, without changing the depreciation method.

Intangible Assets   Again, there are two differences in the measurement of intangibles under IFRS. First, GAAP requires that research and development expenditures be expensed in the period incurred, while IFRS requires that development (but not research) expenditures be capitalized once specific criteria have been met. The main features of these criteria are that the development costs will result in a benefit to the company and that the company will see the project through to its completion. This difference would permit technology-based companies that follow IFRS to report greater amounts for assets from self-developed intangibles than would be possible under GAAP. The larger intangible asset balances under IFRS would be offset by larger Retained Earnings balances. A larger Retained Earnings balance would represent the cumulative difference in R&D expense under IFRS vs. GAAP.

A second difference in accounting for intangibles is in how goodwill is tested for impairment. GAAP requires a revaluation of the current fair value of the identifiable net assets of the business unit associated with the goodwill as well as an estimate of the fair value of the business unit taken as a whole in order to measure the impairment, if any, in goodwill. Hence, GAAP essentially requires a revaluation of the business unit that is as detailed as the valuation made at the time of acquisition. IFRS only requires an estimate of the fair value of the business unit taken as a whole. If the fair value of the business unit taken as a whole has decreased, the decline is assumed to be

---

[10] IFRS 16 defines residual value as the value the entity would *currently* expect to receive for the depreciable asset if it was at the point in its useful life when it would normally be disposed of by the entity. By estimating the *current* residual value, IAS 16 (in theory) avoids requiring a forecast of future residual values, which are not verifiable.

from the value of goodwill, and the impairment charge would be equal to the decline in the fair value. While not always the case, it will generally be true that the impairment charges for goodwill under GAAP will be greater than those required by IFRS. This difference shows that IFRS are somewhat more liberal than GAAP.

There are numerous subtle differences between US GAAP and IFRS involving the measurement of all long-lived assets. While both sets of standards have an overriding test for "impairment" in order to not allow assets to be reported at more than their fair value, differences may result from the application of the same or similar impairment procedures. More advanced study is necessary before one can obtain a reasonably precise estimate of differences in long-term assets due to differences in GAAP.

SUMMARY

Long-term assets result from investing activities. These assets provide the profit-making capability of the business. One analogy you can use in thinking about long-term assets is engines and horsepower. The long-term assets are like an engine and profits are like the horsepower provided by the engine. The goal is to achieve as much horsepower with as small an engine as possible to generate the maximum efficiency (profit per dollar of investment). Growth of a business through additional investments will typically come from the long-term assets that generate the most profit per dollar invested (most horsepower per cubic inch of engine displacement).

The measurement issues that impact both tangible and intangible assets represent significant limitations to the relevance of accounting information for long-term assets. These assets are measured using the historical cost principle and, with the exception of land and indefinite life intangibles, their original historical cost is allocated to the periods of benefit. The allocation of the original cost of long-term assets to the income statement over time is conceptually the same for all wasting assets. Although the terms *depreciation expense*, *depletion expense*, and *amortization expense* are used for productive assets, natural resources, and finite life intangible assets respectively, they all represent methods of systematically allocating an asset's original cost to the periods of benefit. Since the original cost seldom represents the fair value of these assets over the years beyond their original acquisition, we should understand two important implications: 1) the annual expense (i.e., depreciation, amortization, etc.) related to these long-term assets does NOT measure the value actually consumed during the period; and 2) the net book value of these long-term assets reported in the balance sheet does NOT represent an estimate of their fair value.

KEY TERMS

150%-declining balance method   Accelerated depreciation method applying 150% of the straight-line rate to the book value of the asset. *7*

accelerated depreciation methods   Rapid depreciation methods that expense the amount more rapidly than the straight-line method over the same time period; examples are *150%-declining balance*, *double-declining balance*, and *sum-of-the-years'-digits methods*. *5, 6*

accumulated depreciation/depletion/amortization   Total cumulative amount of depreciation, depletion, or amortization expense taken in all prior periods. *4*

acquisition cost   Any cost that is necessary and reasonable to place the asset into its intended useful state. Also called *cost* or *original cost*. *2*

amortization   Process of allocating the cost of an intangible asset to expense over its useful life; only used for intangible assets that have a finite life. *15, 16*

amortization expense   A systematic charge of the cost of an intangible asset to its periods of use; serves the same purpose as depreciation expense. *15, 16*

book value   Original cost minus accumulated depreciation/depletion/amortization. Compare to *fair market value* and *recoverable value*. Also, more generally, the value of an item in the accounting records; also called *net book value*. *5*

brand name   Intangible asset with an indefinite life; also called *trade name*. *14, 19*

capital expenditures   Expenditures that are added to the cost of an existing asset because they are expected to improve the usefulness or extend the life of the original asset. *10*

change in estimate   When new information suggests that the estimate used to measure an asset should be revised; the change impacts operating income in the current and future periods only; it is applied to the book value of the asset at the beginning of the period of change. *19, 20*

copyright   Intangible asset with a finite life—the exclusive usage right of the creator for his or her lifetime plus 70 years. This applies to books, movies, and other creative endeavors. *15, 19*

declining-balance methods   Class of accelerated depreciation methods that apply a percentage between 100% and 200% of the straight-line depreciation rate to the book value of an asset. *7*

depletion (depletion rate)   Process of allocating the cost of a natural resource to expense; generally computed using the units-of-production method. *13*

depletion expense   Expensing a natural resource in a way that is similar to *depreciation* and *amortization*. *13*

depreciable base   The amount of the asset's original cost to be expensed over its life; cost minus salvage value. *4*

depreciation   Cost allocation methods that systematically assign the original cost of a long-term productive asset to the periods of use in a pattern that approximates how the usefulness of the asset is consumed; common methods include straight-line, sum-of-years'-digits, and the declining-balance methods. *4, 6*

depreciation expense   The amount of the original asset cost charged to the income statement in each period; represents the amount of usage of the asset for the period. *4*

double-declining balance method   Accelerated depreciation method applying 200% of the straight-line rate to the book value of the asset. *5-7*

fair market value   An impartial value of what an item is worth to someone else in a market exchange. Also called *fair value*. *9*

finite life intangibles   Intangible assets that can be expected to provide value to the company only over a restricted time period; the time period usually is determined by law (e.g., a patent has a finite life determined by the laws of the country in which the patent is held). *15, 19*

franchise   Intangible asset arising from an agreement to sell a specific product or service; indefinite or finite life intangible asset depending on the contract. *14, 19*

goodwill   The previously unrecorded assets (e.g., scientific talent) of an acquired company recognized as an intangible asset by the acquiring company at the time of purchase; computed as the difference between the price paid for a company and the fair market value of the identifiable net assets acquired; indefinite life intangible not amortized but subject to annual impairment tests. *16-19*

identifiable intangible assets   Specifically identifiable items that have a cost and have future value to the business; can be accounted for as assets such as *patents* and *copyrights*. *14, 19*

impairment   A write down that is required when the recoverable value or fair market value of an asset is less than its book value. *9, 16*

indefinite life intangibles   Intangible assets that are assumed to not be used up in the generation of revenues. These assets must be tested for impairment each year and written down if their *book value* exceeds their *fair market value* or *recoverable value*. *14, 19*

intangible assets   Assets whose value is based on what they represent rather than what they physically are (e.g. patents, goodwill). *2, 14-19*

internally created intangibles   Intangibles providing value to the creating company (e.g. Patents, copyrights, and trademarks); usually recorded at a nominal amount (legal filing fees) relative to their fair (market) value. *14*

license   Intangible asset granting use or permission usually for a finite time. *15, 19*

long-term assets   Those assets providing value to a company over an extended period of time, including tangible and intangible assets; also called *noncurrent assets*. *1*

natural resources   Tangible "wasting" assets that come from nature and are consumed, (e.g. coal, iron, timberlands, etc.). *2, 12-14*

net book value   See book value. *8*

partial-year depreciation   Measured using a daily, nearest month, or half-year approach when assets are bought or sold during the year. *7-8*

patent   Intangible asset with a finite life; the exclusive right to use a product or process for a period of 20 years. *15, 19*

permit   Intangible asset granting use or permission of value to the business, usually granted for a finite time. *15*

productive assets   Long-term tangible assets used in the operation of the business such as machinery, equipment, buildings, and vehicles. *2*

purchased intangibles   Intangible assets obtained from another entity; recorded at their acquisition cost. *14, 19*

recoverable value   The value of a long-term asset that is expected to be received from use; it is compared to book value to determine if impairment has occurred. *8*

replacement cost   The current cost to acquire the asset with similar wear and tear. *9*

research and development (R&D)   Expenditures to develop new or improved products or services; charged to expense as incurred and not capitalized as a long-term asset. *15*

salvage value   The estimated remaining market value of an asset after the completion of its useful life to the business; also called *residual value*. *3*

straight-line method   A method of depreciation that assigns an equal fraction of the original cost less salvage value of an asset to each period of use. *4, 6-7*

sum-of-the-years'-digits method   Accelerated depreciation method that determines expense by first computing the sum of the years' digits, then each year takes the remaining years of useful life at the start of the year divided by the sum of the years' digits and multiplies this fraction by the amount to be depreciated (original cost minus salvage value). *5-7*

tangible assets   Assets whose value is attributed to their physical substance (e.g. productive assets, land, and natural resources). *2*

total asset turnover ratio   Used to evaluate the overall efficiency of the business; sales divided by average total assets. *22-23*

trademark Word or symbol used to identify a product or company; generally an intangible asset with an indefinite life. *14, 19*

unidentifiable intangible assets Intangible assets that are not separately identifiable; goodwill is the only unidentifiable intangible asset. *16-19*

units-of-production method A method of depreciation and depletion that assigns the cost of the long-term asset to income on the basis of the units produced or quantity of asset used relative to an estimated total number of units/quantity. *8*

useful life Estimated amount of time or use that a long-term asset is expect to provide benefit to the firm. *3, 20*

APPENDIX

Long-term Assets and Income Taxes

As noted in Chapter 5, income tax accounting methods will generally differ from the methods and measures used for financial reporting. In this chapter we considered three different classes of assets:

1. Tangible assets, which (except for land) are depreciated;
2. Intangible assets, some of which are amortized; and
3. Natural resources, which are depleted.

Tangible Assets

For income tax purposes, it is common for the allowable depreciable life and method of depreciation to be more aggressive than for financial reporting purposes. The U.S. income tax code generally allows companies to use a depreciable life that is shorter than the real economic life of an asset. This means that many assets that are still being used and depreciated for financial reporting purposes may be fully depreciated for income tax purposes. Because money has more value today than it will a year from today, companies usually have an incentive to minimize their income tax obligations each year. This leads to using the shorter useful life allowed by the tax code whenever possible.

The tax code also allows accelerated depreciation methods for income tax reporting. One of the most common methods used in the tax code is the declining balance method. There are cases where the rules are written to permit the double-declining balance method for an asset over 5 years, while the same asset might be depreciated on a straight-line basis over 8-10 years for financial reporting purposes. These differences are common and should be expected in practice.

Intangible Assets

In general, amortization taken for income tax purposes is similar to depreciation. Various kinds of assets will have specific amortization periods and patterns permitted by the tax code that differ from the usual periods and patterns commonly used in financial reporting.

Natural Resources

Depletion of natural resources is an area where the tax laws allow differences from the cost principle. *In general*, both income tax accounting and financial reporting allow a business to write off only the cost of an asset as an expense. **However,** with natural resources, companies may actually take a tax expense that *exceeds the cost* of the natural resource for certain types of resources!

Taxes and Decision Making

Aside from the LIFO-conformity rule discussed in Chapter 5, there is no necessary link between income tax accounting and financial reporting. However, since the tax laws impact the amount of income tax a company must pay, which is a cash flow requirement, taxes may be a relevant part of making business decisions. In fact, many decisions are made only after considering the "after-tax" consequences of the action.

For example, assume a company is considering buying a machine that would cost $5,000. Before considering this decision the company has taxable income of $30,000. Assume the $5,000 cost of the machine may be deducted for income tax purposes in the current year, and that the income tax rate is 40%. The following comparison shows the **after-tax cost of the machine is only $3,000** ($5,000 – $2,000 income tax savings).

	Do not Purchase Machine	Purchase Machine
Taxable income before machine	$ 30,000	$ 30,000
Less machine deduction	– 0	5,000
Taxable income	$ 30,000	$ 25,000
Times tax rate of 40%	x 40%	x 40%
Income tax due	$ 12,000	$ 10,000

The tax consequences of business decisions are important and we should not ignore them. However, the tax effects of financial reporting are only of secondary interest to our objectives in this text which is why we will not discuss this tax-related topic in greater detail.

Income Taxes and Financial Reporting Rules

This textbook examines the foundations of financial reporting and analysis, which is governed by a generally accepted set of rules (e.g., GAAP or IFRS). These rules are logically related to a framework whose overall objective is to provide relevant information to external users for business decision-making purposes. Understanding the general objective and framework of financial accounting allows us to form expectations about the nature and purpose of financial statement information, even when we do not know the exact rule that governs that data. On the other hand, income tax accounting is very different. In the U.S., the tax code has been developed largely as a social-economic tool that is governed by politicians and frequently influenced by contemporary economic goals, or needs, or even political trends. While income tax laws have an impact on the cash flows of both business entities and individuals, we should understand that determining the amount of income tax in any given period is not based on a logical framework, making analysis more difficult. It is not uncommon for analysts to use pretax income measures from the GAAP-based financial statements to minimize the "noise" created by income taxes. Chapter 7 will deal further with the differences between GAAP and income tax rules.

Review Questions

Test your understanding of the material covered in the chapter by answering the following questions. The correct answers to these questions are shown below.

1. A delivery truck with a 12-year useful life and a $6,000 salvage value was acquired on January 1, 2007 at a cost of $45,000. The straight-line method was used to record depreciation. The truck was sold on January 1, 2014 for $23,500. What amount of gain or loss resulted from the sale of this asset?

    a. A gain of $4,750.
    b. A gain of $1,250.
    c. A loss of $4,750.
    d. A loss of $1,250.

2. In 2013, a machine was acquired for a cash price of $871,200. The machine has an estimated salvage value of $39,600, and it was being depreciated using the units-of-production method and an estimated useful life of 180,000 units. During 2013, 30,000 units were produced on the machine. During 2014 a $79,800 capital expenditure was made to the machine that increased the useful life of the machine by 60,000 units. The salvage value remains the same. What is the new depreciation rate on this machine?

    a. $3.46 per unit.
    b. $2.90 per unit.
    c. $3.68 per unit.
    d. $3.30 per unit.

3. At December 31, 2013, the balances in Equipment and Accumulated Depreciation were $993,300 and $369,600, respectively. At December 31, 2014, the balances were $1,094,400 and $441,800, respectively. Depreciation expense for the year was $89,500 and equipment with a book value of $25,900 was sold. How much equipment was acquired in 2014?

    a. $144,300
    b. $219,600
    c. $101,100
    d. $199,200

Answers: b., c., a.

PROBLEMS

6-1 Long-term Assets

1. Describe the types of costs included in the acquisition cost of a long-term asset. How is that similar to topics you have studied earlier in the course? Differentiate between purchased and self-constructed long-term assets.
2. Explain why the cost of interest is included in the cost of a self-constructed asset during construction but not once the asset is utilized in operations.
3. Describe what determines the depreciation method a firm uses. Differentiate the three methods (straight-line, sum-of-the-years'-digits, declining-balance) noting similarities and differences.
4. Explain why changes in estimated life and salvage value are not made retroactive to the date of acquisition.
5. Define capital expenditures including the judgment factors used to determine whether an item is a capital expenditure or not.
6. Describe the economic impact on the firm of a long-term asset disposal.
7. Provide several examples of identifiable long-term intangibles. How do they differ from unidentifiable long-term intangibles? Provide the example of an unidentifiable intangible asset.
8. Why are impairment tests required of long-term assets?
9. Given a list of asset turnover ratios, which one would you expect to apply to a grocery store? A bridge construction firm? Why?
10. Describe the differences in accounting for long-term assets under GAAP and IFRS.
11. List and explain two inherent challenges presented in accounting for long-term tangible and intangible assets.

6-2 Business Decision Case

As a new internal auditor, you have been assigned a project to evaluate the performance of two mattress-producing plants owned and operated by your parent company. The Cincinnati plant is the newest mattress-producing plant in the U.S., with the most automation and the least amount of labor of any such production facility in the country. It began operations in 2014 and has been producing with near zero defects since the start of operations. The plant in Louisville has a similar capacity to the Cincinnati plant. It has been in operation since 1990 and was bought by your parent company in 1999. The plant manager for Louisville has been in the industry for over 30 years. While the plant is not nearly as automated as Cincinnati, it has produced without significant disruption to production and without the aid of any significant capital expenditures, repairs or replacements for the past decade.

Unfortunately, both plants have been operating at well below capacity due to the reduced demand for new mattresses. Your evaluation of their performance will be used to consider closing down one of the two plants on a temporary basis.

The following brief financial overview of the two plants is provided to you.

($ amounts in millions)	Cincinnati 2015	Cincinnati 2016	Louisville 2015	Louisville 2016
Current assets	$19	$18	$20	$21
Non-current assets	$135	$134	$47	$47
Current liabilities	$10	$10	$10	$11
Interest bearing debt	$100	$99	$13	$12
Revenues	$360	$340	$345	$325
Operating profits	$9	$5	$12	$10

Required:

1. Using the information provided and your understanding from the chapter of long-term tangible assets:
    a. Identify any points in favor of closing down the Cincinnati plant.
    b. Identify any points in favor of closing down the Louisville plant.
2. Describe additional information (qualitative or quantitative) that you would like to have before sending through your final report.

6-3 Acquisition Costs

The following costs were incurred to acquire, install, and operate new machinery:

a.	Delivery charges	$ 19,200
b.	Labor required to install the machinery..................	1,100
c.	Labor to operate the machinery for the first year	66,000
d.	Maintenance for the first year of operation	5,000
e.	Materials required to install the machinery	5,600
f.	Materials used during the first year of operation.....	60,000
g.	Purchase price..	605,400
h.	Sales tax on the purchase price...............................	36,300

Required:

1. Determine the acquisition cost of the machinery.
2. Describe the principle that helped you calculate the acquisition cost.
3. If the firm chose to self-construct the machine, provide examples of the costs that would most likely be incurred and considered part of the machine's acquisition cost.

6-4 Acquisition Costs

In anticipation of having a new headquarters building constructed, a parcel of land is being prepared as a building site. The site currently has an old factory on it that will have to be demolished before the new headquarters can be built. The following information is available concerning recent actions for the building site and the current headquarters building:

a.	Purchase price of the land and factory	$1,000,000
b.	Real estate finder's fee for the site......................................	25,000
c.	Depreciation on the current headquarters building	15,000
d.	Real estate taxes on the current headquarters building	27,000
e.	Cost of a road needed by the equipment that will demolish the factory..	6,000
f.	Cost to demolish the factory	42,000
g.	Real estate taxes on the land for the first year	6,300
h.	Attorney's fees related to the pending sale of the current headquarters building...	3,500

The road for the demolition equipment is temporary and of value during the construction phase. The firm intends for the new headquarters building to be occupied within 18 months.

Required:

1. Determine the acquisition cost of the building site.
2. Describe the principle that helped you calculate the acquisition cost.
3. Explain why the other costs listed above were not included and how you would suggest they be treated in the accounting records.

6-5 Depreciation (Full Year)

A new computer system was acquired on January 1, 2013. The system cost $474,000, has a 5-year useful life, and has an $18,000 salvage value.

Required:

1. Determine the computer system's depreciable base.
2. Compute depreciation expense for 2013 and 2014 using the straight-line method, as well as the accumulated depreciation and the book value at December 31, 2014.
3. Compute depreciation expense for 2013 and 2014 using the sum-of-years'-digits method, as well as the accumulated depreciation and the book value at December 31, 2014.
4. Compute depreciation expense for 2013 and 2014 using the double-declining balance method, as well as the accumulated depreciation and the book value at December 31, 2014.
5. Describe the similarities and the differences among the three methods.

6-6 Depreciation (Partial Year)

On June 1, 2013 some equipment was acquired for $874,800. The equipment has an expected useful life of 9 years and a salvage value of 10% of cost.

Required:

1. Determine the equipment's depreciable base.
2. Compute depreciation expense for 2013 and 2014 using the straight-line method, as well as accumulated depreciation and book value at December 31, 2014.
3. Compute depreciation expense for 2013 and 2014 using the sum-of-years'-digits method, as well as accumulated depreciation and book value at December 31, 2014.
4. Compute depreciation expense for 2013 and 2014 using the double-declining balance method, as well as accumulated depreciation and book value at December 31, 2014.
5. Describe the similarities and the differences among the three methods.

6-7 Depreciation (Partial Year)

On May 1, 2013, a truck was acquired. The truck cost $78,400, has a $2,800 salvage value, and is expected to be driven 140,000 miles over its 7-year useful life. The truck was driven 12,000 miles in 2013 and 20,000 miles in 2014.

Required:

1. Compute depreciation expense for 2013 and 2014 using the units-of-production method, and compute the book value of the truck at December 31, 2014. Do you need to calculate a partial year's depreciation for 2013? Why or why not?
2. Compute depreciation expense for 2013 and 2014 using the 150%-declining balance method, and compute the book value of the truck at December 31, 2014.
3. Assume on June 30, 2015, after driving 12,000 more miles, the truck is sold for $50,000. Update the depreciation records and record the disposal of the truck under each method. Round to the nearest dollar, if necessary.

6-8 Change in Estimate

A company reported $1,362,400 of pre-tax income in 2014, a 30% increase from the $1,048,000 reported in 2013. The Notes to the Financial Statements contained the following item:

Footnote: *In 2014, the company revised the estimated useful life of $21,000,000 of machinery from 10 years to 15 years.*

Required:

1. Compute the amount of pre-tax income the company would have reported for 2014 had it not revised the estimated useful life of the machinery.
2. Compute the percentage increase or decrease in pre-tax income the company would have reported from 2013 to 2014 if it had continued to use the original useful life of the machinery.
3. In your role as a financial analyst, you have been asked to write a brief memo to explain the increase in the company's net income from 2013 to 2014. Prepare a draft of the memo.

6-9 Costs Subsequent to Acquisition

A machine was acquired on January 1, 2010. The machine cost $154,000, has a 9-year useful life, a $5,500 salvage value, and is being depreciated on the straight-line basis. During 2014 the following expenditures were made in connection with this machine:

Annual maintenance on the machine	$ 6,000
Capital improvement on the machine	$45,000
Installation of the capital improvement	$12,000
Labor costs to operate the machine during the current year	$96,000

The capital improvement was installed on January 1, 2014, and it extended the useful life of the machine by an additional 7 years but reduced the salvage value to zero.

Required:

1. Determine the machine's book value at December 31, 2013.
2. Compute the new straight-line depreciation rate for this machine for 2014 and all subsequent years.
3. Compute the book value of this machine at December 31, 2014.
4. Explain why you capitalized the expenditures that you did on January 1, 2014.

6-10 Costs Subsequent to Acquisition

The following transactions related to plant and equipment occurred during the current year. All amounts were paid in cash.

a. Painted the interior of the warehouse at a cost of $27,600.
b. Built an addition to the warehouse for more inventory storage at a cost of $108,300.
c. Repaired the roof of the office building that had been damaged in a storm at a cost of $890.
d. Purchased two new electric motors for production machines at a cost of $63,500. These motors will enable the machines to do more work.
e. Cleaned the carpeting in the office building at a cost of $3,700.
f. Added walls to the entrance of the office building to improve customer traffic flow at a cost of $76,200.

Required:

For each item a. through f. above, identify the item as either a capital expenditure or a maintenance expense. Explain your reasoning for each one using Exhibit 6-4 as a guide.

6-11   Costs Subsequent to Acquisition and Disposal

Equipment was acquired on October 1, 2003 at a cost of $110,000. The equipment was originally expected to have a 15-year useful life and a $2,000 salvage value. The straight-line method of depreciation is used. The following events occurred in recent years:

    a. The equipment was improved at a cost of $23,250 on January 1, 2013. This improvement extended the useful life of the asset by 5 years and reduced the salvage value to zero.

    b. The equipment was sold for cash on June 30, 2014 at a gain of $5,200.

Required:

1. Compute the book value of this equipment at December 31, 2012 (immediately prior to the installation of the improvement).
2. Compute the amount of depreciation expense recorded on the equipment for 2013.
3. Compute the amount of cash that was received from the sale of the equipment on June 30, 2014. Support your answer with the journal entry necessary to record the sale.

6-12   Disposal of Depreciable Assets

Two used assets were disposed of during 2014. The details relating to these assets are as follows:

Asset #1: A building acquired on May 20, 2008 for $6,100,000. This building was being depreciated using the straight-line method, a $1,141,000 salvage value, and a 15-year useful life. The building was sold on January 1, 2014 for $3,200,000.

Asset #2: An aircraft acquired on January 1, 2012 for $2,835,000. This aircraft was being depreciated using the double-declining balance method, a $500,000 salvage value, and a 6-year useful life. The aircraft was sold on April 11, 2014 for cash, and a gain of $45,000 resulted from this transaction.

Required:

1. Determine the gain or loss that resulted from the sale of Asset #1. Support your answer with calculations including the journal entry to record the disposal.
2. Compute the amount of cash that was received from the sale of Asset #2. Support your answer with calculations including the journal entry to record the disposal.
3. Describe the impact on the balance sheet equation from the sale of each asset.

6-13 Effect of Errors

On January 1, 2014, two transactions related to machinery occurred. The transactions and the entries made to record the transactions were:

1. Maintenance on Machine A was performed at a cost of $9,600; the entry to record this transaction was a debit to the Machine A asset account and a credit to Cash for $9,600. Machine A has three years remaining on its useful life and has zero salvage value.

2. A capital expenditure was made to Machine B at a cost of $21,000. This expenditure increased the capacity of the machine to do work but did not increase its useful life. Machine B has a current book value of $120,000, a remaining useful life of three years, and zero salvage value. The entry to record this transaction was a debit to Maintenance Expense and a credit to Cash for $21,000.

Depreciation on both machines is recorded using the straight-line method.

Required:

1. Explain why the journal entries in each transaction were incorrect.
2. Prepare the correct journal entry for each machine and contrast with the journal entries that were made.
3. Determine the effect error 1. had on assets and shareholders' equity at December 31, 2014, 2015, and 2016, and on net income for the fiscal years 2014 through 2016 (ignore income taxes).
4. Determine the effect error 2. had on assets, shareholders' equity at December 31, 2014, 2015, and 2016, and on net income for the fiscal years 2014 through 2016 (ignore income taxes).

6-14 Depletion of Natural Resources – ALCOA

ALCOA, INC., the world's leading producer and fabricator of aluminum, operates a bauxite mine in Clarendon, Jamaica. Assume ALCOA acquired the rights to this mine in 2013 for $48,000,000 and spent an additional $5,080,000 preparing the mine for use. The mine is expected to produce 3,800,000 tons of bauxite over its life and the salvage value of the land is expected to be $3,300,000 once the bauxite has been removed. In 2013, 545,000 tons of bauxite were removed from the mine and 735,000 tons of bauxite were removed in 2014.

Required:

1. Compute the depletion rate per ton of bauxite for this mine and accumulated depletion at December 31, 2014.
2. Assume that in January 2015, ALCOA spent $1,168,000 on a survey that discovered that an additional 80,000 tons of bauxite are recoverable from the mine. The salvage value of the land has increased to $4,200,000. Compute the new depletion rate per ton for this mine.

6-15 Change in Estimate

A freight company has a fleet of five trucks. When these trucks were originally purchased in mid-2003, they cost $270,000 each; and each truck had a life expectancy of 1.5 million miles and no salvage value. At the end of 2013, the average mileage on each of these five trucks had reached 1.25 million miles. On March 23, 2014 these trucks were evaluated; and it was estimated that if maintenance is continued to be performed on the trucks they will actually be useful for an average of 2.0 million miles—0.5 million miles more than originally estimated. Each truck is estimated to have no salvage value after the 2.0 million miles.

Required:

1. Compute the original units-of-production depreciation rate per mile used for each of these trucks.
2. Determine the total book value of the trucks at the end of 2013 using the average mileage and the units-of-production depreciation method.
3. Compute the new units-of-production depreciation rate to be used for the trucks during 2014.
4. Assume the trucks travel an average of 95,000 miles during 2014. Compute the depreciation expense for the five trucks for 2014 as well as the accumulated depreciation and book value at December 31, 2014.

6-16 Analyzing Reported Amounts

The following balances and footnote related were reported at December 31, 2014:

Balance Sheet data:	**2014**	**2013**
Equipment	$527,600	$518,200
Accumulated depreciation	314,200	300,400
Net equipment	$213,400	$217,800
Income Statement data:		
Depreciation expense	$ 16,100	$ 15,800

Footnote: *Equipment is depreciated using the straight-line method assuming a zero salvage value. In 2014, new equipment was acquired and old equipment with a book value of $8,500 was sold for cash. A gain of $6,000 resulted from the sale of the old equipment.*

Required:

1. Set up the three related T-accounts with the beginning, ending and adjusted balances.
2. Compute the cost of the old equipment that was sold during 2014.
3. Compute the cost of the new equipment that was acquired during 2014.
4. Compute the amount of cash received from the sale of the old equipment.
5. Compute the average age of the equipment at December 31, 2014.
6. Compute the percent of the useful life of the equipment that remains at December 31, 2014.
7. Describe the economic impact on the firm from the purchase of the new equipment and the disposal of the old equipment.

6-17 Analyzing Reported Amounts – DEERE & COMPANY

DEERE & COMPANY, the manufacturer of farm and lawn equipment, reported the following information in footnote 16 regarding property and equipment in its 2014 annual report.

At October 31 (*in millions of dollars*)

Equipment Operations	2014		2013	
Land...	$	120	$	123
Buildings & equipment		3,037		2,875
Machinery & equipment.................		5,089		4,931
Dies, patterns, tools, etc.................		1,552		1,492
Other depreciable assets		889		866
Construction in process		530		728
Total at cost	$	11,217	$	11,015
Less accumulated depreciation.......		5,694		5,606
Property & equipment - net	$	5,523	$	5,409

Financial Services				
Land...	$	4	$	4
Buildings & equipment		71		71
All other depreciable assets		37		36
Total at cost	$	112	$	111
Less accumulated depreciation.......		57		53
Property & equipment - net	$	55	$	58

Total property & equipment, net	**$ 5,578**		**$ 5,467**	

From the other information given in the footnote the following data were noted combining Equipment Operations and Financial Services:

Depreciation expense for 2014	$696 million
Additions to property & equipment in 2014	$1,016 million

Required: (Note: *Combine the equipment operations and financial services amounts for this problem.*)

1. Compute the original cost of property and equipment disposed of during 2014 and the amount of accumulated depreciation on the property and equipment disposed of during 2014.
2. Compute the net book value of the assets disposed of during 2014.
3. Compute the amount of <u>depreciable</u> assets at October 31, 2014 at cost less accumulated depreciation (= net depreciable assets).
4. Assume that the fair market value of DEERE's depreciable assets is 45% higher than their reported original cost less accumulated depreciation (see your answer to Requirement 3 above) at October 31, 2014. Discuss the implications of this fact for the GAAP-based measurement of:
   a. Reported total assets; and
   b. Reported net income.

6-18 Transactions Involving Long-term Assets

A table in the Property, Plant, and Equipment (PP&E) footnote in the December 31, 2013 balance sheet reported the following details:

	2013	2012
Land...	$ 200,000	$ 200,000
Office building	3,200,000	3,200,000
Less accumulated depreciation...................	(1,875,000)	(1,687,500)
Warehouse..	1,300,000	1,300,000
Less accumulated depreciation...................	(910,000)	(780,000)
Equipment	7,470,000	7,470,000
Less accumulated depreciation...................	(3,320,000)	(2,490,000)
Property, plant, and equipment, net..............	$6,065,000	$7,212,500

During 2014, the following transactions related to PP&E occurred:

a. Reported uninsured damage to the office building: several windows were broken, and $8,900 was paid to repair the damage.

b. Sold the warehouse for $750,000 on January 1, 2014, receiving $700,000 in cash and a note receivable for the remainder.

c. Performed annual maintenance and repairs on the equipment at a cost of $35,000, paying cash.

d. Completed an addition to the office building on January 1, 2014 at a cost of $235,000. The addition will last only as long as the remaining life of the building (see item e. below), but it increased the salvage value of the building to $300,000. The $235,000 was paid in cash.

e. Recorded the annual straight-line depreciation on the office building on December 31, 2014. The building had been acquired on January 1, 2004 and was originally being depreciated over a 16-year useful life with an original salvage value of $200,000.

f. Recorded the annual straight-line depreciation on the equipment on December 31, 2014. The equipment was acquired on January 1, 2010 and has zero salvage value.

Required:

1. For each item a. through f. above, prepare the journal entry that was made to record the transaction in the accounting records.
2. Prepare the PP&E footnote table at December 31, 2014.

6-19 Goodwill and Intangibles—ORACLE CORPORATION

In 2011 one of the largest acquisitions in recent times took place when ORACLE CORPORATION acquired SUN MICROSYSTEMS for about $7.3 billion. This case illustrates several concepts that are discussed in the chapter. Like the acquisition of Compaq Computer by Hewett-Packard (HP) given in the chapter, this case provides you with the information needed to compare SUN MICROSYSTEMS balance sheets just prior to the acquisition and then the "fair value" view of SUN's balance sheet at the time of the acquisition.

Find the PDF file with the 2011 SUN MICROSYSTEMS excerpts and study its final annual balance sheet as a separate company (i.e., before the purchase) dated June 30, 2011. ORACLE actually completed the purchase transaction of SUN on January 26, 2011.

Now, locate the PDF file with the 2010 ORACLE excerpts and study its May 31. 2010 balance sheet, its fiscal 2010 income statements, and note 2 regarding the acquisition of SUN. These excerpts provide you with the publicly available information regarding this acquisition. They include the GAAP-based financial statements of SUN pre-merger (reporting a net book value of $3,305 million), and ORACLE's view of the $7,295 million fair value of SUN's net assets acquired almost seven months later, at January 26, 2010.

Required:
1. Attempt to prepare a table like the one in Exhibit 6-5 for the HP-Compaq transaction. What are the issues you face trying to prepare such a table?
2. In preparing a table like that in Exhibit 6-5, use one line for all current assets and one line for all current liabilities. Both of these amounts are much lower at January 26, 2010 than at June 30, 2011. Why might that be the case?
3. Examine the amount of "goodwill" reported at fair value by Oracle on January 26, 2010. How does this compare to the amount reported as goodwill by Sun on June 30, 2011? Why might these amounts differ? Did Oracle pay a "goodwill" premium for Sun in excess of the fair value of Sun's recorded net assets?
4. Try to isolate the "intangibles" other than goodwill for Sun at both June 30, 2011 and then at January 26, 2010. What does this analysis suggest about the GAAP-based value of the intangibles at June 30, 2010?
5. Look at Sun's income statement for the year ended June 30, 2011.What is the trend in Sun's income statements for the past three years?

6-20 Goodwill – IHOP Corporation

On November 29, 2007, IHOP Corporation (now DineEquity, Inc.) acquired the operations and assets of 1,976 Applebee's restaurants in 49 states and 18 countries. IHOP paid $1,953.5 million and assumed Applebee's liabilities of $823.1 million. The independent appraisals of the fair market value of the identifiable assets of the Applebee's restaurants along with the approximate book value of the assets recorded by the previous owners are shown below:

	Fair Market Value	Book Value
Total identifiable assets	$2,056.6 million	$930.4 million

Required:

1. Define goodwill as it is used in accounting.
2. Compute the amount of goodwill purchased by IHOP Corporation when the company acquired the Applebee's restaurants.
3. Show how the purchase of the Applebee's restaurants impacted IHOP's balance sheet by recording the transaction in a journal entry. (Use a single account titled "Applebee's Restaurants" to record the identifiable assets.)
4. Comment on why IHOP would pay more than Applebee's book value for the restaurants. Comment on why they would pay more than the fair market value of the identifiable assets.

6-21 Financial Statement Analysis – Coca-Cola

Locate the PDF file with the excerpts from the 2014 10-K of The Coca-Cola Company. Refer to the Consolidated Balance Sheets on page 17 of the file (labeled page 75 of the 10-K, the policy footnote related to Property, Plant and Equipment on page 25 of the file (page 83 of the 10-K) and the numerical details of PP&E in Note 7 on page 26 of the file (page 100 of the 10-K).

Required:

1. Take a few minutes and scan pages 3 through 13 of the file (labeled pages 1 through 11 of the 10-K). Briefly describe something that you learned about Coca Cola (its business, where it operates, something unique that you learned from the 10-K, etc.).
2. Consider the *Consolidated Balance Sheets*: List the major categories of long-term assets and their dollar amounts for the most recent fiscal year.
3. Consider the first paragraph of the *Property, Plant and Equipment footnote*: Describe Coca-Cola's depreciation policy including the estimated useful lives of their assets and total depreciation expense recorded in 2014.
4. Consider the second paragraph of the *Property, Plant and Equipment footnote*: Describe the criteria Coca-Cola uses to determine whether or not to recognize an impairment loss on long-term assets.
5. Consider Note 7. What percentage of the original cost of Coca-Cola's depreciable assets are depreciated as of the end of 2014? Remember to include only the depreciable assets in your analysis.

6-22   Financial Statement Analysis – CISCO SYSTEMS

Locate the PDF file with the excerpts from the 2014 10-K of CISCO SYSTEMS, INC.

Required:

1. Take a few minutes and scan pages 3 through 5 of the file (labeled pages 1 through 3 of the 10-K). Briefly describe something that you learned about CISCO SYSTEMS (its business, where it operates, something unique that you learned from the annual report, etc.).

2. Refer to the *Consolidated Balance Sheets* on page 19 of the file (labeled page 73 of the 10-K). Compute the percentage of total assets represented by each of the non-current assets listed in the balance sheet as of July 26, 2014.

3. Consider the information on "business combinations" completed in 2014 described in Note 3 on page 31 of the file (labeled page 85 of the annual report). Compute the percentage of the total consideration given for these eight companies (four listed specifically and the four in the other category) assigned to: (a) goodwill; and (b) intangible assets.

4. Compute the total asset turnover ratio for fiscal 2014. Most technology companies have a total asset turnover ratio greater than 1.0 because the internally developed assets of these companies are understated by GAAP. Comment on why CISCO's total asset turnover ratio is less than 1.0.

Chapter 6 Study Quiz

For each of the five questions, show and label your calculations and place your answer in the spaces provided.

1. A building was acquired on August 17, 2012, at a cost of $276,000. The building was expected to have a 10-year useful life and a zero salvage value. The straight-line method was used to depreciate the building. On January 1, 2014, the building was sold for $186,000.

   Prepare the journal entry to record the sale.

   Describe the impact of the transaction on the balance sheet equation.

   Calculations:

2. On March 28 of the current year, a machine was purchased for $122,400. The machine has a salvage value of $8,400, and it is expected to operate 10,000 hours over the next 5 years. During the current year, the machine will be used 1,400 hours. The company wishes to use the depreciation method that will give them the lowest depreciation expense on their income statement for the current year ended December 31.

   Describe how much higher or lower depreciation expense will be in the current year if the straight-line method is used instead of the units-of-production method.

   $_____   Higher   Lower   (circle one)

   Explain your answer supporting it with numerical data.

3. A plant asset was purchased on January 1, 2012 that is being depreciated using the straight-line method. The asset has a 10-year useful life with a $20,000 salvage value. $30,000 of depreciation expense was recorded on this asset each year for the years ended December 31, 2012 and 2013. At the beginning of 2014, a capital expenditure was made to the asset that cost $48,000 and extended its useful life. The salvage value remains the same. $24,000 of depreciation expense was recorded on the asset in 2014.

   Determine the remaining useful life of the plant assets from the beginning of 2014 as a result of the capital expenditure.

   _____ years

   Calculation:

4. The Buildings and Accumulated Depreciation accounts had beginning balances of $688,000 and $256,000, respectively. The ending balances in these accounts were $758,000 and $306,000, respectively. During the year, a building costing $100,000 was acquired and a building with a book value of $18,000 was sold.

   Compute depreciation expense for the year. $_____

   Calculation:

5. On January 1, 2010, a copyright for a popular book was acquired for a cash price of $355,500. The copyright is set to expire on December 31, 2024 and it is being amortized over its useful life. During 2013, it was determined that the copyright would not generate any revenues after December 31, 2018.

   Compute the Accumulated Amortization account balance at December 31, 2014.

   $_____

   Calculation:

Chapter 7

Liabilities

LEARNING OBJECTIVES

1. Understand the reporting issues related to current and contingent liabilities.

2. Demonstrate how to account for the time value of money.

3. Apply time value of money concepts to various debt contracts such as leases and bonds.

4. Recognize financial statement disclosures of pensions, other post-employment benefits (OPEBs), and deferred income tax liabilities.

Current liabilities are typically operating accounts necessary to allow business to be conducted without the need for immediate cash payments. Some have suggested that current assets and current liabilities are like the grease needed to keep the gears of business running smoothly. Continuing with this analogy, you should have no more (grease) than necessary to keep things running smoothly. Accounting for current liabilities is relatively straightforward, and easy to monitor, and we spend little time on them in this chapter.

Long-term liabilities are found in the balance sheets of most businesses; and, along with contingent liabilities, they have the greatest interest for analysis and decision-making purposes. Unlike the measurement issues discussed in Chapter 6 for long-term assets, there is little ambiguity involved in the measurement of liabilities. In this chapter, we briefly consider current and contingent liabilities, but the main focus is on the measurement and reporting of long-term, interest-bearing obligations, often referred to as monetary liabilities. **Monetary liabilities** such as notes payable, bonds payable, capital leases, and pensions are fixed claims to a specific amount of the company's cash. These contractual obligations are all interest-bearing liabilities whose amount owed will continually increase by an interest charge simply with the passage of time.

The annual interest expense on monetary liabilities represents a fixed cost of doing business. It represents a "hurdle" that operating profits must exceed in order for shareholders to receive any rewards. Hence, monetary liabilities and their related interest expense represent the primary source of financial risk to shareholders.

CURRENT LIABILITIES

The current liabilities in a typical balance sheet are all operating accounts that are created by the normal business activities. Common examples include accounts payable, wages and salaries payable, taxes payable and perhaps unearned revenues. Sometimes notes payable are found in current liabilities when the cyclical nature of the business requires short-term borrowing to manage operating cash flows. Combined with current assets, current liabilities allow the analyst to measure **working capital**, defined as current assets minus current liabilities. The general idea in managing working capital is to maintain a ratio of current assets to current liabilities that will enable the company to pay its obligations on a timely basis but not have more current assets than necessary.

Accounts Payable

Accounts payable represent the obligations that result from buying goods and services on credit from other businesses. Because of the short-term nature of accounts payable, and the expectation that they will be paid within 30 days, these accounts usually are not interest-bearing obligations. However, some vendors provide financial incentives for prompt payment. For example, a vendor may have credit terms that include interest of 1.5% per month for amounts not paid within 30 days. If paid after 30 days the extra cost to settle the account payable would be recorded as interest expense. Current liabilities that do not have interest or fees associated with them, such as wages payable and many accounts payable are often viewed as "free" liabilities. Working capital managers may sometimes try to maximize the amount of these free current liabilities.

Sometimes vendors offer purchase discounts in order to encourage early payment. For example, a vendor might sell goods or services to a customer on terms of 2/10, n/30. This means that a 2% discount may be taken if the payment is made within 10 days of the sale; otherwise, the net invoiced amount is due within 30 days. Another example is 1/15, n/45, which means that a 1% discount may be deducted from the invoiced amount if paid within 15 days, while the net invoiced amount is due in 45 days.

Modern business practices most often do not offer a discount for early payment, and charging interest on "late" payments is also not common, particularly when your customers and vendors are the same year after year. If a repeat customer pays late and does not pay the late fee are you going to go back to them and force them to pay more? Probably not. Similarly, most customers or businesses who are offered a discount for early payment will take the discount even if they don't pay on time to earn it. Would you initiate a dispute with a repeat customer or vendor for this amount? Again, you probably would not if you plan to do business with them in the future. Hence, discounts and interest associated with payables (and receivables) are confined to certain situations where the business environment might allow it to work without harming future operations.

Notes Payable

Notes payable have many of the characteristics of accounts payable except that notes are formal debt contracts (the company signed a promissory note) and they bear interest. When the current liabilities section of the balance sheet reports notes payable, the notes are usually the currently due portion of a long-term borrowing (e.g., the coming year's payments on a mortgage or other long-term borrowing) or a short-term borrowing that must be repaid within the coming year. As noted, short-term notes are most common in industries with cyclical business.

Sometimes a long-term borrowing (e.g., a note or bond) that is maturing within the next year is reported as a current liability. However, if a company has long-term obligations that are maturing within a year, and *if it intends to replace the borrowing with other long-term debt* and has the ability to do so (that is, it has a sufficient credit rating to permit it to obtain other debt), it is not necessary to reclassify the long-term borrowing as a current liability. Therefore, most interest-bearing debt in the current liability section of the balance sheet will represent short-term operating liabilities.

Interest   When a company borrows money, the lender will require repayment of the borrowed amount (= **principal**) plus interest to compensate the lender for the use of the money and for the risk involved in lending. **Interest** is the amount of money over and above the principal that must be repaid by the borrower. Short-term notes have **simple interest**, and interest is calculated and accrued using the well-known interest relationship:

$$\text{interest} = (\text{principal}) \; x \; (\text{interest rate}) \; x \; (\text{time})$$

The **interest rate** charged by the lender depends upon various characteristics of the borrower, such as the likelihood the borrower will repay the principal plus interest, and the length of time the borrower will have the money. **Risk**, in the context of borrowing and lending, refers to uncertainty in relevant future events, and the interest rate charged will reflect the amount of risk as viewed by the lender. The lender faces interest-rate risk, default risk, and other sources of financial risk when lending money for one or more future periods. **Interest-rate risk** is the risk that interest rates will increase during the period of the loan. If the lender had previously accepted a 6% interest rate when the loan was made and the current interest rate on a comparable loan is 8%, the lender may have accepted too low an interest rate. **Default risk** is the risk associated with non-payment by the borrower. If a company is experiencing financial difficulty, it may be viewed as a risky borrower that might not be able to repay the loan. Borrowers who are considered very risky may not be able to borrow money at all. For borrowers who do qualify for loans, lenders will charge a higher interest rate to those they view as being risky. So, all else being equal, companies that pay the highest interest rates are relatively risky borrowers. The interest rate also tends to increase as the length of time of the borrowing increases. Therefore, both the risk of the borrower and the length of the borrowing period are important factors in explaining the interest rates on debt.

Example On October 1, 2014, $10,000 was borrowed on a 9%, 8-month note payable. The journal entries that would be made to record the receipt of cash, the accrual of interest on the note on December 31, and the payment of the note plus interest on the maturity date would appear as follows:

Journal

Date	Accounts (*Explanation*)	Debit	Credit
Oct. 1	Cash	10,000	
	Note Payable		10,000
	(*To record an 8-month note payable*)		
Dec. 31 2014	Interest Expense*	225	
	Interest Payable		225
	(*To record interest expense for 3 months*)		
May 31 2015	Note Payable	10,000	
	Interest Payable	225	
	Interest Expense**	375	
	Cash		10,600
	(*To record payment of the note plus interest*)		

* $10,000 x .09 x 3/12 = $225
** $10,000 x .09 x 5/12 = $375

Note that the 9% is an <u>annual</u> interest rate. In this text (and generally in business) interest rates are stated in annual percentages. Unless you know otherwise, you should always assume the interest rate is an annual percentage rate.

Estimated Liabilities

Some liability amounts in a balance sheet are not known with certainty at the balance sheet date but can be estimated by the company. Two common examples of estimated liabilities are taxes payable and warranty liabilities.

Taxes Payable Profit-oriented businesses must pay many kinds of taxes, including federal, state and local income taxes, property taxes, federal state and local payroll taxes, and other taxes. When these taxes are unpaid at year-end, they typically appear as separate items in the current liability section of the balance sheet. Accrued taxes, especially income taxes, are estimated liabilities. For one thing, the timing of the recording of taxes necessary to prepare financial statements may not coincide with the actual determination of the tax obligation for the same period of time. Also, it is common for a financially complex company to have ongoing discussions with the Internal Revenue Service (IRS) over its tax returns of past years. Company officials involved in these discussions know the past years that have been settled and the past years that are still undergoing possible adjustment. It is rare for a company to not have some taxes payable at year-end, and if no separate liability is listed for taxes payable, the amount owed is likely to be included in Other Liabilities.

Warranty Liabilities Many companies guarantee their products against defects. These commitments are referred to as warranties, and they usually are provided in an effort to increase sales. Companies must estimate the future costs of warranty claims each period. This estimate is based on the sales for that period, and it is recorded as an expense and an estimated liability in the period of the sales. The features of **warranty liabilities** are:

- The warranty liability is based on an *estimate* of future costs;

- The liability is offset by an expense that reduces net income; and

- The expense must be estimated in the period of the sale in order to offset sales revenue in the period of the sale rather than in some future period when the warranty cost actually is incurred.[1]

For example, assume JOHNSON CONTROLS sells thermostats with a four-year warranty, providing free replacement for any defective product. The company estimates the defect rate at 0.1% (.001) of sales revenue. If JOHNSON CONTROLS had $14,000,000 of sales revenue from thermostats in 2014, the following adjusting journal entry would be made to record the estimated warranty liability:

Journal

Date	Accounts (*Explanation*)	Debit	Credit
Dec. 31 2014	Warranty Expense	14,000	
	Estimated Warranty Liability*		14,000
	(*To record estimated warranty liability*)		

* $14,000,000 sales revenue x .001 = $14,000 estimated warranty liability.

When a customer files a claim for a defective product, JOHNSON CONTROLS reduces the warranty liability account and reduces inventory for the cost of the replacements provided to the customer. If the company had $13,000 of defective thermostats returned for replacement during 2015, the company would provide these customers with new thermostats and record the transaction as follows:

Journal

Date	Accounts (*Explanation*)	Debit	Credit
2015	Estimated Warranty Liability	13,000	
	Inventory – Thermostats		13,000
	(*To record warranty claims*)		

Like the estimation of bad debts, the warranty estimate made in the year of the sale reduces income, while the actual claim for a defective product occurs in a later year and has no impact on net income. The warranty liability in the balance sheet of JOHNSON CONTROLS, for example, would be an estimate of the total expected claims for defective products that will result from all products sold within four years of the balance sheet date.

---

[1] In many ways, warranties are accounted for in a manner similar to bad debts, except that the estimated amount is shown as a liability on the balance sheet and not as a contra asset.

CONTINGENT LIABILITIES

Contingent liabilities are a special class of potential obligations. They arise when a company has a current situation that could result in a liability in the future depending on the outcome of a future event. A classic example would be a lawsuit for an unsafe product the company has sold; no liability exists at the present time because the case has not been resolved yet, but a liability could arise in the future if the company loses the lawsuit. Contingent liabilities are reported in the balance sheet if:

- The amount of the potential liability can be *estimated*, and
- A liability requiring future payment is *probable*.

The amount of the potential obligation must be subject to a point estimate or a range of possible estimates. In the case of an obligation that is subject to a range of possible measures, the low-end of the range is the one that is reported (if it is also probable). For a contingency to be considered *probable*, most practitioners suggest it be more than 80% likely to become a liability. Many contingencies are not reported as liabilities in balance sheets because they are not both able to be *estimated* and *probable*. However, it is common for the footnotes to the financial statements to discuss the contingencies faced by the company that do not meet both of the criteria.

Contingent liabilities can be important for some companies in industries that are exposed to potential obligations, such as environmental cleanup costs and product lawsuits, and analysts must be aware of the potential impact of contingent liabilities on the financial statements when evaluating a business. However, despite the efforts of accounting rule-makers, the fact remains that little accounting information is available on contingent liabilities in the financial statements.

ACCOUNTING FOR THE TIME VALUE OF MONEY

The concept of the time value of money is fundamental to understanding much of accounting and finance. As discussed, the amount of interest on a liability is a function of the principal, the interest rate, and the time the money is held. It also depends on the pattern of the repayment of the principal and interest. We begin with a discussion of the time value of money at a conceptual level by considering three typical liability repayment patterns, and then we explain applications of these patterns to specific liabilities found in financial statements.

Illustrative Repayment Patterns

Assume that $100,000 is borrowed on January 1, 2014. The loan is for three years and carries a 10% interest rate. The three possible repayment patterns are:

1. Principal and interest paid in a single amount at the end of year three (December 31, 2016);
2. Three equal year-end payments with each payment including principal and interest; and
3. Interest paid at the end of each year and principal paid in a single amount at the end of year three (December 31, 2016).

Pattern #1: Principal and Interest Paid in a Single Lump-sum Amount at End Date

Here the borrower will have the use of the cash for three years before any principal or interest is paid. When interest is accrued over more than one time period, it is compounded. **Compound interest** is interest charged on both the unpaid principal and on the accrued unpaid interest. You should always assume that interest is compounded annually unless otherwise indicated. The following time line shows the cash flows for this repayment pattern:

Borrow $100,000	Pay $0	Pay $0	Pay $133,100	
				Time
1/1/14	12/31/14	12/31/15	12/31/16	

The total that must be repaid is $133,100, the $100,000 borrowed plus $33,100 of interest. The interest computations for this pattern are shown in the following **amortization table**:

Amortization Table – Pattern #1

Date	Cash In (Cash Out)	10% Interest Expense*	Change in Balance	Balance of Liability
1/1/14	$100,000		$100,000	$100,000
12/31/14		$10,000	$ 10,000	$110,000
12/31/15		$11,000	$ 11,000	$121,000
12/31/16		$12,100	$ 12,100	$133,100
12/31/16	($133,100)		($133,100)	$ 0
Totals	($ 33,100)	$33,100		

*Annual interest expense is 10% times the balance of the liability owed throughout the period.

Amortization table explanation

A 5-column amortization table such as the one above illustrates how a series of cash payments repays a liability (the amount borrowed) plus interest. The table includes all the information about the liability. The *Date* column lists each of the important dates, starting with the date the loan was taken out. The *Cash In (Cash Out)* column lists each of the cash flows, starting with the initial receipt of the amount borrowed, $100,000 in this case, and ending with the final payment, $133,100 in this case. The net cash flow for this loan is ($33,100) indicating that $33,100 more cash was paid out than was received. This difference between cash inflow and outflow is the total interest on the loan over the three years. The *10% Interest Expense* column shows how the interest is accrued at the end of each year. The *Change in Balance* column describes the increase (or decrease) in the liability each year, and the *Balance of Liability* column shows the balance in the Loan Payable account at each date.

The journal entries that would be made to record the information in this table on the books of both the borrower and the lender are illustrated in Exhibit 7-1.

Exhibit 7-1 Journal Entries for Pattern #1

Date	Borrower			Lender		
	Account	**Debit**	**Credit**	**Account**	**Debit**	**Credit**
1/1/14	Cash	100,000		Loan Receivable	100,000	
	Loan Payable		100,000	Cash		100,000
	(To record loan)			*(To record loan)*		
12/31/14	Interest Expense	10,000		Interest Receivable	10,000	
	Interest Payable		10,000	Interest Revenue		10,000
	(To record interest)			*(To record interest)*		
12/31/15	Interest Expense	11,000		Interest Receivable	11,000	
	Interest Payable		11,000	Interest Revenue		11,000
	(To record interest)			*(To record interest)*		
12/31/16	Loan Payable	100,000		Cash	133,100	
	Interest Payable	21,000		Loan Receivable		100,000
	Interest Expense	12,100		Interest Receivable		21,000
	Cash		133,100	Interest Revenue		12,100
	(To record payment)			*(To record receipt)*		

Note that once you understand the accounting for the borrower (our focus in this chapter), it is easy to understand the accounting for the lender since the journal entries for each transaction are the mirror images of one another.

Pattern #2: Three Equal Year-end Payments This repayment pattern is called an **annuity**. Given the number of periods and the interest rate per period, the equal annual payment that will repay both the principal and interest can be determined. In this example, the equal payment to be made at the end of each year for three years is $40,211.[2] The following time line shows the cash flows for this repayment pattern:

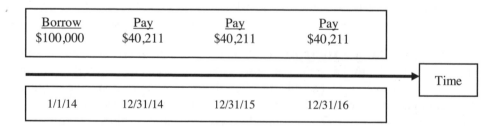

The total cash paid in this case is $120,633 ($40,211 x 3), compared to $133,100 in Pattern #1. This amount is $12,467 less ($133,100 – $120,633) because each of the annual payments pays the accrued interest in each period as well as repaying a portion of the principal. This earlier repayment of the interest incurred and a portion of the principal results in a lower total interest expense. The computations for this repayment pattern are shown in the following amortization table:

---

[2] The calculation of the $40,211 annuity payment is illustrated on page 60. A table of annuity factors is provided on page 81.

Amortization Table – Pattern #2

Date	Cash In (Cash Out)	10% Interest Expense*	Change in Balance	Balance of Liability
1/1/14	$100,000		$100,000	$100,000
12/31/14	($ 40,211)	$10,000	($ 30,211)	$ 69,789
12/31/15	($ 40,211)	$ 6,979	($ 33,232)	$ 36,557
12/31/16	($ 40,211)	$ 3,654**	($ 36,557)	$ 0
Totals	($ 20,633)	$20,633		

* Annual interest expense is 10% times the balance of the liability owed throughout the period.
** Rounded from $3,656 in order to bring ending balance to zero.

The $40,211 payment made on December 31, 2014, covers the interest for 2014 ($10,000) and also repays $30,211 of the principal. In the second year, the interest expense decreases to $6,979 because the balance of the liability has been reduced by part of the payment made on December 31, 2014. We can see that in the case of an annuity repayment pattern, the amount of interest included in each payment declines and the amount of principal in each payment increases over time. The journal entries that would be made to record the information in this table on the books of both the borrower and lender are illustrated in Exhibit 7-2.

Pattern #3: Annual Interest Payments and Repayment of Principal at the End of Year Three This pattern is a combination of the first two. It includes an annuity for the interest payments and a single payment at the end for the principal. The time line on the next page shows this repayment pattern:

Exhibit 7-2   Journal Entries for Pattern #2

		Borrower			Lender	
Date	Account	Debit	Credit	Account	Debit	Credit
1/1/14	Cash	100,000		Loan Receivable	100,000	
	Loan Payable		100,000	Cash		100,000
	(To record loan)			*(To record loan)*		
12/31/14	Loan Payable	30,211		Cash	40,211	
	Interest Expense	10,000		Loan Receivable		30,211
	Cash		40,211	Interest Revenue		10,000
	(To record payment)			*(To record receipt)*		
12/31/15	Loan Payable	33,232		Cash	40,211	
	Interest Expense	6,979		Loan Receivable		33,232
	Cash		40,211	Interest Revenue		6,979
	(To record payment)			*(To record receipt)*		
12/31/16	Loan Payable	36,557		Cash	40,211	
	Interest Expense	3,654		Loan Receivable		36,557
	Cash		40,211	Interest Revenue		3,654
	(To record payment)			*(To record receipt)*		

Borrow $100,000	Pay $10,000	Pay $10,000	Pay $110,000

→ Time

1/1/14	12/31/14	12/31/15	12/31/16

In this case, the year-end payments are only for the 10% interest each year. As a result, the balance of the liability remains at $100,000 until the end of the contract. Since the principal remains at $100,000, the 10% annual interest is the same amount each year ($10,000). The amortization table for this loan would appear as follows:

Amortization Table – Pattern #3

Date	Cash In (Cash Out)	10% Interest Expense*	Change in Balance	Balance of Liability
1/1/14	$100,000		$100,000	$100,000
12/31/14	($ 10,000)	$10,000		$100,000
12/31/15	($ 10,000)	$10,000		$100,000
12/31/16	($ 10,000)	$10,000		$100,000
12/31/16	($100,000)		($100,000)	$ 0
Totals	($ 30,000)	$30,000		

* Annual interest expense is 10% times the balance of the liability owed throughout the period.

The journal entries that would be made to record the information in this table on the books of both the borrower and lender are illustrated in Exhibit 7-3.

Exhibit 7-3   Journal Entries for Pattern #3

Date	Borrower Account	Debit	Credit	Lender Account	Debit	Credit
1/1/14	Cash Loan Payable (To record loan)	100,000	100,000	Loan Receivable Cash (To record loan)	100,000	100,000
12/31/14	Interest Expense Cash (To record interest)	10,000	10,000	Cash Interest Revenue (To record interest)	10,000	10,000
12/31/15	Interest Expense Cash (To record interest)	10,000	10,000	Cash Interest Revenue (To record interest)	10,000	10,000
12/31/16	Loan Payable Interest Expense Cash (To record payment)	100,000 10,000	110,000	Cash Loan Receivable Interest Revenue (To record receipt)	110,000	100,000 10,000

Exhibit 7-4 summarizes our discussion of these three alternative repayment patterns and their effects on cash flows and total interest expense. You should take the time to study the cash flows and interest expense and the graphic depiction of the total cash flows for each pattern to make sure you can explain the logic for each one.

Note that all three patterns depict a 10%, $100,000, three-year loan; nevertheless, the amount of total interest expense varies depending on the repayment pattern used. In Pattern #1, the borrower waited until the end of the contract to pay anything, and this resulted in the greatest amount of interest expense, $33,100. In Pattern #2, the borrower made annual payments that included both the interest for the year as well as some of the principal. This was the fastest repayment plan; and, therefore, the amount of interest expense was the lowest, $20,633. In Pattern #3 the interest payments were made annually with the principal repaid in total at the end in a single amount. This pattern paid the principal and interest faster than Pattern #1 but slower than Pattern #2 resulting in total interest expense of $30,000, which is less than Pattern #1 but more than Pattern #2.

Other Patterns of Loan Repayments   These three cash flow patterns cover about 90% of the borrowing contracts encountered in practice. Of course, a loan contract could be written to require any repayment pattern agreed upon by the borrower and lender, so we might see other patterns in practice. For example, a contract could call for specific payments at specific dates, or it could be open-ended

Exhibit 7-4   Summary of Cash Flows: Three Repayment Patterns

Cash repayment pattern	Interest Rate	Cash Received	Cash Paid	Interest Expense
#1: Single payment at the end	10%	$100,000	$133,100	$33,100
#2: Three equal year-end payments	10%	$100,000	$120,633	$20,633
#3: Three year-end payments plus a single payment at the end	10%	$100,000	$130,000	$30,000

Graphic Depiction

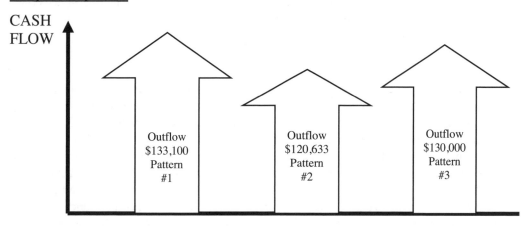

CASH FLOW

Outflow $133,100 Pattern #1

Outflow $120,633 Pattern #2

Outflow $130,000 Pattern #3

and not specify any repayment pattern. A company might enter into a contract to borrow $100,000 and have the contract not stipulate exactly how the loan is to be repaid, other than to require that the principal of $100,000 plus 10% annual interest on any unpaid balance be repaid in full within the next five years. Such a contract would allow any number of repayment schedules.

Present and Future Value Computations

In order to account for a long-term liability, it is necessary to determine the present value of the cash payments that will be made in the future. This text includes present and future value tables that will be used to illustrate all examples involving the time value of money. These tables are provided at the end of this chapter on pages 80 and 81. **Table 7-1** *provides factors for the* **future value** *of a* **present amount**. For example, under the 10% column on the three-period line (n = 3), you will see the factor 1.3310. This is the future value of $1 at the end of three periods at an interest rate of 10% per period compounded annually. That is, a $1.00 investment today will return $1.331 in three years at a 10% annual interest rate. The proof is shown below:

Proof:

$1.00 x 10% = $0.10 interest at the end of Year 1: Balance = $1.00 + $0.10 = $1.10

$1.10 x 10% = $0.11 interest at the end of Year 2: Balance = $1.10 + $0.11 = $1.21

$1.21 x 10% = $0.121 interest at the end of Year 3: Balance = $1.21 + $.121 = $1.331

Notation for all calculations

The notation used in this text is to identify the table, the number of periods, and the interest rate. When combined, these identify a factor as follows: (Table, number of periods, interest rate per period). For example, in the notation for Table 7-1 (p. 80), the future value of a present amount is **(F/P)**. The complete notation to identify the factor of 1.3310 is **(F/P, 3, 10%)**, read as *the future value of a present amount in 3 periods at 10% interest per period*. Note that Pattern #1 above could have used this factor. In Pattern #1, we borrowed $100,000 for 3 periods at 10% interest per period, so we could have used this factor to compute the future amount due to the lender as: (F/P, 3, 10%) x $100,000 = 1.3310 x $100,000 = $133,100.

Table 7-2 (page 81) *provides factors for the* **present value** *of a* **future amount** **(P/F)**. For example, assume that in Pattern #1, we did not know how much money we would be able to borrow, but we did know that the loan would require $133,100 to be repaid at the end of three years and that the interest rate on the loan was 10%. We could compute the present value of the $133,100 by using Table 7-2 and looking on the period 3 row and under the 10% column to find the factor of .7513, written as: **(P/F, 3, 10%)** = .7513. This factor means that the present value of $1 three years in the future at 10% interest per year is $0.7513 (75.13 cents). There is no difference between receiving $1 in three years or $0.7513 today if your interest rate is 10% since investing $0.7513 today at 10% interest would equal $1 at the end of three years.

> **Proof:** $0.7513 \times 1.1 = \$0.82643 \times 1.1 = \$0.909073 \times 1.1 = \$1.00$ (rounded)
>   Year 1   Year 2   Year 3

What is the present value of paying $133,100 at the end of three years? The answer is (P/F, 3, 10%) x $133,100 = .7513 x $133,100 = $100,000. That is, the factors in Table 7-2 can be used to compute the present value today of receiving $133,100 three years from today and the factors in Table 7-1 can be used to compute the future value of $100,000 three years from today. (As you probably can see, the factors in Table 7-2 are the reciprocals of the factors in Table 7-1.)

A Quick Point about Rounding

The factors in all the tables are rounded to four decimal places. Therefore, please understand that making calculations of present and future values with factors from these tables requires that we tolerate minor errors due to rounding and not be confused by them.

Table 7-3 (page 81) *provides factors to determine the* **present value** *of an* **annuity**. These factors can be used to compute the present value of a series of equal payments without having to compute each individual payment. (The factors in Table 7-3 are the summation over time of the factors in Table 7-2.) The notation identifying the factor for the present value of an annuity for three periods at 10% per period is: **(P/A, 3, 10%)** = 2.4869. This factor is interpreted as: $2.4869 is the value today of a promise to receive $1 at the end of each of the next three years, given a 10% annual interest rate. The rationale for this statement can be seen by investing $2.4869 today in an account that earns 10% per year. Such an account will allow you to withdraw $1 at the end of each of the next three years.

Proof:

Beginning of Year 1:	Invest $2.4869 at 10% annual interest.
Preliminary balance end of Year 1:	$2.4869 x 1.1 = $2.73559
Withdrawal at end of Year 1:	$2.73559 − $1 = <u>$1.73559 at the end of Year 1</u>
Preliminary balance end of Year 2:	$1.73559 x 1.1 = $1.909149
Withdrawal at end of Year 2:	$1.909149 − $1 = <u>$0.909149 at the end of Year 2</u>
Preliminary balance end of Year 3:	$0.909149 x 1.1 = $1.00
Withdrawal at end of Year 3:	$1.00 − $1.00 = <u>$0 at the end of Year 3</u>

How do the factors in Table 7-3 apply to our examples? In Pattern #2 we needed to find the amount of the constant annual payment required to repay a $100,000 loan plus 10% annual interest over three years. Consider the following equation, showing that the present value of an annuity factor for 3 periods at 10% interest (P/A, 3, 10%) times the annuity amount ($A) must equal the amount borrowed ($100,000). We can then solve for the annuity amount ($A) required, as follows:

$$(P/A, 3, 10\%) \text{ x } \$A = \text{ Amount borrowed} \qquad [1]$$

(find the present value factor in Table 7-3 for 3 periods at 10% = 2.4869)

$$2.4869 \text{ x } \$A = \$100,000 \qquad [2]$$

$$\$A = \$100,000 \div 2.4869 \qquad [3]$$

$$\$A = \$40,210.704 = \$40,211 \text{ rounded} \qquad [4]$$

When we look at the amortization table for Pattern #2 on page 55 we see that an annuity amount of $40,211 will repay the $100,000 plus 10% interest per year.

Equation [1] above has three components: a present value of an annuity factor (P/A, 3, 10%), an annuity amount ($A), and the amount borrowed. Given any two of these, we can solve for the third. This equation allows us to solve economic puzzles in contracts involving cash flows.[3]

Solving for an Unknown Interest Rate

Assume a loan contract is written without an interest rate. The contract says the lender will give the borrower $99,817.50 today (January 1) in exchange for year-end payments of $25,000 each for the next five years. In order to account for this contract, you must determine the interest rate. What is the Table 7-3 factor that makes equation [1] work? What interest rate does this loan contract imply?

Answer: First, solve for the Table 7-3 factor (P/A, 5, ?%), as follows:

$$(P/A, 5, ?\%) \text{ x } \$25,000 = \$99,817.50$$
$$(P/A, 5, ?\%) = \$99,817.50 \div \$25,000$$
$$(P/A, 5, ?\%) = 3.9927$$

Read across the n = 5 line in Table 7-3 until you find the factor 3.9927 under the 8% interest column. The interest rate implied in this contract is 8% per year.

LONG-TERM LIABILITIES

Repayment patterns #1 through #3 and their related calculations illustrate that using present value tables is a key skill underlying the interpretation of long-term liabilities.

---

[3] In our annuity examples we assume that the series of payments begins at the <u>end</u> of the first year of the contract. These are known as **ordinary annuities** and the tables are designed for this repayment pattern. Some contracts call for the first payment to be made on the date the contract is signed. This initial payment, of course, does not affect the calculation of the liability amount because the liability represents only the payments that must be made in the future.

Exhibit 7-5   Financial Examples of the Basic Cash Flow Patterns

Repayment Pattern	Examples
#1: Repayment in a single amount at the end of the contract	• **Zero-coupon bonds*** • Notes payable • Term loans
#2: Annuity repayment of both principal and interest over the life of the loan	• **Capital leases*** • Mortgage loans • Auto loans
#3: Periodic interest payments with repayment of principal in a single amount at the end of the contract	• **Bonds*** • Debentures • Notes payable • Term loans

* Detailed explanations of these financial instruments are provided in this chapter.

Exhibit 7-5 provides a guide to the various financial instruments that are based on the cash flows illustrated in these repayment patterns.

Zero-Coupon Bonds (Repayment Pattern #1)

Zero-coupon bonds require repayment of principal and interest in a single amount at the end of the contract. The term *zero-coupon* is often mistakenly thought to mean that the bonds pay no interest. Since no one would invest in bonds that pay no interest, this clearly cannot be the case. Zero-coupon bonds, like any borrowing agreement, require a return (interest) to the lender for the use of the money. The borrower will repay more than the amount of money originally borrowed, and this difference is interest. Interest expense is accrued at the end of each period, and since no cash interest payments are made, the interest expense is added to the balance in the liability account to be paid at maturity.

Example   Assume that $1,000,000 of 4-year, zero-coupon bonds were issued on January 1, 2014.[4] The company issuing the bonds received $762,900 in cash (called the **proceeds**). We can use the Present Value of a Single Amount Table (Table 7-2 on page 81) to determine the interest rate for these bonds as follows:

$$(P/F, 4, ?\%) \times \$1{,}000{,}000 \ = \ \$762{,}900$$
$$(P/F, 4, ?\%) \ = \ \$762{,}900 \div \$1{,}000{,}000$$
$$(P/F, 4, ?\%) \ = \ .7629$$

From Table 7-2, on line n = 4, we find the factor of .7629 under the 7% interest rate, so we know the interest rate on these bonds is 7%.

---

[4] The way such bond issuances typically work is that the company wanting cash will issue its bonds through several investment banks each of whom agree to take a percentage of the bonds and sell them to investors.

The $1 million is the **maturity value** or **face value** printed on the bonds. If each bond had a maturity value of $1,000, then there would be 1,000 of these bonds (for a total of $1,000,000), each issued for the cash amount of $762.90. The amortization table to account for this zero-coupon bond issuance is shown below:

Amortization Table – Zero-coupon Bonds

Date	Cash In (Cash Out)	7% Interest Expense*	Change in Balance	Balance of Liability
1/1/14	$ 762,900		$762,900	$ 762,900
12/31/14		$ 53,403	$ 53,403	$ 816,303
12/31/15		$ 57,141	$ 57,141	$ 873,444
12/31/16		$ 61,141	$ 61,141	$ 934,585
12/31/17		$ 65,415**	$ 65,415	$1,000,000
12/31/17	($1,000,000)			$ 0
Totals	($ 237,100)	$237,100		

   * Annual interest expense is 7% times the balance of the liability owed throughout the period.
  ** Rounded from $65,421 to bring the ending balance to the $1,000,000 maturity value.

The journal entries that would be made for this zero-coupon bond are shown in Exhibit 7-6. Track these entries with the amounts in the amortization table above.

Exhibit 7-6   Journal Entries for Zero-Coupon Bond Example

Journal

Date	Accounts (*Explanation*)	Debit	Credit
1/1/14	Cash	762,900	
	Bonds Payable (zero coupon)		762,900
	(*To record issuance of bonds*)		
12/31/14	Interest Expense	53,403	
	Bonds Payable (zero coupon)		53,403
	(*To accrue interest on bonds*)		
12/31/15	Interest Expense	57,141	
	Bonds Payable (zero coupon)		57,141
	(*To accrue interest on bonds*)		
12/31/16	Interest Expense	61,141	
	Bonds Payable (zero coupon)		61,141
	(*To accrue interest on bonds*)		
12/31/17	Interest Expense	65,415	
	Bonds Payable (zero coupon)		65,415
	(*To accrue interest on bonds*)		
12/31/17	Bonds Payable (zero coupon)	1,000,000	
	Cash		1,000,000
	(*To pay off bonds at maturity*)		

At first it might seem odd that a company would be able to sell zero-coupon bonds. Why would creditors be willing to forgo interest payments until the maturity of the bonds? It turns out to be attractive to some creditors in high tax brackets to not receive any interest payments until the bonds mature. This allows them to delay paying the tax, perhaps postponing the tax until a future period when they may be taxed at a lower rate. For tax planning purposes, as well as other motives, there is an active market for zero-coupon bonds.

Capital Leases (Repayment Pattern #2)

A common example of a repayment contract illustrated in Pattern #2 is a capital lease. **Capital leases** (also called *financing leases*) are essentially the purchase of an asset with financing provided by the seller. GAAP requires the **lessee** to report both the leased asset and the lease liability in the balance sheet; and the payments made on capital leases are usually an annuity, including both interest and principal.

Operating Leases

Historically, many industries that require large amounts of tangible assets (e.g., buildings, airplanes, machinery) used *operating leases* as a tool to keep these assets and their related liabilities off their balance sheets. Operating lease contracts were structured to be treated like long-term rental agreements, so that the lessee only had to record rent expense for the periodic lease payments. After decades of work, we should soon see new GAAP designed to eliminate these off-balance-sheet schemes. Both the FASB and IFRS are expected to release new rules by 2016 which will require both operating lease and capital lease contracts to report the present value of their commitments as assets and liabilities. Once their current proposals actually become rules, we should expect a very significant increase in the amount of assets and liabilities on the balance sheets of many companies. Industries that will be heavily impacted include airlines, fast food chains, all major retail chains (e.g., LOWES, MACY'S, STARBUCKS), virtually all transportation companies, and many more.

Capital Lease Example   Assume RYDER (the lessee) acquired a group of trucks with a cash price (market value) of $500,000 from FORD MOTOR COMPANY (the **lessor**) on January 1, 2014, by signing a capital lease contract. The lease calls for a $100,000 payment on January 1, 2014 and five equal year-end payments, starting on December 31, 2014 at 8% annual interest. Notice that RYDER has use of the trucks forever but pays the lease obligation over five years. The annuity payment to repay the $400,000 borrowed ($500,000 cost of the trucks minus the $100,000 initial payment) is computed as follows:

$$(P/A, 5, 8\%) \times \$A \;=\; \$400,000 \quad \text{[See Table 7-3]}$$
$$(3.9927) \times \$A \;=\; \$400,000$$
$$\$A \;=\; \$400,000 \div 3.9927 \;=\; \$100,182.83 \text{ (rounded to } \$100,183)$$

This lease allows RYDER to obtain new assets from FORD, who is providing both the trucks and the financing. The lessee (RYDER) must account for both the lease liability and the long-term asset (trucks), along with the related interest expense and depreciation expense. Since the liability is equal to the total value of the trucks less the initial $100,000 paid on January 1, 2014, we know that the life of the trucks is equal to or greater than the term of the lease.

The total cash paid for the January 1, 2014 "down payment" and the five year-end lease payments is $600,915 [$100,000 + (5 x $100,183)] for assets with a market value of $500,000. So the total interest expense for this lease is $100,915 ($600,915 − $500,000). The amortization table for this capital lease liability is shown below:

Amortization Table – Capital Lease

Date	Value In (Cash Out)	8% Interest Expense*	Change in Balance	Balance of Liability
1/1/14	$500,000 ($100,000)		$400,000	$400,000
12/31/14	($100,183)	$ 32,000	($ 68,183)	$331,817
12/31/15	($100,183)	$ 26,545	($ 73,638)	$258,179
12/31/16	($100,183)	$ 20,654	($ 79,529)	$178,650
12/31/17	($100,183)	$ 14,292	($ 85,891)	$ 92,759
12/31/18	($100,183)	$ 7,424**	($ 92,759)	$ 0
Totals	($100,915)	$100,915		

> * Annual interest expense is 8% times the balance of the liability owed throughout the period.
> ** Rounded from $7,421 to bring the ending balance to zero.

This illustration of an annuity is characterized by decreasing amounts of interest expense (computed as 8% of the unpaid balance) and increasing amounts of principal (change in balance owed). The amount of interest decreases each year because the unpaid principal balance (= **carrying value** of the liability) decreases each year. This decreasing-interest/increasing-principal effect is also observed for home mortgages, car loans, and many other annuity contracts where the borrowing is repaid with a series of equal payments. Exhibit 7-7 shows the journal entries that would be made to account for the lease liability on RYDER's books. In addition, the leased assets (trucks) would be depreciated by RYDER using one of the methods described in Chapter 6.

Exhibit 7-7   Journal Entries for RYDER's Capital Lease

	Journal				Journal		
Date	Accounts	Debit	Credit	Date	Accounts	Debit	Credit
1/1/14	Trucks	500,000		12/31/16	Interest Expense	20,654	
	Lease Liability		400,000		Lease Liability	79,529	
	Cash		100,000		Cash		100,183
12/31/14	Interest Expense	32,000		12/31/17	Interest Expense	14,292	
	Lease Liability	68,183			Lease Liability	85,891	
	Cash		100,183		Cash		100,183
12/31/15	Interest Expense	26,545		12/31/18	Interest Expense	7,424	
	Lease Liability	73,638			Lease Liability	92,759	
	Cash		100,183		Cash		100,183

No Initial Payment

Sometimes capital leases do not require a payment when the lease is signed. For example, if the lease signed by RYDER called for no payment on January 1, 2014, and five equal year-end payments starting December 31, 2014, the required annuity payment would be $125,229 [$500,000 borrowed ÷ 3.9927 (P/A, 5, 8%)], and total interest expense would be $126,145 [(5 x $125,229) – $500,000]. The amount being financed in this case would be $500,000, versus the $400,000 borrowed when a $100,000 payment was made on the date the lease was signed. The annuity payments would repay the $500,000 principal plus the 8% interest over the five years. As before, the asset would be reported at its fair market value (cash equivalent price) of $500,000 at the inception of the contract and depreciated over its useful life.

Bonds (Repayment Pattern #3)

Bonds are debt contracts that can have a variety of terms and conditions.[5] The bond contract stipulates the timing and amount of the cash flows that the issuing company promises to pay to the bond holder (creditor). Bonds have a **stated interest rate** (or **face interest rate**) printed on the face of each bond which may or may not be the interest rate the bonds return. They also have a maturity (face) value printed on each bond and a maturity date stating when they will be repaid. A typical bond might be described as follows:

> *A $1,000, 10%, 5-year bond dated January 1, 2014, paying interest annually on December 31 of each year, due on December 31, 2018.*

This contract indicates that, for each bond, the issuer will pay $100 ($1,000 x the stated interest rate of 10%) each December 31 from 2014 to 2018 and will also pay an additional $1,000 at maturity (December 31, 2018). Companies often issue several million dollars of bonds in a public offering, usually selling them through investment banks. Balance sheets often list bonds, loans, and notes under the heading *Long-term Debt*.

Bond offerings are traded in the market after they are issued at whatever the market determines is the right price. This is the price at which the bond issuer is willing to sell and the bond purchaser is willing to buy. After the issuance, the market price of the bond may increase or decrease depending on changes in the market rate of interest for investments with similar risk. Also, the risk of the issuing company may change due to its performance after the issuance, resulting in a change in the market value of its bonds. However, it is important to understand that the accounting records of the issuing company will not be affected by changes in the price of the bond after it is issued. The issuing company will continue to account for the original amount received and will continue to pay the stipulated interest payments and the face value of $1,000 each at maturity.

---

[5] A bond may be secured with assets that the cash is used to obtain, or it may be unsecured, backed only by the credit worthiness of the issuer. The term **debenture** generally is used to identify an unsecured bond issue. Secured bond issues generally are made clear by a formal name printed on the bond such as *First Mortgage Bond*, indicating the bonds are backed by an asset (e.g., a building) that was purchased with the cash raised by the bond issue.

Interest Rates and Bond Premium and Discount   The bond described on the prior page should be viewed as a contract between the issuing company and the creditors (bond purchasers). For each bond, the contract offers the purchaser a $100 cash payment each year and $1,000 at maturity. If the purchasers feel that 10% is a fair return, then they will be willing to pay $1,000 each for the bonds. But what would happen if the purchasers decided 10% was not a sufficient return on the bond? Alternatively, what would happen if the purchasers decided that the bond was such an attractive investment that they would be willing to accept less than 10% interest? In either case, the bond could still be sold, but it would not sell at the maturity value of $1,000. *Only when a bond has a stated interest rate that is also considered by the purchasers (the market) to be an acceptable market interest rate will a bond sell for its maturity (face) value.*

Bonds with a stated interest rate *above* the acceptable rate to the market will sell above their maturity value and are called **premium bonds**. In this case, the purchasers bid the price of the bond up above its maturity value of $1,000 because of the superior cash interest payments. Bonds with a stated interest rate *below* the market interest rate will sell at a price that is less than maturity value and are called **discount bonds**. In this case, the purchasers will still buy these bonds; but they are only willing to pay an amount less than $1,000 for them.

Note that both premium and discount bonds result from an unwillingness of the market to accept the stated interest rate on the bond. Yet the issuer of the bond does not change the bond contract, which stipulates that the issuer will pay $100 interest each year-end and $1,000 at maturity. By bidding the price up or down, the purchasers effectively change the interest rate on the bond without the issuer changing the contractual cash payments. The **market interest rate** (= **yield** or **effective interest rate**) is the rate that purchasers are willing to accept in purchasing a bond, and knowing the market rate will allow us to determine what the bond can actually be sold for.

Bonds Issued at a Premium   To illustrate the nature and reporting of premium bonds, assume that on January 1, 2014 a company issued $100,000 of 10%, 5-year bonds. The bonds pay interest annually on December 31 and were sold to yield a market interest rate of 9%. If creditors were willing to accept 9%, and since the cash flows stipulated in the bond could not be revised, how much were the purchasers willing to pay for this bond? To answer this question, we must understand that *the purchasers will pay the present value of the future cash flows they will receive.* The future cash flows of a bond such as this one are (1) the stream of annual cash interest payments plus (2) the repayment of principal at maturity. Both of these cash flows must be discounted to their present value at the <u>market interest rate</u>. From the current bond contract, we know the cash flows are:

Interest: $10,000 ($100,000 x 10%) each December 31, from 2014 through 2018

Principal: $100,000 at December 31, 2018 (in 5 years)

The answer to how much the market is willing to pay for a 9% return on $100,000 of 10% bonds can be found using present value factors from Table 7-3 for the annual interest payments (the annuity) and from Table 7-2 for the repayment of the principal in 5 years (the single amount), as follows:

Interest: (P/A, 5, 9%) $10,000 = (3.8897) x $10,000 = $ 38,897 [Table 7-3]
Principal: (P/F, 5, 9%) $100,000 = (.6499) x $100,000 = 64,990 [Table 7-2]

Total cash received from the bond issuance $ 103,887

The bonds, therefore, were sold at 103.887 (103.887% of face value), and the premium on this bond issue was $3,887 ($103,887 cash received minus the $100,000 face amount that will be repaid at maturity). This is the additional amount (or principal) above the bond's face value that the issuer was able to borrow since the purchaser required a lower return than the bond's stated interest rate. The amortization table for this bond issuance is shown below.

Amortization Table – Premium Bonds

Date	Cash In (Cash Out)	9% Interest Expense*	Change in Balance	Balance of Liability
1/1/14	$103,887		$103,887	$103,887
12/31/14	($ 10,000)	$ 9,350	($ 650)	$103,237
12/31/15	($ 10,000)	$ 9,291	($ 709)	$102,528
12/31/16	($ 10,000)	$ 9,228	($ 772)	$101,756
12/31/17	($ 10,000)	$ 9,158	($ 842)	$100,914
12/31/18	($ 10,000)	$ 9,086**	($ 914)	$100,000
12/31/18	($100,000)		($100,000)	$ 0
Totals	($ 46,113)	$46,113		

* Annual interest expense is 9% times the balance of the liability owed throughout the period.
** Rounded from $9,082 to bring the ending balance to the $100,000 face value.

If you study the amortization table for the premium bond case, you will see that the interest expense reported each year-end is *the market interest rate of 9%* times the balance in the Bonds Payable account.[6] However, the cash interest payment each year is *the stated interest rate of 10%* times the face amount of the bonds (10% x $100,000 = $10,000), which is greater than the interest expense each year. To the extent that each $10,000 cash interest payment exceeds the 9% interest expense, the excess is a repayment of the $3,887 premium reducing the balance in the Bonds Payable account.

---

[6] Note that the *interest expense* is based on the <u>market</u> rate of 9%, not the stated rate of 10%. The stated rate of 10% is used only to compute the amount of the annual cash interest payment.

Each $10,000 cash payment not only will pay the interest expense of the year, but also will repay some of the original amount borrowed. When the interest payment is recorded in the accounting records, we amortize the premium by the difference between the cash interest payment and the interest expense recognized. By amortizing (reducing) the premium with the excess of the cash payments over the interest expense each year, the final contractual cash payment of $100,000 will exactly equal the remaining balance in Bonds Payable. The journal entries that would be made over the five-year life of the bond are shown in Exhibit 7-8.

Bonds Issued at a Discount Discount bonds arise when the stated interest rate on the bonds is below the required market interest rate. As a result the market will bid the price of the bonds down below the maturity value to yield the effective interest rate. Each year's cash interest payment then will be less than the amount of interest expense, and the balance in Bonds Payable will grow each year by that shortfall.

To illustrate this, assume that on January 1, 2014, $100,000 of 10%, 5-year bonds were issued. The bonds pay interest annually on December 31. Assume the required interest rate in the market at this time was 11%. To get the required 11% market interest rate on these bonds, the market bid only $96,299 for the bonds ($962.99 for each $1,000 bond), computed as follows:

Interest: (P/A, 5, 11%) $10,000   = (3.6959) x $10,000 = $ 36,959   [Table 7-3]

Principal: (P/F, 5, 11%) $100,000 = (.5934) x $100,000 =   59,340   [Table 7-2]

Total cash received from bond issuance $ 96,299

The bonds sold at 96.299 (96.299% of face amount), and the total discount for this bond issue was $3,701 ($100,000 face amount minus the $96,299 cash received). The following amortization table describes the cash flows and interest expense for this bond

Exhibit 7-8   Journal Entries for Premium Bond Example

Journal				Journal			
Date	Accounts	Debit	Credit	Date	Accounts	Debit	Credit
1/1/14	Cash	103,887		12/31/17	Interest Expense	9,158	
	Bonds Payable		103,887		Bonds Payable	842	
					Cash		10,000
12/31/14	Interest Expense	9,350					
	Bonds Payable	650		12/31/18	Interest Expense	9,086	
	Cash		10,000		Bonds Payable	914	
					Cash		10,000
12/31/15	Interest Expense	9,291					
	Bonds Payable	709		12/31/18	Bonds Payable	100,000	
	Cash		10,000		Cash		100,000
12/31/16	Interest Expense	9,228					
	Bonds Payable	772					
	Cash		10,000				

issuance. Note that the annual cash interest payments are always less than the interest expense that was incurred so the difference must be added to the Bonds Payable liability account as we amortize the discount.

Amortization Table – Discount Bonds

Date	Cash In (Cash Out)	11% Interest Expense*	Change in Balance	Balance of Liability
1/1/14	$ 96,299		$ 96,299	$ 96,299
12/31/14	($ 10,000)	$10,593	$ 593	$ 96,892
12/31/15	($ 10,000)	$10,658	$ 658	$ 97,550
12/31/16	($ 10,000)	$10,731	$ 731	$ 98,281
12/31/17	($ 10,000)	$10,811	$ 811	$ 99,092
12/31/18	($ 10,000)	$10,908**	$ 908	$100,000
12/31/18	($100,000)		($100,000)	$ 0
Totals	($ 53,701)	$53,701		

* Annual interest expense is 11% times the balance of the liability owed throughout the period.
** Rounded from $10,900 to bring the ending balance to the $100,000 face value.

The principal payment of $100,000 at the end of the five years is the original amount borrowed ($96,299) plus the unpaid portions of each annual interest expense, totaling $3,701 at the end of the bond's life. The $50,000 (nominal) cash interest payments were $3,701 short of the total interest expense of $53,701 on this bond, but this shortfall was made up by paying $100,000 face amount at maturity instead of the $96,299 actually borrowed. Note that the net cash out in the Cash In (Out) column is $53,701, the same as the sum of the interest expense in the next column of the table. The journal entries that would be made over the five-year life of the bond are shown in Exhibit 7-9.

Exhibit 7-9   Journal Entries for Discount Bond Example

	Journal				Journal		
Date	Accounts	Debit	Credit	Date	Accounts	Debit	Credit
1/1/14	Cash	96,299		12/31/17	Interest Expense	10,811	
	Bonds Payable		96,299		Cash		10,000
					Bonds Payable		811
12/31/14	Interest Expense	10,593					
	Cash		10,000	12/31/18	Interest Expense	10,908	
	Bonds Payable		593		Cash		10,000
					Bonds Payable		908
12/31/15	Interest Expense	10,658					
	Cash		10,000	12/31/18	Bonds Payable	100,000	
	Bonds Payable		658		Cash		100,000
12/31/16	Interest Expense	10,731					
	Cash		10,000				
	Bonds Payable		731				

Bonds Issued Between Interest Dates   It is not uncommon for the issuance of new bonds to take place over several months. This means that investors will buy the bonds on many different dates, none of which is an interest payment date. To account for these different dates, it is understood by all purchasers and sellers that bonds are always sold with accrued interest added to the selling price to the date of the sale/purchase.

For example, if a 6%, $10,000 bond, dated January 1, 2014 paying semiannual interest on June 30 and December 31 each year, is issued at the quoted price of 100 on May 1, 2014, it means that it is issued for 100% of its face value (= $10,000) plus four months accrued interest (interest earned from January 1 to May 1). In this example the accrued interest at May 1 would be $200 ($10,000 x 6% x 4/12 = $200). The bond could be purchased on May 1 for $10,200 ($10,000 + $200). When the next interest payment is made on June 30, the seller will eliminate the $200 accrued interest payable and the purchaser will eliminate the $200 accrued interest receivable. This $200 interest is not reported as an expense or revenue by either the seller or the buyer. Exhibit 7-10 illustrates the journal entries that would be required to record the sale/purchase transaction, along with the June 30 interest payment.

It is easy to be confused by why the purchaser should have to pay the seller for accrued interest on the date of issuance just because it is not an interest payment date. Why not just pay 100% for the bond on May 1 and then receive interest for only two months on June 30? The answer lies in the contractual terms of the bond. The bond contract calls for semiannual interest of $300 to be paid each June 30 and December 31. If the first interest payment was only for $100, the bond contract would have to be modified. And if the bonds were originally issued on 35 different dates within the first six months, each date would require a different contract for the first interest payment. To keep things simple, and permit the fixed cash flow contract of the bond to be issued on any date, the *bonds are sold at some percent of maturity value plus accrued interest to that date*.

In this example, we see the seller receives $200 of interest from the purchaser on May 1, and the purchaser then is paid $300 interest on June 30 (only $100 of which the purchaser has earned), thereby getting the $200 back. The $200 can be viewed as

Exhibit 7-10   Journal Entries for Issuance of Bond Between Interest Payment Dates

Seller				Purchaser			
Date	Accounts	Debit	Credit	Date	Accounts	Debit	Credit
5/1/14	Cash	10,200		5/1/14	Interest Receivable	200	
	Bonds Payable		10,000		Bonds Investment	10,000	
	Interest Payable		200		Cash		10,200
	(To sell bond at 100%)				*(To buy bond at 100%)*		
6/30/14	Interest Expense	100		6/30/14	Cash	300	
	Interest Payable	200			Interest Receivable		200
	Cash		300		Interest Revenue		100
	(To pay interest)				*(To receive interest)*		

a short-term loan to the seller that is repaid on the first interest payment date. In any case, we should see that a system of always trading bonds at a percentage of their face value plus accrued interest permits the bond contract to remain uniform for all bondholders, regardless of when they purchased the bond. And, once the bonds are issued, exchanges between purchasers and sellers in the bond market are greatly enhanced by always including accrued interest to the date of the sale.

Computing the Balance in Bonds Payable at a Future Date The balance in a long-term liability account is always equal to the present value of the future cash flows, discounted at the original market interest rate. To illustrate this point for bonds payable, consider once again the discount bond amortization table shown on page 69. At the end of 2014, the balance in the Bond Payable account will be $98,281. This is the balance with two interest payments plus the repayment of the principal remaining. This balance can be computed directly as the present value of the remaining contractual cash flows as of December 31, 2014 as follows:

Interest: (P/A, 2, 11%) $10,000   = (1.7125) x $10,000 = $ 17,125   [Table 7-3]

Principal: (P/F, 2, 11%) $100,000 = (.8116) x $100,000 =   81,160   [Table 7-2]

Balance at December 31, 2014 $ 98,285[7]

This example illustrates that *the carrying value for an interest-bearing liability in the financial statements is always the present value of the cash flows that remain to pay off the liability.*

Semiannual and Quarterly Interest

We have used annual cash flows in our examples. It is also common to find contracts that call for monthly cash flows, quarterly cash flows, or semiannual cash flows. We will work with semiannual cash flows in some of the homework assignments. For these applications, we will adopt the usual convention of *always stating interest rates in (nominal) annual percentages*. For example, if a rate is stated as "10% interest paid semiannually," we interpret that to mean that 5% interest will be paid twice during the year. If a rate is stated as "10% interest paid quarterly," we interpret that to mean that 2.5% interest will be paid four times during the year.

Other Bond Features Bonds can contain a variety of features to make them more attractive to the investor or issuer. Variable interest rates, the right to buy back the bond at a predetermined price, and the right to participate in superior earnings are all possible features of bond contracts. A feature of **convertible bonds** that makes them attractive is the ability to convert the bond into shares of common stock after some specified time at a specified exchange rate. For example, assume a company issues a $1,000 bond that matures in ten years and pays 8% annual interest. Further assume the bond is convertible into 10 shares of common stock after two years. At the time of issuance, assume the common stock is selling for $85 per share, so the conversion feature does

---

[7] The difference of $4 ($98,285 – $98,281) is due to rounding of the present value factors.

not seem to be worth anything. However, after two years assume the stock is selling for $120 per share. The bond holder can now convert the $1,000 bond into 10 shares of common stock worth $1,200 (10 shares x $120). The option to convert to common stock is attractive to investors in two ways: 1) if the stock goes up in value, the bondholder can share in the upside potential; and 2) if the stock value drops, the bondholder will not lose anything and will still receive 8% interest as well as $1,000 at maturity. In fact, investors will accept a lower interest rate on convertible bonds because of this feature. This feature is attractive to the issuer also since the issuer will get to deduct the interest expense until the bond is converted to common stock, and will typically pay less interest than what investors would have demanded on a non-convertible bond. So both issuers and investors may have incentives that make convertible bonds attractive.

Accounting rules in the U.S. currently require that convertible bonds be reported in the balance sheet as debt. However, when we analyze convertible bonds we see that they are really made up of two parts: 1) a straight bond and 2) an option to buy common stock. Some have argued that convertible bonds should be separated into their two parts and reported as both debt and equity, but U.S. rules currently do not permit this separation.

Pensions and Other Post-Employment Benefits

Many companies that deal with organized labor have commitments to their employees for retirement benefits. The benefits are given to employees after they retire from the company and can be in the form of defined pension plans and/or health care and other benefits. All of the benefits given to the employees once they retire are earned by the employees during their working years. Therefore, all retirement benefits should be viewed as a form of deferred compensation. As a result, the company must expense these benefits during the years of service when they are earned, not during the retirement period when they are actually paid. For U.S. labor-intensive industries these private company retirement obligations can be enormous.[8] For example, at the end of 2014 FORD MOTOR reported liabilities of over $9 billion for pensions and over $6 billion for health care! These $15 billion in interest bearing liabilities are, in effect, the present value of the unpaid benefits that employees will receive during retirement.

Defined benefit pension plans are plans that define the payment the company promises to provide the employee once they retire (for example, 50% of pre-retirement salary). The employer must put aside enough money during the employees' years of service to pay for these benefits. The company will put the money into a separate account (usually a trust) that is referred to as the pension fund, which is owned by the employees. If the amount of money put into the pension fund is not sufficient to meet the estimated obligations to all employees, a liability will be reported on the employer's balance sheet (e.g., $9 billion for FORD). When pension plans are over-funded, the employer's balance sheet will show the over-funded amount as an asset.

---

[8] Note that outside of the U.S. most countries have government as the responsible party for pensions and health care of retirees, not publicly-traded companies, putting US entities at a significant disadvantage in terms of total labor costs to the companies.

Although defined benefit pension plans are becoming less popular, they are still very important in industries like heavy manufacturing with large amounts of union-organized labor. Most companies will have a number of different plans to account for, typically one for each different labor union. Each plan is accounted for separately, so when we see a balance sheet that has both a pension asset and a pension liability it means that some of the pension plans are over-funded (assets) and others are under-funded (liabilities).

In addition to, or in place of, defined benefit pension plans, employers often have **defined contribution pension plans**, called 401(a) plans. In these plans, the employer defines the *current* contribution (instead of the *future* benefit) that will be made to each employee. These contributions are reported as a part of wage and salary expense, and once they are paid into the employee's retirement account, the employer has no further obligation to make payments. The risks and rewards of managing these individual pension accounts rest with the employee once the employer makes their defined contribution.

Of course, there are also companies that have no pension plans, and in such cases it is up to the individual employees to plan for their own retirement. Individual employee retirement plans are often referred to as 401(k) plans, or IRAs (Individual Retirement Accounts), and the U.S. Tax Code permits individuals to set aside money in these retirement accounts on a before-tax basis, meaning the individuals will not have to pay income tax on these retirement savings until they withdraw them after they retire. In addition to these three types of private pension plans, virtually all employees are eligible for the U.S. government's social security benefits for retirees.

We should understand that, from an accounting viewpoint, defined *benefit* pension plans represent a potentially significant liability that impacts both income and the balance sheet of U.S. labor intensive industries. These pension liabilities are real interest-bearing liabilities *that should be thought of as a loan from the employees of the company*. The employer will eventually have to pay the pension liability, plus interest, for any amounts owed to the pension fund. In defined benefit plans all of the risk of the pension funds' performance remains with the employer, since the employer remains responsible for the defined future retirement benefits for all employees. Hence, pensions are an important liability to consider when reading and evaluating U.S. corporate financial statements.

In addition to pension plans, many employers also promise their employees other benefits during their retirement period. Examples include health insurance and life insurance. These other benefits are generally known as **other post-employment benefits (OPEBs)**. Unlike pension benefits, OPEBs usually are not funded during the service period of the employees, even though they must be expensed during the service period and are earned during the service period.[9] As a result, estimated liabilities for OPEBs tend to be very large for the exact same set of companies that have large defined benefit pension plans. The amount of the reported liability is the present value of the

---

[9] The reason retirement health insurance benefits are not paid for during the employee service period is that health insurance companies will usually not sell polices more than one year in advance. Therefore, it is not possible for an employer to buy a health insurance policy today to cover the health insurance of an employee 2, 5, or 15 years from today.

expected future cash flows that the company estimates will be required to pay the benefits that have been earned by the employees. Like defined benefit pensions, these benefits will require future cash payments during the employees' years of retirement and should be viewed as interest-bearing loans from the employees. OPEB liabilities will increase each year by the implied interest rate used to compute their present-value, as well as the additional benefits earned by the employees each year. Cash payments towards the liability will, of course, reduce these liabilities.

Key Points to Remember

Several key points should be noted about interest-bearing liabilities:

1. The balance in an interest-bearing liability at any point in time is always the present value of the remaining future cash outflows, discounted at the effective (market) interest rate at the time of issuance.

2. The total amount of interest always equals the difference between the cash paid by the issuer and the cash (or other value) received by the issuer. The net cash effect may be seen in the cash in (out) column of each amortization table and is always equal to the total in the interest expense column.

3. Stated interest rates, known by several other names (e.g. nominal), are not usually equal to the required market interest rates, also known by several other names (e.g. effective). Knowing which interest rate to use for measurement and analysis is essential to understanding interest-bearing assets and liabilities.

4. We use the usual convention of stating interest rates in annual percentages. In addition, we make the assumption that an annual interest rate can be converted into a semiannual rate by dividing by two so that the tables based on whole interest percents may be used to solve all problems and examples in the text. Keep in mind however that, in reality, semiannual and quarterly interest rates are not the same as simply dividing annual interest rates by two or by four because of compounding effects.

Debt versus Equity and the Risk-Return Tradeoff

The first point in the list of four key points above is extremely important to understand. The role of accounting information for valuation purposes calls for a deep understanding of this fact. The value of any debt security (capital lease, bond, note, etc.) at any point in time is simply the present value of the remaining cash flows. In the case of most debt instruments, these cash flows are highly predictable. For example, unless there is a default, a bond will pay interest on the scheduled dates and will repay the principal at maturity. This makes debt securities relatively low-risk investments. Some debt instruments like pensions and OPEBs are a little more uncertain, but accounting routinely generates the estimates needed to record these obligations. The greater the uncertainty regarding the future cash flows the greater will be the risk of the debt security.

This fundamental principal of valuation based on the present value of future cash flows pertains to stocks (i.e., "equities") as well as debt instruments. In the case of equity securities, the future cash flows are not scheduled by contract like they are for monetary liabilities. The more uncertain future cash flows for equities stem from either dividend payments or stock price increases. And, as noted at the start of the chapter, shareholders cannot receive dividends or positive returns until profits exceed the fixed interest costs associated with monetary liabilities. Hence, equity securities are considered to be much more risky than debt securities.

Deferred Income Taxes

Another long-term liability that is common in balance sheets is the **deferred income taxes** liability. This liability does not represent a real obligation of the company. It does not represent a real claim against the assets as of the balance sheet date. Furthermore, if the company reporting the deferred tax liability were to file for bankruptcy and/or go out of business, no payment would be required for this liability. It exists in order to allow the income tax payable to the IRS for a given year (based on the company's income tax return) to differ from the amount of income tax expense reported in the GAAP income statement for that same year. Keep in mind that the taxable income in the company's income tax return will typically be much different than the pre-tax income per GAAP. In order to accommodate a current liability for income tax payable that is different from the recognized income tax expense in the financial statements, GAAP essentially plugs the difference to an asset (when the payable exceeds the expense) or a liability (when the expense exceeds the payable). The deferred income tax assets and liabilities are created to allow the tax expense and the tax payable to differ in any given year.

To illustrate why a deferred tax account is needed, assume a company expenses an asset in 2014 for tax purposes, while for financial reporting purposes it expenses this asset over 2014 and 2015. Assume the difference is that GAAP-based pretax income is $1,000 higher in 2014 and $1,000 lower in 2015 as a result of the difference in depreciation expense. If the income tax rate is 40%, the difference between income tax expense on the income statement and the income tax obligation on the tax return will be $400 (40% x $1,000). In the first year the actual income tax due to the IRS will be $400 less that the amount of the income tax expense reported in the income statement, so a deferred income tax liability will be reported for the $400 difference. In 2015, this liability will be satisfied because the income tax obligation to the IRS will be $400 more than the income tax expense reported in the income statement. In reality, of course, the deferred income tax liabilities for most corporations persist over a number of years and continue to be reported in the financial statements.

The deferred income taxes that appear in the balance sheet as liabilities, and sometimes as assets, are not real in an economic sense. You should think of the deferred income tax accounts that appear in the balance sheet as bookkeeping vehicles to permit financial reporting numbers to differ from those reported for income tax purposes, and you should not consider them to be real liabilities or assets when conducting analysis of financial statements. Because of this, many analysts delete deferred income tax amounts from the balance sheet for decision-making purposes and plug the Retained Earnings account for any difference.

LIABILITIES AND BUSINESS DECISIONS

Liabilities represent financial risk that is the primary source of risk to investors and shareholders of most businesses. While operating risk is also important, it is not uncommon for financial risk to be highly related to operating risk. Operating risk stems from large investments in plant and equipment. And it is typically large quantities of plant assets that lead to the need for large amounts of long-term monetary liabilities.

The decision concerned with how to finance the required plant assets needed to operate a business is one of the most important in determining the riskiness of a company. There are basically three ways to finance a company's assets, and the same three alternatives for obtaining resources needed to obtain new assets to sustain or grow the business. These three sources of capital are:

1. Sale of stock;
2. Debt; and
3. Earnings that are retained in the business (versus paid to owners).

More debt or other interest-bearing obligations used to finance the assets of the entity results in higher risk, all else being equal. Debt and other interest-bearing obligations tend to be the most common source of significant amounts of new capital for most businesses. Seasoned equity offerings (i.e., stock offerings for an existing publicly traded company) are not common; and while earnings are an ideal source for major capital requirements, earnings alone are generally insufficient.

Investors at all levels need to be well versed in how to assess the risk of a company and to understand the fundamental nature of the relationship between risk and return. This basic understanding of the tenants of investing leads to understanding that there is no such thing as the optimal level of risk, or the optimal mix of interest-bearing obligations for financing the assets of the entity. While decisions related to how to finance the company, or how much risk to take in making investments in stocks and debt securities are extremely important and interesting, there is no way to judge (ex-ante) these decisions. Of course, after the fact, everyone has 20-20 hindsight!

INTERNATIONAL FINANCIAL REPORTING STANDARDS

There are, for the most part, no differences in the basic accounting treatment of liabilities between IFRS and U.S. GAAP. Perhaps the most important difference to note here is in the impact of pensions on comprehensive income. While the pension **liability** would be essentially the same under US GAAP and IFRS, the disclosure of the income consequence would differ. The annual change in pensions would be reported entirely in net income under IFRS; while under US GAAP, some portion of the change in pensions would be reported in comprehensive income.(below the net income amount). The IFRS treatment of all changes in pension liability as a part of employee compensation expense for the period is actually preferred to the treatment in the US. Chapters 8 and 9 both discuss and illustrate the elements of comprehensive income in more detail.

While there are other less important differences between US GAAP and IFRS concerning the reporting of liabilities, these details go beyond the scope of this introductory text and will be covered in more advanced textbooks. It is sufficient to understand that, with very rare exception, the measurement and reporting of liabilities is the same under US GAAP and IFRS. Furthermore, there are few, if any, measurement issues pertaining to liabilities. The reported liabilities tend to provide an unbiased measure of the real economic obligations of the business entity under both sets of rules.

SUMMARY

There are very few measurement issues related to liabilities, and in general the liability section of the balance sheet reports the essential obligation of the entity at relevant and reliable amounts. The reported amounts of most liabilities are known with certainty, such as the amounts due on accounts payable and the amounts due on notes or bonds payable. Other current liabilities such as taxes payable and warranty liabilities are not known precisely and can only be estimated in the financial statements. However, the estimation process is usually reliable, resulting in relevant information about these estimated obligations.

Contingent liabilities are a special category of liabilities; they represent possible liabilities that require the resolution of future events for a final determination of whether they do in fact represent a liability. These liabilities can include items such as an environmental action by the government or a lawsuit by consumers that could result in an obligation in the future. Contingent liabilities are recorded in the balance sheet if the amount of the loss can be estimated and the loss is probable; otherwise the contingency will only be described in the footnotes.

A company's most important category of liabilities is their long-term, interest-bearing liabilities. Bonds (notes) and capital leases are commonly found in financial statements. These liabilities are accounted for using time value of money concepts, and they generally conform to one of the three common repayment patterns described in the chapter. The guiding principle is that all long-term liabilities are reported in the current balance sheet at the present value of the future cash flows required to pay them off.

KEY TERMS

annuity A series of equal cash payments made over a specified period of time. *54, 59*

amortization table A table that illustrates how a series of cash payments repays a liability (the amount borrowed) plus the interest. *53, 55-56, 62, 64, 67, 69*

bonds Debt contracts that can have a variety of terms usually requiring fixed semiannual or annual interest payments and a stated payment at maturity; unsecured bonds are called debentures. Also see *zero-coupon bond* and *convertible bond*. *65-72*

capital lease A contract where the lessee records an asset based on the value of the leased property and a liability for the amount that must be paid in the future to obtain the asset. Also called *financing lease*; *sales-type lease*; *lease purchase contract*. *63-64*

carrying value The balance owed on a long-term liability. *64*

compound interest Interest that is computed on unpaid accrued interest. For example, if you borrow $100 at 10% with principal and interest due in two years, the interest for the first year is $10 ($100 x 10%) and the compound interest for the second year is $11 [($100 + $10 accrued interest) x 10%]. Compare to *simple interest*. Assume all interest is compounded annually unless otherwise stated. *53*

contingent liability A potential liability that depends upon a future event for a final judgment as to whether it is an actual liability or not. If the potential liability is both able to be estimated and probable, it will be recorded in the balance sheet. If it is able to be estimated or probable but not both, it will be described in the footnotes. *52*

convertible bond Bond that may be converted into a predetermined number of shares of common stock after a predetermined period of time. *71*

debenture An unsecured debt contract. See *bond*. *65*

default risk Risk associated with non-payment by the borrower. *49*

deferred income taxes Balance sheet accounts that permit the amount of income tax expense reported in the income statement to differ from the actual income tax obligation. Deferred income taxes may appear as both assets and liabilities. *75*

defined benefit pension plans Pension plans where the employer assumes the responsibility for funding an amount necessary to provide the employees with a stipulated amount of benefits during their retirement period. *72*

defined contribution pension plans Pension plans where the employer is responsible for contributing a specified amount to the employees' pension accounts. *73*

discount bond A bond sold for less than its face value because the market requires a higher return (market interest rate) than the bond's stated interest rate. *66, 68-69*

effective interest rate The market interest rate. *66*

face interest rate The stated interest rate printed on the face of the debt contract. *65*

face value The value printed on the face of a debt contract; see *maturity value*. *62*

future value The value that an investment today will grow to at a stipulated future date at a specified interest rate. For example, the notation for the future value of an amount invested for five years at 10% annual interest is (F/P, 5, 10%). *58, 80*

interest The amount of cash paid to the lender in excess of the amount borrowed. The difference between the sum of the cash paid and the amount of cash received. Represents interest expense to the borrower and interest income to the lender. *49*

interest rate Annual percentage used to compute interest. Ambiguous term as it may refer to a *stated rate* or a *market rate*. *49*

interest rate risk Risk associated with the possibility that interest rates will increase during the period of the loan. *49*

lessee The renter or property acquirer in a lease contract. *63*

lessor The party providing the property to the lessee in a lease contract. *63*

market interest rate   The interest rate that purchasers are willing to accept in purchasing a bond. The market interest rate times the sum of the accumulated unpaid principal plus accrued interest equals interest expense for the borrower (and interest income for the lender); also called *effective interest rate*; *true interest rate*; *real interest rate;* and *yield. 66*

maturity value   The amount of cash due to the lender at the maturity of a bond, note or other similar instrument. Also known as the *face value* since this is the amount printed on the face of the bond or note; see *face value. 62*

monetary liabilities   Fixed claims to a specified number of dollars. Monetary liabilities are reported at their present value, which equals the dollar amount of the claim at that date. *47*

operating lease   A contract allowing the lessee to treat the lease as a rental agreement and to not record the leased asset or the liability to make lease payments. *63*

ordinary annuity   Series of equal payments that begin at the *end* of the first year. *60*

other post-employment benefits (OPEBs)   Retiree benefits other than retirement income that an employer promises employees during their retirement period (e.g., health care benefits). *73*

pensions   See *defined benefit pension plans* and *defined contribution pension plans.*

premium bond   A bond sold for more than its face value because the market is satisfied with a lower return (market interest rate) than the bond's stated interest rate. *66-68*

present value   The value today of one or more future cash payments given the market interest rate. For example, the notation for the present value of an amount at the end of 10 years at 8% annual interest is (P/F, 10, 8%). *58-59, 82*

principal   The amount of debt that must be repaid, not including interest. Usually, the amount borrowed or the value of the property acquired in a capital lease. *49*

proceeds   The total amount of cash received for a bond issue, including accrued interest for bonds issued between interest dates. *61*

risk   Uncertainty regarding future events. In the context of borrowing/lending, risk refers to the uncertainty of future events such as changes in the market rate of interest over the term of the loan and the uncertainty that the borrower will be able to repay the loan. The interest rate varies depending on the amount of risk, with higher risk contracts demanding a higher interest rate. *49*

simple interest   Interest computations that do not account for compounding. For example, if you borrow $100 at 10% for two years the simple interest is $10 per year or $20 total for two years. Compare to *compound interest. 49*

stated interest rate   The rate printed on the face of a borrowing/lending contract. This rate times the maturity (face) value of the contract equals the periodic cash interest payments that must be made. Also called the *face interest rate; nominal interest rate; coupon interest rate. 65*

warranty liabilities   The estimated future cost of yet to be filed claims from past sales of products/services that were sold with a warranty. *51*

working capital   Current assets minus current liabilities; the general idea is to maintain a ratio of current assets to current liabilities that will enable the company to pay its obligation on a timely basis but not have more current assets than necessary. *48*

yield   The interest rate required by the market. See *market interest rate. 66*

zero-coupon bond   A bond that does not pay periodic interest to the holder but instead repays both principal and accumulated interest as a single amount at maturity. *61*

APPENDIX

Future Value and Present Value Tables

Table 7-1 presents the factors for computing the future value of a single amount invested today. Future value is the amount to which the single amount will grow in **_n_** periods at a specified interest rate, compounded each period. The formula is:

$$\text{Future Value} = \text{Present Amount} \times (1 + \text{interest rate})^n$$

Table 7-2 presents the factors for computing the present value of a future amount. (These are the reciprocals of the factors in Table 7-1.) Present value is the current value of a future single payment that will be made **_n_** periods away at a specified interest rate that is compounded each period. The formula is:

$$\text{Present Value} = \text{Future Amount} \times [1 \div (1 + \text{interest rate})^n]$$

Table 7-3 presents the factors for computing the present value of a series (annuity) of future equal payments. (These factors are the sum over **_n_** periods of the present value factors in Table 7-2.) Present value of an annuity is the current value of an annuity of future payments over **_n_** periods at a specified interest rate, compounded each period. The formula is:

$$\text{Present Annuity Value} = \text{Annuity Amount} \times \Sigma[1 \div (1 + \text{interest rate})^n]$$

Table 7-1 (F/P, n, i)   Future Value of a Single Amount Invested Today

n	4%	5%	6%	7%	8%	9%	10%	11%	12%
1	1.0400	1.0500	1.0600	1.0700	1.0800	1.0900	1.1000	1.1100	1.1200
2	1.0816	1.1025	1.1236	1.1449	1.1664	1.1881	1.2100	1.2321	1.2544
3	1.1249	1.1576	1.1910	1.2250	1.2597	1.2950	1.3310	1.3676	1.4049
4	1.1699	1.2155	1.2625	1.3108	1.3605	1.4116	1.4641	1.5181	1.5735
5	1.2167	1.2763	1.3382	1.4026	1.4693	1.5386	1.6105	1.6851	1.7623
6	1.2653	1.3401	1.4185	1.5007	1.5869	1.6771	1.7716	1.8704	1.9738
7	1.3159	1.4071	1.5036	1.6058	1.7138	1.8280	1.9487	2.0762	2.2107
8	1.3686	1.4775	1.5938	1.7182	1.8509	1.9926	2.1436	2.3045	2.4760
9	1.4233	1.5513	1.6895	1.8385	1.9990	2.1719	2.3579	2.5580	2.7731
10	1.4802	1.6289	1.7908	1.9671	2.1589	2.3674	2.5937	2.8394	3.1059
11	1.5395	1.7103	1.8983	2.1049	2.3316	2.2504	2.8531	3.1518	3.4786
12	1.6010	1.7959	2.0122	2.2522	2.5182	2.8127	3.1384	3.4984	3.8960
13	1.6651	1.8856	2.1329	2.4098	2.7196	3.0658	3.4523	3.8833	4.3635
14	1.7317	1.9799	2.2609	2.5785	2.9372	3.3417	3.7975	4.3104	4.8871
15	1.8009	2.0789	2.3966	2.7590	3.1722	3.6425	4.1772	4.7846	5.4736
16	1.8730	2.1829	2.5403	2.9522	3.4259	3.9703	4.5950	5.3109	6.1304
17	1.9479	2.2920	2.6928	3.1588	3.7000	4.3276	5.0545	5.8951	6.8661
18	2.0258	2.4066	2.8543	3.3799	3.9960	4.7171	5.5599	6.5435	7.6900
19	2.1068	2.5269	3.0256	3.6165	4.3157	5.1417	6.1159	7.2633	8.6128
20	2.1911	2.6533	3.2071	3.8697	4.6609	5.6044	6.7275	8.0623	9.6463

Table 7-2 (P/F, n, i) Present Value of a Single Amount Received or Paid in the Future

n	4%	5%	6%	7%	8%	9%	10%	11%	12%
1	.9615	.9524	.9434	.9346	.9259	.9174	.9091	.9009	.8929
2	.9246	.9070	.8900	.8734	.8573	.8417	.8264	.8116	.7972
3	.8890	.8638	.8396	.8163	.7938	.7722	.7513	.7312	.7118
4	.8548	.8227	.7921	.7629	.7350	.7084	.6830	.6587	.6355
5	.8219	.7835	.7473	.7130	.6806	.6499	.6209	.5934	.5674
6	.7903	.7462	.7050	.6663	.6302	.5963	.5645	.5346	.5066
7	.7599	.7107	.6651	.6228	.5835	.5470	.5132	.4817	.4524
8	.7307	.6768	.6274	.5820	.5403	.5019	.4665	.4339	.4039
9	.7026	.6446	.5919	.5439	.5002	.4604	.4241	.3909	.3606
10	.6756	.6139	.5584	.5084	.4632	.4224	.3855	.3522	.3220
11	.6496	.5847	.5368	.4751	.4289	.3875	.3505	.3173	.2875
12	.6246	.5568	.4970	.4440	.3971	.3555	.3186	.2858	.2567
13	.6006	.5303	.4688	.4150	.3677	.3262	.2897	.2575	.2292
14	.5775	.5051	.4423	.3878	.3405	.2993	.2633	.2320	.2046
15	.5553	.4810	.4173	.3625	.3152	.2745	.2394	.2090	.1827
16	.5339	.4581	.3936	.3387	.2919	.2519	.2176	.1883	.1631
17	.5134	.4363	.3714	.3166	.2703	.2311	.1978	.1696	.1456
18	.4936	.4155	.3503	.2959	.2502	.2120	.1799	.1528	.1300
19	.4746	.3957	.3305	.2765	.2317	.1945	.1635	.1377	.1161
20	.4564	.3769	.3118	.2584	.2145	.1784	.1486	.1240	.1037

Table 7-3 (P/A, n, i) Present Value of an Ordinary Annuity Received or Paid in the Future

n	4%	5%	6%	7%	8%	9%	10%	11%	12%
1	.9615	.9524	.9434	.9346	.9259	.9174	.9091	.9009	.8929
2	1.8861	1.8594	1.8334	1.8080	1.7833	1.7591	1.7355	1.7125	1.6901
3	2.7751	2.7232	2.6730	2.6243	2.5771	2.5313	2.4869	2.4437	2.4018
4	3.6299	3.5459	3.4651	3.3872	3.3121	3.2397	3.1699	3.1024	3.0374
5	4.4518	4.3295	4.2124	4.1002	3.9927	3.8897	3.7908	3.6959	3.6048
6	5.2421	5.0757	4.9173	4.7666	4.6229	4.4859	4.3553	4.2305	4.1114
7	6.0021	5.7864	5.5824	5.3893	5.2064	5.0330	4.8684	4.7122	4.5638
8	6.7328	6.4632	6.2098	5.9713	5.7466	5.5348	5.3349	5.1461	4.9676
9	7.4353	7.1078	6.8017	6.5152	6.2469	5.9953	5.7590	5.5371	5.3282
10	8.1109	7.7217	7.3601	7.0236	6.7101	6.4177	6.1446	5.8892	5.6502
11	8.7605	8.3064	7.8869	7.4987	7.1390	6.8052	6.4951	6.2065	5.9377
12	9.3851	8.8633	8.3839	7.9427	7.5361	7.1607	6.8137	6.4924	6.1944
13	9.9857	9.3936	8.8527	8.3577	7.9038	7.4869	7.1034	6.7499	6.4235
14	10.5631	9.8986	9.2950	8.7455	8.2442	7.7862	7.3667	6.9819	6.6282
15	11.1184	10.3797	9.7123	9.1079	8.5595	8.0607	7.6061	7.1909	6.8109
16	11.6523	10.8378	10.1059	9.4467	8.8514	8.3126	7.8237	7.3792	6.9740
17	12.1657	11.2741	10.4773	9.7632	9.1216	8.5436	8.0216	7.5488	7.1196
18	12.6593	11.6896	10.8276	10.0591	9.3719	8.7556	8.2014	7.7016	7.2497
19	13.1339	12.0853	11.1581	10.3356	9.6036	8.9501	8.3649	7.8393	7.3658
20	13.5903	12.4622	11.4699	10.5940	9.8181	9.1285	8.5136	7.9633	7.4694

Test your understanding of the material covered in the chapter by answering the following questions. The correct answers to these questions are shown below.

1. On January 1, $1,000,000 of 11%, 8-year bonds were issued to yield a market interest rate of 9%. Interest is payable annually on December 31. What amount of cash was received from the issuance of these bonds?

    a. $1,110,728
    b. $943,651
    c. $1,000,032
    d. $897,049

2. On January 1, $500,000 of 8% bonds were issued to yield a market interest rate of 10%. Interest is payable <u>semiannually</u> on June 30 and December 31. A total of $461,384 in cash was received. What was the balance in the Bonds Payable account at July 1 of the first year?

    a. $459,839
    b. $467,552
    c. $458,315
    d. $464,453

3. On January 1, 2014, a 6-year, 10% capital lease was signed. The lease calls for a $100,000 payment on January 1, 2014 and five year-end payments of $100,000 each starting on December 31, 2014. What was the total interest expense reported for this lease for the <u>year</u> ended December 31, <u>2015</u>?

    a. $44,117
    b. $31,699
    c. $37,908
    d. $34,117

Answers: a, d, b

PROBLEMS

7-1 Liabilities

1. Who should be held responsible for the failure to take advantage of a purchase discount—the Accounts Payable Department or the Purchasing Department? Why?
2. Describe the three components of the basic interest calculation equation.
3. Why do estimated liabilities exist? How is the warranty liability similar to the allowance for doubtful accounts? Explain your answer.
4. Describe the criteria for a contingent liability to be reported on the balance sheet. If it is not reported on the balance sheet, where would we often find reference to it?
5. Explain why short-term borrowing is often critical for cyclical businesses.
6. Describe three different repayment patterns illustrated in the chapter and give an example of a borrowing contract for each.
7. Why might an investor choose to purchase zero-coupon bonds?
8. How are capital leases different from operating leases? Describe the challenges this could present to investors.
9. Differentiate among bonds issued at face value, for a premium, and at a discount. What are their similarities and differences?
10. Why require a portion of the interest to be prepaid by the bond purchaser when the bond is issued between interest dates?

7-2 Business Decision Case

The Precision Casting Company (PCC) is a closely-held, family-controlled corporation that is considering alternative ways to grow its business. (You are a third generation member of the family who controls PCC.) The existing business has been in operation for the past eighteen years and has recently experienced a major increase in the otherwise steady increase in demand for product since its inception. The growth in demand has made it clear that without additional plant assets PCC will not be able to keep up with demand. Also, due to the pressure on the existing capacity, the efficiency of operations and losses due to mechanical breakdowns has hurt profitability as well as customer relations.   The recent balance sheet and income statement data are provided in the table below:

(all $ in millions)	2017	2016
Balance Sheet Data:		
Plant and equipment (net)	$260	$266
Total assets	$581	$580
Long-term debt	$240	$245
Equity	$160	$163
Income Statement Data:		
Sales	$725	$685
Operating income	$18	$32
Interest expense	$12	$12.25

PCC's Board of Directors is considering ways to obtain new capital to help the company meet growing demand. Some venture capital and investment bankers have discussed PCC's situation with the Board and feel PCC has the ability to issue additional stock to obtain the additional $250 million in capital needed for the expansion of operations. A public equity offering of $250 million would need to be offered at a per share price that would represent a 75% equity stake in the company. PCC's bankers also feel that financing the $250 million expansion could be done with additional long-term bank debt, but at a slightly higher interest rate than the current debt. The CFO has presented the Board with three alternative ways to obtain an additional $250 million in capital, as depicted in the table below:

(all $ in millions)	Sell Stock	Issue Debt	50% Stock 50% Debt
Additional capital	$250	$250	$250
Annual interest cost	none	$15	$7.5

PCC's Board of Directors is a high-functioning board with the best interests of the investors (including your family) and PCC's employees always considered. To test your knowledge of the issues, you have been asked to evaluate the options and compare your recommendation against what the Board recommends.

Required:

1. Briefly list the key advantages and disadvantages of each of these three options.
2. Which option would you recommend? Explain.

7-3 Liability Transactions

The following transactions related to liabilities occurred during 2013 and 2014:

a. On April 1, 2013, acquired $48,000 of equipment on a 6%, 4-year note payable. The note requires annual payments on March 31 of each year of the accrued interest for that year plus one-quarter of the principal.
b. On September 1, 2013, borrowed $20,000 on a 5%, 9-month note payable with principal and interest due in a single amount at maturity.
c. On December 31, 2013, recorded accrued interest on the 6% and 5% notes.
d. On December 31, 2013, made the adjusting entry to record estimated warranty expense at 0.2% of total sales of $15,000,000.
e. On March 31, 2014, made the first payment of principal and interest on the 6% note payable.
f. On April 15, 2014, made the entry to record that $5,600 of replacement parts had been sent to customers under the terms of the company's warranty agreement.
g. On May 31, 2014, paid the 5% note plus interest.

Required:

1. For each item a. through g. above, prepare the journal entry that was made to record the transaction in the accounting records.
2. Describe the economic impact on the firm from each transaction.

7-4   Future Values and Present Values with Annual Compounding

(Note: *Remember, interest rates are stated in annual percentages.*)

Part A: Compute the future value of the following single amounts:

1. $20,000 at the end of 5 years at 8% interest compounded annually.
2. $20,000 at the end of 5 years at 10% interest compounded annually.

Part B: Compute the present value of $20,000 single amount:

1.   At 8% interest compounded annually
     a.   At the end of 5 years
     b.   At the end of 10 years

2.   At 10% interest compounded annually
     a.   At the end of 5 years
     b.   At the end of 10 years

Part C: Compute the present value of the following ordinary annuities:

1.   Annual payments of $10,000 each for 6 years at 9% interest.
     a.   Same calculation but change the years to 3 years. And then 9 years.
     b.   Describe what you notice about the present value amounts. What is the impact of time on the present value amount? Why?
2.   Annual payments of $5,000 each for 7 years at 8% interest.
     a.   Same calculation but change the interest to 4%. And then 12%.
     b.   Describe what you notice about the present value amounts. What is the impact of on the present value amount with a change in the interest rate? Why?

7-5   Time Value of Money

You have won $1,000,000 in the state lottery! The winnings are to be paid to you in 20 annual payments of $50,000 each starting one year from today. You take the winning ticket to the bank and ask them what they are willing to pay you today in exchange for the twenty annual $50,000 payments.

Required:

1.   Assume the bank wants to earn a 6% interest rate. Compute the amount of cash they are willing to give you today in exchange for the ticket.
2.   Now assume the bank is willing to give you $623,110 cash today for the ticket. Compute the interest rate the bank will earn on this transaction.
3.   Now assume the bank will pay you $456,425 today, which will allow them to earn a 9% interest rate. Further assume you can take this cash and invest it at 10% interest compounded annually. Compute how much this investment will be worth in 20 years assuming you do not withdraw any cash until then.
4.   Describe what you notice about the impact interest rates have on present and future values.

7-6   Time Value of Money

It is January 1, 2015. You have decided to take a world tour beginning one year from now. You have savings of $90,000 invested in a bank account that earns 8% per year. To travel for four years you will need to withdraw $20,000 on December 31, 2015, $20,000 on December 31, 2016, $20,000 on December 31, 2017 and $20,000 on December 31, 2018.

Required:

1. Compute the amount of money you will have in your bank account on December 31, 2018, immediately after withdrawing the last $20,000 and beginning the last year of your world tour.
2. Compute the amount you would be willing to pay on January 1, 2015 for a bank account earning 8% that would allow you to withdraw $20,000 per year as described above, leaving a zero balance after the last withdrawal on December 31, 2018.
3. Compute the maximum amount you could withdraw at the end of each of the four years given the amount you currently have available and the 8% interest rate it is currently earning assuming you will have a zero balance in your account at December 31, 2018 after the last withdrawal (round to the nearest dollar).

7-7   Time Value of Money

You want to purchase and refurbish a house in the city. The house has a cash price of $220,000. A bank is willing to lend you the $220,000 and will require you to repay $29,891 at the end of each of the next 10 years starting one year from today.

Required:

1. Compute the total amount of cash you will repay the bank.
2. Compute the total amount of interest you will pay the bank.
3. Compute the interest rate you are paying on the borrowed money.
4. Assume the average annual home appreciation rate for the area in which the house is located is 5%. Compute the expected market value of the house in 10 years.

7-8   Applying Time Value of Money Concepts to a Business Decision

New equipment for your business has a cash price of $600,000. The manufacturer is willing to sell the equipment for a down payment of $60,000 and six annual year-end payments of $106,389 beginning one year from today. A bank will lend you $600,000 with no down payment and ten year-end payments of $85,426 per year beginning one year from today.

Required:

1. Prepare a schedule of the cash flows for each alternative.
2. Utilizing the annuity present value tables, compute the interest rate in each of the two financing arrangements.
3. Determine the total interest costs for each alternative.
4. Prepare an amortization schedule for each alternative.
5. Present arguments for and against each alternative for acquiring the equipment supporting your arguments with data from the previous requirements.

7-9   Time Value of Money

Your parents have won $5,000,000 in the state lottery! They are scheduled to collect their money on December 15, 2014. They were told the $5,000,000 will be paid out in 20 installments at the rate of $250,000 per year with first payment of $250,000 being made on December 15, 2014 and the next 19 payments of $250,000 coming each subsequent December 15. However, your parents would like to get the value of the lottery win as soon as possible to retire and are wondering if there are other options available to them.

As a student of business, you meet with your parents to discuss their situation. You know that the state's promise to pay them $250,000 in 20 annual installments is a sound one. You have a friend in the banking business who has told you that the bank is currently lending money to its best customers on long-term loans of from 15 to 20 years at the rate of 5% per year. Your friend is confident that the bank would be willing to give your parents the initial $250,000 payment plus the present value of the 19 future payments discounted at 5% per year if they sign over the lottery ticket to the bank.

The state also tells your parents that they are willing to give them $3,039,525 in cash on December 15, 2014 instead of the $250,000 payment and annuity of $250,000 for the next 19 years.

Required:

1.   Your parents ask you if they should take the cash offer from the state or the offer from the bank. Explain to them how you suggest they analyze the two options to maximize the funds they receive for the ticket.
2.   Calculate the proceeds your parents would receive if they choose to sell their ticket to the bank.
3.   Before you calculate your answer to this question, predict whether the interest rate implied in the cash option from the state is greater or less than 5%. Determine the interest rate the state is using to compute the present value of the payments.
4.   What would you suggest to your parents to allow them to cash in on their lottery win today? Explain your answer making sure to include supporting calculations.

7-10   Applying Time Value of Money Concepts to a Business Decision

You and some friends have formed a band. You need to purchase a set of speakers for your concerts. The speakers have a cash price of $50,000. Thus far you and your friends have been investing your earnings in conservative investments that earn 5% annually. If you buy the speakers outright, you will use your savings, essentially borrowing from yourselves at 5%. The speaker store is willing to sell the speakers to the group for a $5,000 initial payment and five additional year-end payments of $10,683 each beginning one year from today.

Required:

1.   Determine the present value of each of the two alternatives: (1) purchase the speakers with their current savings; or (2) finance $45,000 of the purchase.
2.   Provide and explain your recommendation to your fellow band members.

7-11 Bond Issuance

On January 1, 2014, $2,000,000 of 9%, 15-year bonds were issued. The bonds pay interest annually on December 31. The bonds were priced to yield a market interest rate of 8%.

Required:

1. Describe the cash flows the bonds will pay (and investors will receive) over the 15 years.
2. Will cash received from the bond issuance be greater or less than the bond's face value? Explain your answer.
3. Compute the amount of cash received from issuing these bonds and the total interest cost over the life of the bonds.
4. Prepare an amortization schedule for the first three annual interest payments.
5. Predict the carrying value of the bonds at the end of year 12.

7-12 Bond Issuance

On January 1, 2014, $6,000,000 of 10%, 10-year bonds were issued. The bonds pay interest semiannually on June 30 and December 31. The bonds were priced to yield a market interest rate of 8%.

Required:

1. Describe the cash flows the bonds will pay (and investors will receive) over the 10 years.
2. Will cash received from the bond issuance be greater or less than the bond's face value? Explain your answer.
3. Compute the amount of cash received from issuing these bonds and the total interest cost over the life of the bonds.
4. Compute interest expense for the first five interest payments of the bonds. An amortization schedule would be help for organizing your data.
5. Prepare the journal entries to record the interest payments on June 30 and December 31, 2014.
6. Now assume the bonds were issued at 104 on March 1, 2014 rather than January 1, 2014. Compute the total amount of cash received and show the journal entry that was made to record the issuance of the bonds.

7-13 Bond Issuance

On January 1, 2014, $4,000,000 of 7%, 20-year bonds were issued. The bonds pay interest annually on December 31. The bonds were priced to yield a market interest rate of 9%.

Required:

1. Describe the cash flows the bonds will pay (and investors will receive) over the 20 years.
2. Will cash received from the bond issuance be greater or less than the bond's face value? Explain your answer.
3. Compute the amount of cash received from issuing these bonds and the total interest cost over the life of the bonds.
4. Prepare an amortization schedule for the first three annual interest payments.
5. Predict the carrying value of the bonds at the end of year 16.

7-14   Bond Issuance

On January 1, 2014, $8,000,000 of 10%, 10-year bonds were issued. The bonds pay interest semiannually on June 30 and December 31. The bonds were priced to yield a market interest rate of 12%.

Required:

1. Describe the cash flows the bonds will pay (and investors will receive) over the 10 years.
2. Will cash received from the bond issuance be greater or less than the bond's face value? Explain your answer.
3. Compute the amount of cash received from issuing these bonds and the total interest cost over the life of the bonds.
4. Compute interest expense for the first five interest payments of the bonds. An amortization schedule would be helpful to organize your data.
5. Prepare the journal entries to record the interest payments on June 30 and December 31, 2014.
6. Now assume the bonds were issued at 96 on March 1, 2014 rather than January 1, 2014. Compute the total amount of cash received and show the journal entry that was made to record the issuance of the bonds.

7-15   Interpreting Bond Amounts

The following table summarizes bonds payable at December 31, 2014 and 2013:

Bonds	2014	2013
$300,000 of 5% bonds due on December 31, 2022	$281,367	$279,596
$400,000 of 7% bonds due on December 31, 2023	$427,208	$429,443

The bonds pay interest annually on December 31. No bonds were sold or retired in 2013 or 2014.

Required:

1. Set up two Bonds Payable T-accounts—one for the 5% bonds and one for the 7% bonds.
2. Determine the annual cash interest payment for each bond. Using that information and the T-accounts, recreate the journal entries that were prepared to record those interest payments on December 31, 2014.
3. Compute the effective (market) interest rate for each bond (round to the nearest percent).
4. Describe what you know about the bond issuances contrasting the stated and market interest rates as well as cash received at issuance and the bonds' face values.
5. Given that you have computed the effective interest rate for each bond, confirm (using calculations) the carrying values given above for each bond at December 31, 2014 and 2013. *Remember that the carrying value of a long-term liability is the present value of the remaining future cash flows.*

7-16   Zero-coupon Bonds

On January 1, 2014, $40,000,000 of 20-year, zero-coupon bonds were issued. The market interest rate on these bonds was 8% on the issue date, compounded annually.

Required:

1. Describe the timing of the cash flows related to the bonds (both inflows and outflows).
2. Determine the amount of cash received from issuing these bonds.
3. Record the interest expense that was accrued on December 31, 2014 and 2015.
4. Compute the total amount of interest expense over the life of these bonds.

7-17   Capital Lease

On January 1, 2014, a plant asset with a cash price of $230,000 was purchasing on a 4-year, 8% capital lease. Note that the asset is being purchased which means that ownership of the plant asset is passing to the lessee. The lease calls for a $50,000 payment on January 1, 2014 and three equal year-end payments, starting on December 31, 2014.

Required:

1. Determine the amount of the annuity payment required to cover both interest and repayment of the principal over the term of this lease.
2. Prepare an amortization table for this lease.
3. Prepare the journal entry that was made to record the second lease payment on December 31, 2014.
4. Explain why this is a capital lease rather than an operating lease.

7-18   Capital Lease

On January 1, 2014, an opera company signed a 20-year capital lease to acquire a new opera house. The lease calls for a $100,000 payment on January 1, 2014 and 19 year-end payments of $100,000 each starting on December 31, 2014. The cash price of the opera house was $1,215,800.

Required:

1. Determine the present value of the 20 lease payments.
2. Determine the interest rate of this capital lease.
3. Compute the total amount of interest expense over the life of the lease.
4. Determine the balance of the lease liability that would be shown on the December 31, 2027 balance sheet.

7-19 Capital Lease

On January 1, 2014, a machine was purchased on a 4-year, 6% capital lease. The lease calls for a $10,000 payment on January 1, 2014; a $12,000 payment on December 31, 2014; a $14,000 payment on December 31, 2015; and a $16,000 payment on December 31, 2016.

Required:

1. Determine the cash price of the machine at January 1, 2014.
2. Prepare the journal entry that was made to record the first lease payment and the acquisition of the machine.
3. Compute the total amount of interest expense over the life of the lease.
4. Compute the amount of the lease liability that will be shown on the December 31, 2015 balance sheet.

7-20 Reading Financial Statements – JCPENNEY

Locate the PDF file with excerpts from the 2014 annual report of JCPENNEY. Refer to the *Consolidated Statements of Operations* and the *Consolidated Balance Sheets* on pages 7 and 9 of the file (labeled pages 61 and 63 of the 10-K).

Required:

1. It is often of interest to analysts to determine the average borrowing rate for an entity. Sometimes the entity of interest only provides balance sheets and income statements and the average rate of interest must be estimated using these data only. Consider only the "long-term debt" in the balance sheet and net interest expense on statement of operations and estimate the average borrowing rate for JCPENNEY for the past year.
2. Now consider Footnote 10 related to long-term debt on page 16 of the file (labeled page 76 of the 10-K). As we can see, current disclosures for large public companies include the weighted average interest rate. Identify the rate for JCPENNEY'S long-term debt and explain why your calculation in requirement 1 is different.
3. Like most companies, JCPENNEY reports a long-term liability identified as "other". Consider footnote 7 on page 15 of the file (labeled page 73 of the 10-K) and describe the composition of the other liabilities of $526 million.
4. For many industries, such as the retail industry sector of JCPENNEY, assets used for operations are not owned but are simply leased on a long-term operating lease basis. Recall that operating leases do not get recorded as assets or liabilities, but are simply treated like rental arrangements. Consider the portion of footnote 13 containing the schedules of minimum future operating and capital leases and note payable payments on page 18 of the file (labeled page 83 of the 10-K). Answer the following questions:
   a. What is the total future cash flows committed for operating leases?
   b. What percentage of the future cash flow commitments in these contracts is beyond five years into the future?
   c. Might this be of concern to current or future investors? Explain.

7-21   Operating vs. Capital Lease

On January 1, 2014, an aircraft was acquired on a 10-year lease. Given the terms of the lease contract, ownership passed to the lessee. The lease required a $1,000,000 payment on January 1, 2014 and nine year-end payments of $1,000,000 each starting on December 31, 2014. The cash price of the aircraft was $7,515,200. The company expects to use the aircraft over the next twenty years and will depreciate it on a straight-line basis over that time period with an estimated salvage value of $0.

Required:

1. Determine the interest rate on this lease agreement.
2. Compute the total amount of expense recorded over the life of the lease if it were an operating lease.
3. Compute the total amount of depreciation expense and interest expense over the life of the lease if it were a capital lease.
4. Assume the lease is accounted for as an operating lease. Prepare the journal entries to record: (a) the signing of the lease on January 1, 2014; (b) any necessary adjustment on December 31, 2014: and (c) the $1,000,000 payment on December 31, 2014.
5. Assume the lease is accounted for as a capital lease. Prepare the journal entry to record: (a) the signing of the lease on January 1, 2014; (b) the adjustment for depreciation expense on December 31, 2014; and (c) the $1,000,000 payment on December 31, 2014.
6. Describe the economic impact of these transactions on the firm.

7-22   Financial Statement Analysis – MACY'S

Locate the PDF file with the 2014 10-K of MACY'S, INC. Consider the *Consolidated Balance Sheets* on page 53 of the file (labeled F-6 of the 10-K) and footnote 4 on Properties and Leases on page 62 of the file (labeled F-15 of the 10-K).

Required:

1. Reference the Business Overview on pages 7 and 8 of the file (labeled pages 2 and 3 of the 10-K). Briefly describe MACY'S, INC. (its business, where it operates, something unique that you learned from the annual report, etc.).
2. Refer to footnote 4 and identify the total minimum lease payments for capital leases and the present value of those minimum lease payments at the end of the most recent fiscal year. Describe what the present value of those lease payments represents.
3. Refer again to footnote 4 and identify the total minimum payments for operating leases at the end of the most recent fiscal year. Compute the ratio of present value to cash flow for the capital leases. Assume this same ratio holds for the operating leases and compute the present value of the future operating lease payments.
4. The present value of the operating lease amounts is not recorded in the financial statements as either an asset or a liability. Assume that the present value of the future operating lease payments from requirement 3 is a close approximation of the unrecorded leased assets and the unrecorded lease liability. Compute the percentage increase in *Property and Equipment – net* (see *consolidated balance sheets*) that would result if this amount were recorded as an asset in the balance sheet. Compute the percentage increase in *Long-term Debt* (see *consolidated balance she*ets) that would result if the lease liability were recorded in the balance sheet.

Chapter 7 Study Quiz

For each of the five questions, show and label your calculations and place your answer in the spaces provided.

1. During the year, a lawsuit was filed against a company for unsafe working conditions. Management and the attorneys feel that it is not likely that the company will lose the case. The lawsuit is for $1,000,000. The plaintiff who filed the lawsuit has offered to settle the lawsuit for $600,000. Management estimates this lawsuit would be settled for $300,000.

    Determine the amount of contingent liability reported for this lawsuit in the current balance sheet.

    $_____

    Explain why you chose the answer you did.

2. The following alternatives are available to purchase an asset at 10% annual interest:

    a. Pay $10,000 down and $10,000 at the end of each year for the next ten years.
    b. Pay no money down and pay $185,500 ten years from now.
    c. Pay $71,500 now.

    Which payment method(s) would you select based on present values? Support your answer with calculations.

    Method:_____

    Supporting calculations:

3. On January 1, $1,000,000 of bonds payable with a 9% stated interest rate were issued to yield a market rate of 10%. The bonds pay interest annually on December 31 and were sold at a discount of $48,644.

   Compute the amount of discount amortized at the first December 31 interest payment (rounded).

   $_____

   Calculation:

4. Sometime last year, $800,000 of 12%, 12-year bonds payable were issued between interest dates. The bonds are dated January 1 and pay semiannual interest on June 30 and December 31. The bonds were priced at 103% of face value plus accrued interest. A total of $864,000 in cash was received on the issue date.

   Determine the date on which these bonds were issued.

   $_____

   Calculation:

5. On January 1, 2014, equipment was purchased on a 4-year, 7% capital lease. The lease calls for a $5,000 payment on January 1, 2014; a $10,000 payment on December 31, 2014; a $15,000 payment on December 31, 2015; and a $20,000 payment on December 31, 2016.

   Compute amount recorded as a lease liability on January 1, 2014.

   $_____

   Calculation:

Chapter 8

Shareholders' Equity

LEARNING OBJECTIVES

1. Understand the elements that make up contributed capital and earned capital.
2. Explain how cash dividends and treasury stock transactions are reflected in the financial statements; define stock dividends and stock splits.
3. Read and interpret the information reported in a statement of shareholders' equity.
4. Compute and interpret the earnings per share (EPS) measure.

Shareholders' equity is the balance sheet amount that represents the net assets of the business. It is often referred to as the **book value** of the entity. In this chapter we examine the two principal components of shareholders' equity (SE) that are reported in the comparative balance sheets: 1) *capital contributed* by the owners; and 2) *earned capital*. To increase the net assets of the business, the entity can either issue more stock (i.e., increase the amount of contributed capital) or keep earnings (profits) in the business (i.e., increase earned capital). Along with the issuance of debt, increases in earned capital and contributed capital provide the three ways a company can finance the growth of the business. It is important for financial statement users to understand what drives increases and decreases in book value (net assets). Changes in net assets (book value) from additional earnings (or losses) communicate good news (or bad news) while changes due to levels of debt or stock outstanding generally require additional analysis to determine why the new resources are needed and how they will be employed.

THE ESSENCE OF SHAREHOLDERS EQUITY

The first paragraph above contains the essential information regarding shareholders' equity. Study this paragraph and understand it above all else that you might learn from this chapter. The details regarding shareholders' equity that follow, while necessary to explain some of the fine points impacting SE, are far less important in terms of your ability to read and evaluate financial statements. Do not allow these details to overwhelm you, which they are capable of doing. Once you have completed this text in sequence, you should be able to look back on this chapter and see that the first paragraph above is really THE salient point of the entire chapter. Your deeper understanding of the measurement and reporting of assets and liabilities will help you to see that SE is essentially a plugged amount making the balance sheet balance.

CONTRIBUTED CAPITAL

Contributed capital is represented by the accounts that result from stock transactions. These accounts report the par value of the stock as well as any amounts received in excess of the par value. Common stock is the most frequently encountered form of contributed capital but there are other forms of stock as well. All shares of stock are effectively legal contracts between the entity and its shareholders; and, like all contracts, the actual terms and features of stocks may vary somewhat in practice.

Common Stock

Common stock is generally the **voting stock** of the business; holders of the common stock own the business, effectively governing all important decisions.[1] The financial statements in the corporation's annual report are addressed to these shareholders. Net income is an accounting measure of the change in common shareholders' equity for the period that resulted from *non-owner* related transactions. The shareholders effectively run the company by electing representatives who serve as their **board of directors**. The board of directors oversees all important decisions on behalf of the shareholders and (in theory) is independent of the managers of the entity. This board is responsible for all important decisions including: hiring and firing top managers, determining executive compensation, naming the independent outside auditors, monitoring the financial performance of the entity and all of its major operating objectives such as growth through mergers and acquisitions or divestures, and declaring dividends. The most essential condition for effective corporate governance by the board of directors is for the board to be independent. When corporations are involved in scandals or unethical practices it may often be traced back to an ineffective or non-independent board of directors.

Common stock's most important feature, distinguishing it from other types of stock is a **voting right**. Because the common shareholders elect the board of directors, they are the most important stakeholders in the business.[2] In addition to a voting right, the common shareholders usually have a **preemptive right,** allowing them to maintain a proportionate share of ownership of the company. For example, if a shareholder purchased a 2% interest in the total amount of stock a corporation was authorized to issue, then the corporation could not reduce that ownership percentage without the approval of the majority of the shareholders. Finally, common shareholders have a **dividend right**, the right to share in any distributions of earnings (= dividends). If there is only one class of common stock, each common shareholder will receive one vote per share and will receive any dividends declared by the board of directors in proportion to the number of shares held.

---

[1] When a company is incorporated, the state approving its existence as a corporation will authorize the corporation to issue a certain number of shares of stock. Other things like the purpose of the business must also be recorded. While these features may later be changed, they will normally require the approval of both the shareholders and the state of incorporation.

[2] While common stock is usually voting stock, it is not necessarily the case that all common stock is voting. Some companies have multiple classes of common stock, such as Class A and Class B Common. Whenever more than one class of stock is present, it is important to determine the actual rights and responsibilities conveyed to the holder of each type of share.

In addition to being viewed as the primary owners of the business, the common shareholders also are viewed as the capital providers who take on the most risk. In the event that a corporation goes bankrupt or otherwise ceases to exist, all liabilities and other claims must be settled before the common shareholders receive any payout. Finally, the corporate form of business offers the common shareholders **limited liability,** meaning that they cannot lose more than what they have invested in the company from their stock purchases. In partnerships and proprietorships, the owners are usually liable for more than just the amount of assets they place in the business, and if the company fails they could lose personal assets to unpaid creditors.

Buying and Selling Shares of Stock

The common stocks of *closely-held corporations* may be _privately_ bought or sold at any time a buyer and seller agree, as long as there are no restrictions stipulated in the shares.[3] The common stocks of *publicly-traded corporations* may be transferable at any time on the stock market. Publicly-traded corporations usually hire a **transfer agent**, who keeps track of exactly who owns each share of common stock at any point in time. This information is necessary so the corporation can communicate with shareholders, make dividend payments, etc. The transfer agent usually is listed at the end of the annual report.

Preferred Stock

Preferred stock is found in the balance sheets of about 10-11% of large, public companies.[4] The term *preferred* usually means that these shareholders receive their dividends before the common share-holders receive any dividends. Preferred stocks usually receive a fixed dividend per period, and the dividends often are designated as **cumulative dividends**, meaning that if a preferred dividend is not paid in one period, it must be paid in a future period along with the future period's dividend before the common shareholders can receive any dividends in that future period. Cumulative dividends are not a liability to the company until they are actually declared, but the notes to the financial statements should indicate if there are any unpaid cumulative dividends (called **dividends in arrears**). Preferred stock usually is not voting stock.

Why have Preferred Stock?

Accounting rule makers are currently looking carefully at the nature of preferred stock. It has been suggested that the economic features of preferred stock make it more like a permanent debt security than an equity security. It may very well be eliminated from shareholders' equity if the current thinking persists. And when the features of preferred stock include the ability of the buyer or the entity to refund or cancel the shares, it is even more like debt.

---

[3] Closely-held companies often require that sales of shares be first offered back to the entity, and sometimes a sale of ownership will require approval of some or all of the other owners.
[4] Percentages referred to in this chapter are from *Accounting Trends & Techniques* (New York, NY: American Institute of CPAs, 2011).

Par Value and Capital in Excess of Par

Stocks are usually reported in the balance sheet at their par value. **Par value** is a nominal amount that is less than the original issue price of the stock. It is interpreted as the minimum investment per share and in most states the stock cannot be issued at a price below par value.

Par value has virtually no relevance. From a bookkeeping viewpoint, the company records the par value amount in the Common Stock or Preferred Stock accounts. The amount received at the time of issuance in excess of the par value will be entered in a separate shareholders' equity account called **Capital in Excess of Par** (or *Capital Surplus*, or **Additional Paid-in Capital**, or some similar title). Therefore, par value stocks will have two account balances reported in the shareholders' equity section of the balance sheet: one for par value and one for the amount received in excess of par. The sum of these accounts represent the total <u>contributed</u> capital. Common and preferred shares that do not have par value are referred to as **no-par stocks**, and the entire amount from the issuance of these stocks is reported in a single account (e.g., "no-par common" or "no-par preferred" stock) in the balance sheet.

Example Assume a company issued 800,000 shares of $1 par value common stock for $12 per share on June 21, 2014, receiving $9,600,000 cash (800,000 shares x $12 per share). The amount that would be recorded in the Common Stock account would be $800,000 (800,000 x the $1 par value). The other $11 per share ($12 issue price – $1 par value) would be recorded in the Capital in Excess of Par account. The entry to record the issuance of these shares would be:

Journal

Date (2014)	Accounts (*Explanation*)	Debit	Credit
June 21	Cash	9,600,000	
	Common Stock (800,000 x $1)		800,000
	Capital in Excess of Par (800,000 x $11)		8,800,000
	(To record the issuance of 800,000 shares of $1 par value common stock at $12 per share)		

When a corporation begins operations, before it goes public, it is common for consideration other than cash to be received in exchange for shares of stock. For example, land, buildings, and other assets, or even services, may be contributed in exchange for shares of stock. The individuals who plan to manage the business usually contribute these assets, but sometimes unrelated parties will help start the business by turning over assets or providing services to the business in exchange for ownership shares. These transactions are recorded at the fair market value of the stock given up or the fair market value of the assets or services acquired, whichever is more easily determined. In addition, new companies often turn to **venture capital firms**, which provide capital to promising start-up companies in exchange for an ownership interest. Most start-up companies are organized as **closely-held companies** with relatively few shareholders. These initial investors often hope the business will grow to the point where they can take the company public.

Balance Sheet Presentation of Contributed Capital

The contributed capital portion of the shareholders' equity section of the balance sheet will provide the reader with the following information:

- The number of shares of each class of stock **authorized** to be issued by the corporation's articles of incorporation from the state where it is registered;

- The number of shares of each class of stock **issued** (sold to the public);

- The number of shares of each class of stock **outstanding** (held by the public—the difference between issued and outstanding being shares that have been repurchased by the corporation and held in the treasury);

- The par value of each class of stock (if applicable); and

- The total amount of the capital in excess of par value received from all issuances of stock (if applicable).

Consider the amounts shown in Exhibit 8-1, from the December 31, 2013 balance sheet of E.I. DU PONT DE NEMOURS AND COMPANY (known as DUPONT).

As we can see, DUPONT has both preferred and common stock. The preferred stock has a cumulative dividend and is a no-par stock, so none of the Additional Paid-in Capital (DUPONT's name for capital in excess of par) pertains to the preferred stock. Of the 23 million preferred shares authorized, fewer than 3 million have been issued in two series. One series was issued when a $4.50 per share dividend was required to attract investors. The second series was issued when the required dividend was $3.50 per share. These stocks are callable at the option of DUPONT at the amounts shown ($120 and $102, respectively). The average issue price of each series can be determined by dividing the amount in each stock account by the number of shares in each series. This suggests that the average issue price for each series was $100 ($167 million divided by 1,672,594 shares = $100 per share, and $70 million divided by 700,000 shares = $100). Note that the call price for each series is above the issue price of $100.

Exhibit 8-1   Contributed Capital Example – DUPONT

Stockholders' Equity (*dollars in millions*)	2013	2012
Preferred stock, without par value – cumulative; 23,000,000 shares authorized; issued at December 31, 2013 and 2012:		
$4.50 Series – 1,673,000 shares (callable at $120)	$ 167	$ 167
$3.50 Series – 700,000 shares (callable at $102)	70	70
Common stock, $.30 par value, 1,800,000,000 shares authorized;		
Issued at December 31, 2013 – 1,020,057,000		
Issued at December 31, 2012 – 1,013,164,000	306	304
Additional paid-in capital	10,632	10,107

Example Assume DUPONT called the 700,000 shares of $3.50 Preferred Stock at $102 on January 1, 2014. How would the financial statements be impacted? The book value of the stock would be removed from the accounts and the cash would be recorded. ***The income statement cannot be impacted by transactions involving the company's own stock*** (= no gain or loss), so any additional amount needed to balance the transaction would be taken from Retained Earnings. The redemption of the shares would be recorded as follows:

Journal

Date (2014)	Accounts (*Explanation*)	Debit	Credit
January 1	Preferred Stock	70,000,000	
	Retained Earnings	1,400,000	
	Cash (700,000 x $102)		71,400,000
	(*To record the redemption of 700,000 shares of preferred stock at $102 per share*)		

Assume that instead of being callable, the preferred stock was convertible into common stock at the rate of 15 shares of common stock for each share of preferred stock. How would the conversion of the 700,000 shares of the $3.50 Preferred Stock into common stock impact the financial statements? When a conversion occurs, the book value of the preferred stock is removed from the Preferred Stock account and that same dollar amount is entered in the common stock accounts. Again, no gain or loss would be recorded. The par value would be entered in the Common Stock account and the excess amount would be entered in the Additional Paid-in Capital account. The conversion would be recorded as follows:

Journal

Date (2014)	Accounts (*Explanation*)	Debit	Credit
January 1	Preferred Stock	70,000,000	
	Common Stock (700,000 x 15 x $.30)		3,150,000
	Additional Paid-in Capital		66,850,000
	(*To record the conversion of 700,000 shares of preferred stock into 10,500,000 shares of $.30 par value common stock*)		

The DuPONT common stock is a par stock, and it has a par value of $.30 per share. The amount reported in the common stock account is the par value of the stock times the number of shares issued ($.30 x 1,020,057,000 shares issued as of December 31, 2013 = $306 million rounded). As was done for the preferred shares, the average issue price of the common shares can be computed. We divide the combined amount in the Common Stock account ($306 million for 2013) and the Additional Paid-in Capital account ($10,632 million for 2013) by the number of shares issued (1,020,057,000 for 2013). This results in an average issue price of $10.72 per share ([$306 million + $10,632 million] ÷ 1,020,057,000 shares).

Dividends

Shareholders choose to invest their dollars in a corporation with the plan to gain economic returns either through the receipt of dividends (maintaining their ownership interest), or through the sale of the stock for a price greater than the purchase price (reducing or eliminating any ownership interest) or a combination of the two. An investor's tax position can play a role in which type of return the investor prefers. Cash dividends are usually subject to income tax at an ordinary tax rate which is most often higher than the capital gains tax rate which is usually in effect when the stock itself is sold.

Cash Dividends Cash distributions of a corporation's earnings are called **cash dividends**. As discussed earlier in the chapter, preferred stock shareholders have priority to a specific amount of the total dividends when declared. The common stock shareholders receive the residual amount quoted as a dollar amount per share of common stock. The following three dates relate to cash dividends, two of which require recording transactions:

- The **declaration date** is the point in time that the board of directors declares that a cash dividend will be paid. Recall that dividends are not required like interest costs are. It is only at the declaration date that the dividend becomes a legal obligation of the business and recorded as an increase in dividends payable and a decrease in retained earnings.

- Because ownership of publicly-traded stock can frequently change, the **date of record** is administratively used to identify the specific shareholders who will receive the dividend. Shareholders who hold this stock at the end of the business on this date receive the cash dividend. Only the outstanding shares of stock are eligible to receive a cash dividend. This is a clerical date only where no economic event occurs; therefore, no journal entry is recorded on this date.

- The **payment date** is when the dividend obligation is actually paid (reducing liabilities) to those shareholders of the date of record.

Stock Splits and Stock Dividends   When a company divides its outstanding shares of stock into smaller ownership interests, a **stock split** occurs. For example, a 2-for-1 stock split means that everyone holding a share of stock before the split will hold two shares of stock after the split. If the stock has a par value, it is reduced accordingly. If the par value before a 2-for-1 split was $5 per share, after the split the par value would be $2.50 per share, with twice as many shares outstanding (and the dollar amounts in all the shareholders' equity accounts would remain the same). The old $5 par value shares are replaced with the new $2.50 par value shares.

A **stock dividend** occurs when a company issues additional shares of stock to its existing shareholders on a pro rata basis as a dividend. For example, a 10% stock dividend would result in issuing one additional share of stock for every 10 shares held by each investor. These newly issued shares typically come from previously authorized but unissued stock. The important thing to understand about stock splits and stock dividends is that they do not change the book value of the entity and they have no substantive impact on the entity. The best analogy to explain the impact of splits and dividends is to see that, before a split or dividend, each owner has a defined "piece of the pie" (i.e., owner has stock representing a 3% ownership interest). After the stock split or dividend, the owner's slice of the pie is simply cut into smaller slices, but still represents the same piece of the pie (i.e., owner will still only own 3% of the company after the split or dividend).

---

[5] For additional insight on this topic, see E. Fama and K. French (2001) "Disappearing dividends: changing firm characteristics or lower propensity to pay?" *Journal of Financial Economics*, pp. 3-43; and D. Skinner, "The evolving relation between earnings, dividends, and stock repurchases," *Journal of Financial Economics*, March 2008, pp. 582-609.

Treasury Stock

Treasury stock appears in the balance sheets of approximately two-thirds of U.S. publicly-traded corporations. It represents the amount a company has paid for repurchases of its own shares in the open market that it plans to reissue at some time in the future.[6] The repurchased shares are almost always common shares, and only very rarely are preferred shares repurchased and held in the treasury. Treasury stock is shown as a contra shareholders' equity amount more than 95% of the time, although it can be reported in other ways as well.[7]

To illustrate the accounting for treasury stock transactions, assume that Sunrise Corporation bought 20,000 shares of its common stock on the stock market on December 20, 2014, when the market price was $4.00 per share. The treasury shares would have been recorded at cost as shown in the following entry:

Journal

Date (2014)	Accounts (*Explanation*)	Debit	Credit
December 20	Treasury Stock (20,000 x $4)	80,000	
	Cash		80,000
	(*To record repurchase of stock for the treasury*)		

Later, when the shares are resold, the business ***cannot report a profit or loss*** on the sale because this is a transaction with the company's owners. Any change in net assets that results from a treasury stock transaction is *not reported in the income statement*, but is directly entered into a contributed capital account (usually the Capital in Excess of Par account). For example, assume that Sunrise resold 10,000 of treasury shares on January 19, 2015, for $4.20 a share. The entry to record this sale of treasury stock would have been:

Journal

Date (2015)	Accounts (*Explanation*)	Debit	Credit
January 19	Cash (10,000 x $4.20)	42,000	
	Treasury Stock (10,000 x $4)		40,000
	Capital in Excess of Par		2,000
	(*To record the resale of treasury stock above cost*)		

---

[6] While buying back a company's own stock in the market is commonly practiced in the U.S., it is not legal in many other countries, including Canada.

[7] Occasionally, the cost of the treasury shares is deducted from the common stock and the capital in excess of par accounts.

If the resale of the 10,000 treasury shares had been at $3.80 per share, the entry to record the resale would have been:

Journal

Date (2015)	Accounts (*Explanation*)	Debit	Credit
January 19	Cash (10,000 x $3.80)	38,000	
	Capital in Excess of Par (or Retained Earnings)	2,000	
	Treasury Stock (10,000 x $4)		40,000
	(To record the resale of treasury stock below cost)		

That is, when treasury stock is sold for less than was paid to acquire it, the Capital in Excess of Par account is used to absorb the difference. If Capital in Excess of Par does not exist, Retained Earnings is used.

Summary   The two important aspects of treasury stock to keep in mind are:

1. The business cannot report gains or losses in income from purchases and sales of its own stock; and

2. The details of how treasury stock is reflected *within* the shareholders' equity section of the balance sheet may vary slightly from one company to another, but the impact on shareholders' equity *in total* is always the same; treasury stock reduces total shareholders' equity by the cost of the treasury shares.

Employee Stock Options

A common reason corporations purchase treasury stock is to have shares on hand to issue to employees who are exercising **stock options**. A stock option is a right to acquire a share of stock at a stipulated price for a stipulated period of time. For example, assume that Sunrise Corporation granted stock options to employees on January 1, 2015, when its common stock was selling for $2 per share. The options give the employees the right to acquire 200 shares of the company's common stock at $2 per share between January 1, 2017 and December 31, 2017. On the surface, it seems the employees received nothing on the date the options were *granted (grant date = January 1, 2015)*. Employees value these options, however, and hope the company's performance will drive the stock price up and make the stock options valuable ("in the money") by January 1, 2017 when they are exercisable. The options encourage employees to remain with the company, and they give them incentives to work towards increasing the value of the company's stock.[8]

---

[8] Accounting rules around the world require stock-based compensation to be recorded in the income statement as a part of wages and salaries expense between the date of grant and the exercise date using option pricing models to estimate the amount of the employee benefit. The notes to the financial statements normally reveal how much expense was recorded each year for stock-based compensation. The methods used to record stock-based compensation are beyond the scope of this text.

EARNED CAPITAL

Corporations earn capital through profitable operations, and those profits not paid to shareholders in dividends are retained and used to "grow the business." The principal account devoted to earned capital is **Retained Earnings**, although other terms are used such as *Reinvested Earnings* and *Retained Deficit* (for companies that have losses that exceed their cumulative earnings).

Another account representing earned capital that may be reported in the shareholders' equity section of the balance sheet is *Accumulated Other Comprehensive Income (AOCI)* This account summarizes the cumulative effect of certain transactions that result in a change in net assets but are not reported as a part of net income.

Retained Earnings

We have consistently noted that Retained Earnings measures the *cumulative amount of net income reported throughout the life of the business minus the amount of dividends declared and paid throughout the life of the business*. With the discussion of accounting for stock transactions, we now see that retained earnings can be impacted by transactions other than net income and cash dividends. For example, **callable preferred stock** transactions, stock dividends, and treasury stock transactions all have the ability to *reduce* retained earnings. While net income and cash dividends will normally explain all the changes in retained earnings from one year-end to the next, we should understand that certain other transactions may also have an impact.

Accumulated Other Comprehensive Income (AOCI)

Besides the transactions that impact net income, there are several other types of transactions that change the net assets of the business. When added to net income, the impact of these additional transactions produce a measure called **comprehensive income**. Comprehensive income is *a complete measure of the change in net assets from all non-owner related transactions of the business*. The other components of comprehensive income (that is, components other than net income) are:

1. Unrealized gains and losses on securities held as investments;
2. Gains and losses on derivative securities not included in net income;
3. Gains and losses on the translation of the financial statements of foreign subsidiaries into U.S. dollars; and
4. Minimum pension liability adjustments.

These other transactions give rise to gains (or profits) and losses that are just as economically relevant as the profits or losses reported in net income. However, as we briefly mentioned in Chapter 2, current accounting rules stipulate that these four categories of gains and losses are not included in net income but are reported separately in comprehensive income.

Accumulated Other Comprehensive Income (AOCI) is the balance sheet account that reports the cumulative amount of these other elements of comprehensive income. In that way, it is similar to retained earnings. AOCI is reported in the balance sheet by over 97% of publicly-held companies. We address the details of comprehensive income in Chapter 9 when we discuss the measurement of net income. Here we simply note that other comprehensive income is a measure of the change in the net assets of a business from non-contributed capital sources that is not included in net income and, therefore, not added to retained earnings.[9]

The complete shareholders' equity section of the December 31, 2013 balance sheet of DuPont is reproduced in Exhibit 8-2. The accounts representing the items we have just discussed (treasury stock, retained earnings, and accumulated other comprehensive income) are shaded.

As you can see, the total change in shareholders' equity for DuPont in 2013 was an increase of $1,495 million ($10,088 – $8,593). This is an increase of *over 17%* of total net assets of one of the largest corporations in the U.S. Observe the following:

- Most of the increase was in "Reinvested Earnings" (Retained Earnings).
- The accumulated loss in Accumulated Other Comprehensive Income (Loss) decreased slightly in 2013.
- The negative balance of $8,646 in AOCI at the end of 2013 points out the importance of Other Comprehensive Income (to be discussed in Chapter 9).
- The changes in all shareholders' equity accounts for the last three years can be found in the Statement of Changes in Shareholders' Equity provided by most corporations as a fourth formal financial statement (along with the balance sheet, income statement, and statement of cash flows).

Exhibit 8-2   Complete Shareholders' Equity Example – DuPont

Stockholders' Equity (*dollars in millions*)	2013	2012
Preferred stock, without par value – cumulative; 23,000,000 shares authorized; issued at December 31, 2013 and 2012:		
$4.50 Series – 1,673,000 shares (callable at $120)	$ 167	$ 167
$3.50 Series – 700,000 shares (callable at $102)	70	70
Common stock, $.30 par value, 1,800,000,000 shares authorized; Issued at December 31, 2013 – 1,020,057,000		
Issued at December 31, 2012 – 1,013,164,000	306	304
Additional paid-in capital	10,632	10,107
Reinvested earnings	14,286	13,422
Accumulated other comprehensive income (loss)	(8,646)	(8,750)
Common stock held in the treasury, at cost	(6,727)	(6,727)
Total shareholders' equity	**$ 10,088**	**$ 8,593**

[9] The illogical nature of the display and location of other comprehensive income components is confusing and can only be explained by understanding the social-political nature of the standard setting process. Future accounting rule changes will likely integrate these components into the income statement in a more logical way.

THE STATEMENT OF SHAREHOLDERS' EQUITY

The **statement of shareholders' equity** (the third "flow" statement) reports all the changes in the shareholders' equity accounts of a business for the past three years. In the DuPont example in Exhibit 8-3, we see that DUPONT reported: net income of $2,788 million; other comprehensive income of $104 million; declared $1,603 million of cash dividends on its common and preferred stock ($1,593 + $10); issued $631 million of common stock during the year; and purchased and retired $400 million of treasury shares. Details of the components of net income and other comprehensive income (OCI) are found in those separate statements, as we will discuss in Chapter 9. Any details or further clarification of the other changes in shareholders' equity will typically be provided in the footnotes to the financial statements.

Future accounting rule changes are apt to change the nature of shareholders' equity. It is likely that net income and OCI will be reported in a single statement, eliminating the need for AOCI as a separate equity account. Also, there is discussion that all but voting common stock will be eliminated from shareholders' equity.[10] The most important information for users is to be able to determine what changes in shareholders' equity, if any, were from non-owner related transactions.

Exhibit 8-3   Statement of Shareholders' Equity – DUPONT

Consolidated Statements of Equity (*dollars in millions*)

Item	Preferred Stock	Common Stock	Additional Paid-in Capital	Reinvested Earnings	Accumulated Other Comprehensive Income (Loss)	Treasury Stock	Total
Balance 12/31/12	$237	$304	$10,107	$13,422	$ (8,750)	$(6,727)	$8,593
Acquisition of non-controlling interest			(25)				(25)
Net income				2,788			2,788
Other comprehensive income					104		104
CS dividends ($1.70/share)				(1,593)			(1,593)
PS dividends				(10)			(10)
CS issued		4	627				631
TS repurchased						(400)	(400)
TS retired		(2)	(77)	(321)		400	0
Balance 12/31/13	$237	$306	$10,632	$14,286	$ (8,646)	$(6,727)	$10,088

---

[10] Some have argued that non-voting preferred stock is essentially debt, an appealing concept.

FINANCIAL STATEMENT ANALYSIS

Earnings Per Share

Earnings per share (EPS) is the most widely cited and most frequently predicted accounting measure. Considered by most analysts to be the bottom line measure of how a company performed for a period of time, it is, essentially, net income divided by the number of shares of common (voting) stock outstanding. More specifically, we find that EPS has two common definitions:

- Basic EPS; and
- Fully diluted EPS.

All businesses must report basic EPS. Companies that have securities (such as **convertible preferred stock**) or contracts (such as employee stock options) that would dilute (reduce) the basic EPS computation if they were converted into common stock will also report a fully diluted EPS measure. Both measures report the net income of the company on a per-share-of-common-stock basis.

Basic EPS   **Basic EPS** is defined as the net income available to the common shareholders divided by the weighted average number of common shares *outstanding* during the period for which the earnings are measured (i.e., treasury shares are not included). For example, assume that a corporation had 500,000 shares of common stock outstanding at the beginning of the year and issued another 300,000 shares of common stock on April 1. The company also has 200,000 shares of cumulative convertible no-par preferred stock outstanding. The preferred stock has a $.25 per share annual dividend. Net income for the year was $800,000. Basic EPS in this case would be computed as follows:

Computing Basic EPS:

$$= \frac{\textbf{Net income available to common shareholders}}{\textbf{Weighted average number of common shares outstanding}}$$

$$= \frac{\$800,000 - [(\$.25 \ \times \ 200,000 \ \text{shares})]}{[500,000 \ \text{shares} \ \times \ 3/12] \ + \ [800,000 \ \text{shares} \ \times \ 9/12]}$$

$$= \frac{\$750,000}{725,000 \ \text{shares}}$$

$$= \ \$1.03 \ \text{(rounded)}$$

Notice that the $800,000 of net income is reduced by the $50,000 preferred stock dividend ($.25 x 200,000 shares) before it is divided by the weighted average number of shares of common stock. EPS is the amount of net income per share *available to the common shareholders* and the preferred dividend amount is not available to the common shareholders since the preferred dividend must be paid before any common dividends could be paid.

The computation of basic EPS is used in nearly all countries to express the net income of the company on a per-share basis. It is a simple computation for companies that have no preferred stock and do not change the number of shares of common stock outstanding.

Fully Diluted EPS   Companies having convertible securities that could become shares of common stock in the future are said to have **complex capital structures**. The capital structures are considered complex because it is unclear how many shares of common stock effectively exist. For example, assume that in addition to the information provided above, you learned that the corporation's preferred shares are trading at $8 per share. Further assume that you find the common stock is selling for $10 per share, and that the 200,000 shares of preferred stock are convertible into 200,000 shares of common stock at the end of the next year. If the market price of common stock remains above that of the preferred stock, what is likely to happen at the end of the next year? Unless the preferred shareholders are very attracted to the $.25 dividend, they are likely to convert their shares of preferred stock into shares of common stock. This would impact EPS since there would be an additional 200,000 shares of common stock outstanding.

To make sure the common shareholders understand the potential for these other securities to reduce reported EPS in the future, GAAP requires companies with complex capital structures to report a second EPS number, called **fully diluted EPS**, in any case where the sum of these other securities have the ability to reduce the basic EPS number by 3% or more.

Fully diluted EPS is defined as net income to the common shareholders adjusted for other dilutive securities divided by the weighted average number of shares of common stock *plus common stock equivalents* (represented by the other dilutive securities). When we see EPS reported in the financial press, we should assume they are fully diluted EPS measures unless otherwise stated.

SHAREHOLDERS' EQUITY AND DECISION MAKING

In each chapter we have tried to provide some focus on the decision-making implications of accounting information.   Understanding and using accounting information is often simply a first step towards making an important business decision. Hence, it is important to keep in mind that the role of accounting and its relevance as a subject should be linked in some way to important economic decisions related to the business entity. For example, understanding that the increase in net assets of a business during the past year was 80% due to operating income is important, but it is not yet clear how this understanding is linked to a business decision. However, if you are a bank lender and your loan decision is based on how much growth in net assets is from operating profit retained in the business we are one step closer to understanding how accounting information might impact an important business decision.

If we focus on the business decision as a starting point, we will find how various decision makers use their analysis and understanding of accounting information to help them in making their decisions. Also, we must be realistic in our expectations of what is to be gained by our understanding of how accounting information impacts decision making. Understanding alone does not make the decision. Our understanding of accounting reduces, but does not eliminate, the uncertainty in making important business decisions. But our ability to understand and evaluate accounting information will help us avoid certain typical decision errors and leads to more informed decisions.

This chapter discusses the components of shareholders' equity. While most of this material is descriptive in nature, calling for very little analysis per se, simply understanding the nature and content of the components of shareholders' equity should help us to make better business decisions. Consider the decision case in the assignment material as an example of how we might use this understanding to make a better business decision.

INTERNATIONAL FINANCIAL REPORTING STANDARDS

The main difference between IFRS and GAAP in reporting shareholders' equity is in the reporting of redeemable (convertible) preferred stock. Under GAAP, all preferred stock is currently required to be reported in shareholders' equity, regardless of any conversion or redemption features. However, IFRS require redeemable preferred stock to be treated as debt. And non-redeemable preferred stock that has conversion characteristics that give the investor the right to receive cash or its equivalent at their discretion is treated as debt as well. Finally, like convertible bonds, convertible preferred stock is reported as two elements under IFRS: (1) a straight preferred stock portion; and (2) a common stock option portion.

It is also possible that statements prepared under IFRS could have an account that represents the holding gains recognized on the revaluation of assets. Recall from Chapter 6 that IFRS allows the revaluation of certain long-term assets such as land and buildings from historical cost to their current cost. Although rare in practice, when long-term assets are written up to their estimated fair value, the offsetting balance sheet impact is to increase a shareholders' equity account. The title of that account could be something like "gains on appraisal" or "appraisal capital"

SUMMARY

The shareholders' equity section of the balance sheet reports the contributed capital and earned capital of the business. This is the one section of the financial statements that is affected by the organizational form of the company. Because we focus on corporate financial reporting throughout this text, the elements that are contributed capital of interest to us include common stock, preferred stock, capital in excess of par, stock splits, cash dividends, stock dividends, and treasury stock. These elements report the details of the shareholders' claim on the assets of a corporation.

Retained earnings and accumulated other comprehensive income are the accounts that report the earned capital of the business. These amounts belong to the shareholders and they represent the accumulated profits or losses from all non-owner related transactions. Earned capital represents the increase in the shareholders' wealth from all business activities.

Basic earnings per share (EPS) is net income divided by the weighted average number of common shares. Fully diluted EPS provides an expected EPS measure based on the assumption that all dilutive securities have been converted to common stock. When we see an EPS number reported in a source other than the annual or quarterly report of the entity, we should assume it is fully diluted EPS unless otherwise noted. EPS is generally considered the most important and most commonly reported measure of the company's performance.

KEY TERMS[11]

accumulated other comprehensive income   A cumulative summary of the components of comprehensive income beyond net income that is reported in the shareholders' equity section of the balance sheet. See *comprehensive income*. *105-106*

additional paid-in capital   See *capital in excess of par*. *98*

authorized shares   Maximum number of shares allowed to be issued per the corporate charter. *99*

basic EPS   Earnings per share computed by dividing net income (earnings) available to the common stockholders by the weighted average number of shares of common stock outstanding during the period. *108*

board of directors   Group elected by the shareholders to represent them in overseeing the management of the company. The board of directors appoints the managers of the company. *96*

book value   The value of a financial statement item in the accounting records; also called *net worth*. See *book value of the business*. *95*

book value of the business   Common shareholders' equity (total shareholders' equity minus any preferred stock accounts). In a company with only common stock, book value is simply net assets (total assets minus total liabilities). *95*

callable preferred stock   Preferred stock that may be redeemed by the issuing company, usually after a specified date and at a specified price. *105*

capital in excess of par   The amount of value received from the issuance of stock that is in excess of its par value; also called *additional paid-in capital* and *capital surplus*. *98*

cash dividends   Distribution of a corporation's earnings in the form of cash. *101*

closely-held company   A company whose ownership shares are not publicly traded. *98*

common stock   Corporate ownership shares that typically carry voting privileges, the right to share in dividends that are declared, a preemptive right, and the right to share in the residual assets upon the liquidation of the business; also called *capital stock* and *voting stock*. *96-97*

complex capital structure   A capital structure that consists of common shares of stock plus other securities, such as preferred stock, bonds, and stock options that could be converted into common shares under certain conditions. *109*

---

[11] The definitions provided here are common definitions. However, please understand that many of these terms cannot be defined in a completely uniform manner since ownership contracts may be written in a variety of ways. You might, for example, see voting preferred stock, although it would be unusual. Also, you might see a class of common stock that does not receive any dividends but has multiple votes per share, but again it would be unusual.

comprehensive income   A complete measure of income that includes all changes in net assets from non-owner related events and transactions. Comprehensive income includes net income and adds to it the impact of several other items such as unrealized gains and losses on securities held as investments and gains and losses on the translation of the financial statements of foreign subsidiaries into U.S. dollars. (This topic also is discussed in Chapter 9.) *105*

contributed capital   The total value received from all shareholders for their shares of stock. Total shareholders' equity consists of contributed capital and earned capital. *96-99*

convertible preferred stock   Preferred stock that may be converted into common stock at the option of the shareholder. *108*

cumulative dividends   A feature of preferred stock indicating that if annual dividends are not paid the dividends accumulate and must be paid before common shareholders can receive any dividends. Cumulative dividends that have not been paid do not represent a liability to the corporation until they have been declared. *97*

date of record   Date used to determine the specific shareholders who will receive the dividend; an administrative date only; no accounting transaction occurs. *101*

declaration date   Date when the board of directors decides a dividend will be paid; at this date the dividend is a legal obligation of the business. *101*

dividend right   The right of shareholders to receive distributions of earnings in the form of dividends when declared by the board of directors. *96*

dividends in arrears   The amount of unpaid cumulative dividends on preferred stock at a given date. Dividends in arrears are not a liability to the company. *97*

earned capital   The cumulative amount of increases in net assets from all prior periods from all non-owner related transactions. Total shareholders' equity consists of earned capital plus contributed capital. *95*

earnings per share (EPS)   Net income (earnings) expressed on a per share of outstanding common stock basis. See *basic EPS* and *fully diluted EPS. 108*

fully diluted EPS   Net income to common shareholders adjusted for other dilutive securities divided by the sum of the actual weighted average shares of common stock outstanding plus the number of shares of common stock equivalents represented by securities with the potential to be converted to common stock (e.g., convertible preferred stock). *109*

issued shares   The number of shares of stock that have been sold to the public. See *authorized shares* and *outstanding shares. 99*

limited liability   An attribute of corporate ownership. The liability (possible loss) of corporate shareholders is limited to the greater of the amount they invested in the stock or its par value. *96*

no-par stock   Stock that does not have a par value. *98*

outstanding shares   The number of shares held by the public. Equal to the issued shares minus treasury shares. *99*

par value   An arbitrary amount assigned to each share of stock; the total is sometimes called legal capital. Par value is typically a small fraction of the original issue price of the stock. Sometimes called *stated value. 98*

payment date   Date the cash dividend is paid and the liability is reduced. *101*

preemptive right   The provision in a stock contract that allows current shareholders to maintain their proportionate share of ownership if additional shares are issued. *96*

preferred stock   Typically non-voting stock that serves much like permanent debt. It often has a specified dividend amount or rate, and the dividend is often cumulative. *97*

retained earnings   The principal account devoted to earned capital; measures the change in net assets from non-owner related transactions. *105*

statement of shareholders' equity   Financial statement that provides details on the changes in all shareholders' equity accounts. *107*

stock dividend   A distribution of additional shares of stock by the company to its existing shareholders accompanied by a transfer of retained earnings to the stock accounts; essentially, an increase in the number of shares of stock offset by a proportional decrease in the market value per share such that the total value of the company is the same before and after. Also called *stock splits effected in the form of a stock dividend*. *102*

stock options   Securities that, under certain specified conditions, may be converted to common stock. For example, an employee might be granted a stock option to buy a share of stock in the company for $14 per share between December 1, 2014 and December 1, 2014. The option is said to be "in the money" if the market price of the stock exceeds $14 per share, allowing the employee to buy the stock at the lower price. *104*

stock split   A dividing of all existing shares of stock and its various terms. For example, a "2-for-1" stock split of a $1.00 par value stock would exchange each share of $1.00 par stock for two shares of $0.50 par value stock. Stock splits have the same effect as a stock dividend and are sometimes implemented like a stock dividend. *102*

transfer agent   Individual or organization that maintains the records of who owns each share of outstanding stock for a public corporation. This is essentially an up-to-date mailing list for those who should receive corporate communications (e.g., dividends). *97*

treasury stock   A company's own stock that has been repurchased and is being held for future use. This is a contra (negative) equity amount and is not considered an asset. Income is not impacted by the purchase or resale of treasury stock; also called *treasury shares*. *103-104*

venture capital firms   Financial firms that provide capital to promising start-up companies in exchange for an ownership interest. *98*

voting right   The right of shareholders (generally the common shareholders) to vote for members of the board of directors. *96*

voting stock   Typically this is the common stock of a company. Sometimes there are multiple classes of common stock with different voting rights. *96*

Review Questions

Test your understanding of the material covered in the chapter by answering the following questions. The correct answers to these questions are shown below.

1. There are 10,000 shares of 3%, $100 par value preferred stock outstanding which had been sold at par. The preferred stock can be converted into $1 par value common stock at the rate of 7 common shares for each preferred share. 5,000 shares of the preferred stock were converted during the current year. What effect did this transaction have on the financial statements?

   a. Common Stock decreased by $35,000.
   b. There was a Gain on Conversion of Preferred Stock of $15,000.
   c. Common Stock increased by $500,000.
   d. Capital in Excess of Par increased by $465,000.

2. On January 1, 2014, the balance sheet of a company showed $160,000 in Common Stock, $160,000 in Capital in Excess of Par, and $72,000 in Retained Earnings. On July 1, 2014, the company purchased 2,000 shares of its own stock from the market for $24 per share. On October 1, 1,000 of these shares were resold for $32 per share. On November 1, one-half of the remaining shares were sold for $16 per share. There were no other stock transactions. What was total stockholders' equity on the December 31, 2014 balance sheet?

   a. $344,000
   b. $392,000
   c. $384,000
   d. $380,000

3. Net income for the year was $1,038,500. At January 1, there were 180,000 shares of common stock outstanding. On April 1, an additional 45,000 shares of common stock were issued. On October 1, another 50,000 shares of common stock were issued. The company's fiscal year end is December 31. What amount was reported as basic earnings per share for the year?

   a. $4.59
   b. $3.08
   c. $4.28
   d. $5.27

Answers: d., c., a.

PROBLEMS

8-1 Shareholders' Equity

1. Describe the two main components of shareholders' equity and the details within each.
2. Differentiate between preferred stock and common stock. Why might an investor choose one over another?
3. Differentiate between authorized, issued and outstanding shares of stock.
4. Dividends can be in the form of cash or stock. Why might an investor prefer one over the other? Why might a corporation declare a stock dividend rather than a cash dividend?
5. How are cash dividends calculated for preferred stock shareholders? For common stock shareholders?
6. Describe the impact of a stock dividend on an individual shareholder's ownership interest in the corporation.
7. Define treasury stock and how treasury stock transactions impact the financial statements. When treasury stock is reissued by the corporation, how are "gains" or "losses" reported?
8. When computing EPS, why should the denominator be the weighted average number of common shares outstanding rather than a simple average?
9. Differentiate between basic and fully diluted EPS.

8-2 Business Decision Case

Consider the following four possible components of Other Comprehensive Income (OCI) which are reported after the measurement of Net Income in GAAP based financial statements.

1. Unrealized gains and losses on securities held as investments;
2. Gains and losses on derivative securities not included in net income;
3. Gains and losses on the translation of the financial statements of foreign subsidiaries into U.S. dollars; and
4. Minimum pension liability adjustments.

Details regarding these four components of comprehensive income and how they are measured and what they represent were briefly discussed in Chapter 7 (pensions), or will be considered further in Chapter 9 and future courses. What we do know from Chapter 8 is that these four possible components of OCI impact the net assets of the business, and help explain changes in the net assets from non-owner related transactions and events. As a result, changes in OCI have the same impact on net assets as does net income.

As discussed in the chapter, the current requirements for earnings per share (EPS) measurements focus completely on net income and ignore any impact from OCI. We also know that EPS is one of the most widely cited and important measurements of a company's performance. EPS is the measure that is typically forecasted by hundreds of analysts each quarter, and is considered the "holy grail" by some financial statement users.

Required:

Upon learning more about pension accounting as discussed in Chapter 7, you have come to realize that pension expense is basically the same as wages and salaries. Also, further study has revealed that the pension component of OCI is basically a correction/adjustment to the pension expense recorded as a part of operating income. Further assume that you are involved in several types of decision making analyses where EPS is the key piece of accounting information employed. How might your realization of the nature of pensions in OCI be of use to you in your decisions?

1. Upon learning more about foreign exchange and translation gains and losses as measured in the third component of OCI (listed on the previous page), you have come to realize that the company has a great deal of control over their exposure to gains and losses from translation. The Treasurer's function in most companies is responsible for managing how exposed (or hedged) the business is from these translation gains and losses. In looking at the executive pay formula for a company with a large translation component to OCI you learn that they pay a cash bonus each year to the CEO, CFO, CIO, COO, and Treasurer based on EPS performance. Can you suggest how this executive pay scheme might be improved?

8-3 Common and Preferred Stock

The following transactions related to stock occurred:

a. Issued 1,500,000 shares of Class A, no-par common stock for $8.25 per share.

b. Issued 1,500,000 shares of Class B, $1 par value common stock for $8.25 per share.

c. Issued 10,000 shares of Series A, 5%, $120 par value convertible preferred stock for $120 per share.

d. The owners of 2,000 shares of the Series A, 5%, $120 par value convertible preferred stock converted their shares into Class B, $1 par value common stock. The preferred stock is convertible at the rate of 25 shares of common stock for each preferred share.

e. Issued 12,000 shares of Series B, 6%, $50 par value preferred stock in exchange for the assets of a company that was going out of business. The book value of the acquired assets was $440,000 at the date of the exchange and the fair market value was $650,000 total.

Required:

1. For each item a. through e. above, prepare the journal entry that was made to record the transaction in the accounting records.
2. After recording all five transactions, determine the total contributed capital.
3. Assume the company wishes to declare a $0.50 per share cash dividend to the common shareholders. Determine the total cash dividend that would be declared and the amount of that total that would be received by each of the preferred stock series.

8-4 Common and Preferred Stock

The shareholders' equity section of a balance sheet reported the following amounts:

(dollars in millions)
Shareholders' Equity

Preferred stock – $7.50, no-par value, cumulative dividend; 480,000 shares issued...............................	$ 72.0
Common stock, 520,000,000 shares issued	442.0
Capital in excess of par	4,680.0
Retained earnings..	7,857.2
Total shareholders' equity	$ 6,114.7

Required:

1. Determine the average per share issue price of the preferred stock.
2. Determine the par value per share and the average issue price per share of the common stock. How do you know the capital in excess of par applies to the common stock only?
3. During the year the company declared and paid the preferred stock dividend and declared and paid a $0.60 per share cash dividend on the common stock. Compute the amount of cash that was paid to each class of shareholder for these dividends. Assume there were no preferred stock dividends in arrears.

8-5 Common and Preferred Stock

The shareholders' equity section of a balance sheet reported the following amounts:

(dollars in millions)
Shareholders' Equity

Preferred stock – $2.50, no-par value, cumulative dividend; 400,000 shares issued	$ 34.4
Common stock, 20,000,000 shares issued...............	30.0
Capital in excess of par	335.0
Retained earnings	2,692.8
Treasury stock (400,000 common shares)...............	(18.6)
Total shareholders' equity	$ 3,073.6

Required:

1. Compute the average issue price per share of the preferred stock.
2. Compute the par value per share and the average issue price per share of the common stock. How do you know the capital in excess of par applies to the common stock only?
3. Compute the average price per share paid for the treasury shares. How many shares of common stock are outstanding?

8-6 Preferred Stock and Debt

Consider the following two items found in the balance sheet of a large corporation:

1. Bonds – 20 year life – maturity date June 30, 2032, 3.5% interest per year paid semiannually; and

2. Preferred Stock – 4% dividend - $100 par value – callable at 115% of par value after December 31, 2023 – redeemable for cash at 95% of par value after December 31, 2028.

Accounting rule makers are currently considering the economic differences between such instruments. Assume both the bonds and preferred shares are publicly-traded instruments. Looking at these two instruments, we can see that the bonds were issued in 2012. However, we do not know when the preferred shares were issued. The timing of the issuance and the risk class of the issuing entity at the time of issuance determine the effective interest rate and the resulting issue price of the two instruments. Without knowing the issue price of the bond or the preferred stock, we cannot know if the nominal rate of return (3.5% for the bond and 4% for the stock) is the same as the effective rate of return at issuance. Furthermore, we do not know what has happened to the effective interest rate required on either instrument since their issuance. Without consideration of these issues that might allow you to compare the two instruments from the standpoint of risk and return, consider the following questions:

Required:

1. From the viewpoint of the investor who might hold one or both of these instruments, what are the substantive economic differences between these two instruments?
2. From the viewpoint of the shareholders' of the voting common stock of the issuing entity, what are the substantive economic differences between these two instruments?
3. Would you be in favor of a balance sheet that classified the preferred stock as debt? Briefly explain your reasoning.

8-7 Treasury Stock

The following transactions concerning common stock occurred during the first year of a company's life:

January 1	Issued 50,000 shares of $5 par value stock for $62 per share; 300,000 shares are authorized.
April 15	Purchased 8,000 of the shares in the market for $68 per share.
July 20	Sold 3,000 of the treasury shares for $70 per share.
September 25	Sold 2,000 of the treasury shares for $53 per share.

Required:

1. For each of these transactions, prepare the journal entry that was made to record the transaction in the accounting records.
2. Prepare the balance sheet excerpt of the shareholders' equity section related to the above transactions immediately after the last transaction (9/25). Show as much detail as possible.

8-8 Treasury Stock

The January 1 balances in the shareholders' equity amounts were:

Shareholders' Equity	
Common stock, $1.50 par value,	
1,836,000 shares issued at year end	$ 2,754,000
Capital in excess of par	21,114,000
Retained earnings	37,180,000
Total shareholders' equity	$61,048,000

On April 1 the company purchased 120,000 shares of the common stock for the treasury at $20 per share. On June 1 they sold 65,000 of the treasury shares for $23 per share. On September 15, they sold 10,000 of the treasury shares for $15 per share. Net income was $1,360,000 and $459,000 of cash dividends were declared and paid during the year.

Required:

1. For each of the treasury stock transactions described above, prepare the journal entry that was made to record the transaction in the accounting records.
2. Show how the shareholders' equity section of the balance sheet would appear at the end of the year.

8-9 Financial Statement Analysis: E. I. du Pont de Nemours & Company

Locate the PDF file with the excerpts from the 2014 10-K of DUPONT. Refer to the *Consolidated Balance Sheets* and *Consolidated Statements of Equity* on pages 15 and 16 of the file (labeled pages F-6 and F-7 of the 10-K), and Footnote 16 on pages 18 and 19 of the file (labeled page F-28 and F-29 of the 10-K).

Required: Answer the following questions.

1. Briefly describe DU PONT (its business, where it operates, something unique that you learned from the annual report, etc.).
2. What is the weighted average price paid for treasury shares held at the end of 2014?
3. What was the change in treasury stock during 2014?
4. How many additional shares of stock were issued during 2014?
5. What was the average issue price of the new shares issued during 2014?
6. When a mature company like DUPONT has a new stock offering to the public, it is called a "seasoned equity offering" and it usually is a very significant event associated with a major expansion or acquisition(s) by the mature company. It may increase the shares of stock outstanding by 50-100% or more. Do you think DUPONT had a seasoned equity offering during 2014? What do you think might have caused the increase in the number of shares outstanding?
7. Now consider the *Consolidated Statements of Comprehensive Income* on page F-4. What was comprehensive income attributable to DUPONT for 2014?
8. Refer again to DUPONT'S *Consolidated Statements of Equity* on page F-7. What was the total dividends declared for the shareholders during 2013? How much did each class of shareholders receive (preferred and common)?

8-10 Treasury Stock

A start-up company recently purchased 1,000 shares of its own stock from the market to be used to provide shares to employees who are exercising stock options under an incentive program. The employees accepted the stock options instead of cash salaries. The company reported the following balance sheet at December 31, 2014:

Start-up Corporation
Balance Sheet
December 31, 2014
(dollar amounts in thousands)

Assets			Liabilities & Shareholders' Equity		
Cash.............................	$	8	Accounts payable.............	$	120
Accounts receivable		220	Wages payable		144
Treasury stock		190	Notes payable		300
Land		540	Contributed capital		500
Building & equipment....		600	Retained earnings		494
....			Total liabilities &		
Total assets....................		$ 1,558	shareholders' equity.......		$1,558

Required:

1. Is this presentation of treasury stock in accordance with GAAP?
2. Comment on the theoretical merits of reporting Treasury Stock as an asset.

8-11 Treasury Stock and Cash Dividends

During the current year a company went public and reported the following chronological transactions related to stock:

   a. Issued 200,000 shares of $1 par value common stock for $40 per share.
   b. Issued 5,000 shares of 7%, $100 par value preferred stock for $105 per share.
   c. Purchased 12,000 of the common shares from the market at $44 per share.
   d. Sold 4,000 of the treasury shares for $41 per share.
   e. Declared and paid a $.75 cash dividend on the outstanding common shares and the required preferred stock cash dividend.
   f. Sold the remaining treasury shares for $46 per share.

Required:

For each item a. through f. above, prepare the journal entry that was made to record the transaction in the accounting records.

8-12 Balance Sheet Analysis

The comparative balance sheets of the Rockport Company were prepared at the end of 2014. During 2014, Rockport declared and paid cash dividends to shareholders in the amount of $6 million dollars. This was the first dividend paid by the company since its incorporation in 2004.

Rockport Company
Comparative Balance Sheets
December 31,
(in millions)

Assets	2014	2013
Current assets:		
Cash	$ 70	$ 66
Other current assets	196	174
Total current assets	$266	$240
Plant and equipment (net)	648	650
Investment	64	54
Total assets	$978	$944

Liabilities and Shareholders' Equity		
Current liabilities:		
Payables	$ 60	$ 90
Other current liabilities	108	118
Total current liabilities	$168	$208
Debt and other long-term liabilities	450	446
Total liabilities	$618	$654
Shareholders' equity:		
Common stock	$230	$220
Capital in excess of par	120	110
Retained earnings (deficit)	10	(40)
Total shareholders' equity	$360	$290
Total liabilities and shareholders' equity	$978	$944

Required:

1. Compute the total amount of the change in net assets from the end of to 2013 to the end of 2014.
2. Indicate the amount of the change in net assets computed in Requirement 1 above that is attributable to *owner-related* transactions.
3. Indicate the amount of the change in net assets computed in Requirement 1 above that is attributable to *non-owner related* transactions.

8-13   Treasury Stock

Consider the information in problem **8-12** for Rockport Company. Focus your attention on the shareholders' equity section of the balance sheet. Assume the following additional facts explain all of the changes in Rockport's contributed capital for 2014.

    a. On February 11, 2014 Rockport purchased 400,000 shares of its common stock for $20 per share. On September 15, 2014 Rockport sold the 400,000 treasury shares in the market for $24 per share.

    b. On November 30, 2014 Rockport issued 1 million shares of previously unissued stock to their employees in exchange for $18.40 cash per share.

Required:

1. Prepare the journal entries that were made to record the two treasury stock transactions in item a.
2. Prepare the journal entry that was made to record the issuance of the 1 million shares of stock to the employees in item b. *Remember, only the information described above related to Rockport's contributed capital during 2014.*
3. Compute the par value of the common stock.
4. Compute the number of shares of common stock that were issued and outstanding at the end of 2014.

8-14   Error Analysis

On January 5, 2015, Maltese Corporation's new accountant discovered errors related to the following two transactions which were recorded during 2014. The transactions and the journal entries made to record the transactions were:

    a. On March 1, Maltese issued 2,000 shares of $8.25 no-par preferred stock for $120 per share. Maltese recorded the transaction as an increase of $240,000 to Cash; and increase of $16,500 to Preferred Stock—Par; and an increase of $223,500 to Contributed Capital in Excess of Par.

    b. On April 25, Maltese sold 1,000 shares of its common stock held in treasury for $67 per share. The stock was originally purchased during 2013 for $54 per share. To record the sale of the treasury stock, the impacts on the Cash and Treasury Stock accounts were appropriately recorded and a gain on sale of treasury stock of $13,000 was recognized.

Required:

1. Explain why the journal entries in each transaction were incorrect.
2. Prepare the correct journal entry for each transaction and contrast with the journal entries that were made.
3. Determine the effect error a. had on assets liabilities and shareholders' equity at December 31, 2013 and 2014, and on net income for the fiscal years 2013 and 2014 (ignore income taxes).
4. Determine the effect error b. had on assets, shareholders' equity at December 31, 2014, 2015, and 2016, and on net income for the fiscal years 2014 through 2016 (ignore income taxes).

8-15 Earnings per Share

Part A:

The following activity relating to the shares of common stock occurred during the current year:

Date	Share Activity	Total Shares Outstanding
January 1	—	108,000
April 1	Issued 36,000 shares	144,000
June 1	Repurchased 24,000 shares	120,000
November 1	Reissued 18,000 shares	138,000

Required

Compute the weighted average number of shares of common stock for the current year.

Part B:

For the year ended December 31, $374,400 of net income was reported. Assume that in addition to the common shares described in **Part A**, the company has 3,900 shares of $3, no-par value convertible preferred stock issued and outstanding. The preferred stock is convertible into common stock at the rate of 6 common shares for each preferred share.

Required:

1. Compute basic earnings per share.
2. Compute fully diluted earnings per share.
3. Are the shares of the convertible preferred stock dilutive? Explain.

Part C:

Now assume $374,400 of net income was reported for the year ended December 31, but that the company does not have any convertible preferred stock outstanding. Instead, assume the company has convertible bonds outstanding. These bonds are convertible into 20,000 shares of common stock. The after-tax cost of interest on these bonds would have increased net income by $23,100 had the bonds been converted into common stock and the interest not paid. Assume the same common share activity described in **Part A**.

Required:

1. Compute basic earnings per share.
2. Compute fully diluted earnings per share.
3. Are the convertible bonds dilutive? Explain.

8-16   Earnings per Share

Part A:

The following activity relating to the shares of common stock occurred during the current year:

Date	Share Activity	Total Shares Outstanding
January 1	—	3,000,000
July 1	Issued 720,000 shares	3,720,000
October 1	Repurchased 1,200,000 shares	2,520,000

Required:

Compute the weighted average number of shares of common stock for the current year.

Part B:

For the year ended December 31, $5,362,000 of net income was reported. Assume that in addition to the common shares described in **Part A**, the company has 200,000 shares of 5%, $100 par value convertible preferred stock issued and outstanding. The preferred stock is convertible into common stock at the rate of 8 common shares for each preferred share.

Required:

1. Compute basic earnings per share.
2. Compute fully diluted earnings per share.
3. Are the shares of the convertible preferred stock dilutive? Explain.

Part C:

Now assume $5,362,000 of net income was reported for the year ended December 31, but that the company does not have any convertible preferred stock outstanding. Instead, assume the company has convertible bonds outstanding. These bonds are convertible into 500,000 shares of common stock. The after-tax cost of interest on these bonds would have increased net income by $360,000 had the bonds been converted into common stock and the interest not paid. Assume the same common share activity described in **Part A**.

Required:

1. Compute basic earnings per share.
2. Compute fully diluted earnings per share.
3. Are the convertible bonds dilutive? Explain.

8-17 Statement of Shareholders' Equity

The following statement of shareholders' equity (in thousands) was reported at December 31, 2014:

Item	Common Stock	Preferred Stock	Capital in Excess of Par	Retained Earnings	Treasury Stock
Balance 12/31/13	$49,200	$2,400	$25,600	$109,000	$ (720)
Net income				31,200	
Cash dividend				(21,400)	
Preferred stock conversion	200	(1,000)	800		
Treasury stock purchased					(660)
Stock dividend	200		4,000	(4,200)	
Balance 12/31/14	$49,600	$1,400	$30,400	$114,600	$(1,380)

Required:

For each item listed, describe its impact on total shareholders' equity.

8-18 Statement of Shareholders' Equity

The following statement of shareholders' equity (in thousands) is shown without descriptions for the items:

Item	Common Stock	Preferred Stock	Capital in Excess of Par	Retained Earnings	Treasury Stock	Total Shareholders' Equity
Balance 12/31/13	$28,000	$4,000	$14,000	$17,320	$(500)	$62,820
a.				5,200		5,200
b.	2,000		200			2,200
c.		1,000				1,000
d.				(2,600)		(2,600)
e.					(1,400)	(1,400)
f.			200		400	600
Balance 12/31/14	$30,000	$5,000	$14,400	$19,920	$(1,500)	$67,820

Required:

For items a. through f., describe the transaction that most likely caused each change in the shareholders' equity accounts. Revenues for the year were $47,000 thousand and expenses were $41,800 thousand.

8-19   Reading Financial Statements – BEMIS COMPANY

Locate the PDF file with the excerpts from the 2014 annual report and 10-K of BEMIS COMPANY, INC.

Required:

1. Take a few minutes and scan the first 15 pages of the annual report. Briefly describe BEMIS, INC. (its business, where it operates, something unique that you learned from the annual report, etc.).
2. Reference the *Consolidated Balance Sheet* on page 21 of the file (labeled page 30 of the annual report/10-K). Answer the following questions.
    a.   Identify the amount of *total stockholders' equity* at the end of the two most recent fiscal years. Explain what caused the decrease over the year.
    b.   Identify the *par value of the common stock*.
    c.   Compute the book value per share for the most recent fiscal year.
    d.   How many shares of common stock were being held in the treasury at the end of the most recent fiscal year? Compute the average price paid for the treasury stock.
3. Assume the company's stock was selling for $40 per share at the end of the most recent fiscal year. Compute the price-to-book ratio and the price-to-earnings ratio at that year end.
4. Identify BEMIS' transfer agent. Describe the responsibilities of the transfer agent. *(Refer to the description in the chapter on page 97 regarding where you will find the listing for a corporation's transfer agent.)*

8-20   Financial Statement Analysis – UNITED PARCEL SERVICE

Locate the PDF file with the excerpts from the 2014 annual report and 10-K of UNITED PARCEL SERVICE, INC. (UPS).

Required:

1. Take a few minutes and scan the first 9 pages of the annual report. Briefly describe UPS (its business, where it operates, something unique that you learned from the annual report, etc.).
2. Consider the 2014 *Consolidated Balance Sheet* (page 14 of the file and labeled page 62 of the 10-K): Based on the information on this page, identify the <u>average</u> number of shares of common stock <u>issued</u> throughout 2014 (combine the Class A shares and Class B shares into a single common stock number) and the <u>average</u> number of shares of common stock <u>outstanding</u> throughout 2014. Remember, all numbers are in millions.
3. Consider the 2014 *Statement of Consolidated Income* (page 15 of the file and labeled page 63 of the 10-K): Based on the per share data provided, estimate the weighted average number of common shares that were outstanding during the year.
4. Consider *Footnote 13* (page 17 of the file and labeled page 108 of the 10-K): What were the average number of common stock shares outstanding used for the basic EPS calculation? What may have caused the slight difference in your numbers between requirements 2 and 3?
5. Identify UPS' transfer agent. Describe the responsibilities of the transfer agent. *(Refer to the description in the chapter on page 97 regarding where you will find the listing for a corporation's transfer agent.)*

Chapter 8 Study Quiz

For each of the five questions, show and label your calculations and place your answer in the spaces provided.

1. At January 1, the following balances were reported in the shareholders' equity accounts:

Preferred stock – $100 par value	$ 110,000
Common stock – $1 par value	550,000
Capital in excess of Par	429,000
Retained earnings	418,000
Total	$ 1,507,000

During the year, 10,000 shares of common stock were issued in exchange for a patent with a market value of $61,600, a parcel of land valued at $154,000 was received in exchange for shares of preferred stock, the common stock was split 2 for 1, $123,200 of cash dividends were declared and paid, $649,000 of net income was reported, and 33,000 shares of the common stock were purchased for the treasury at $3 per share.

Determine total shareholders' equity at 12/31. $_____

Calculation:

2. One thousand shares of $3, no-par value cumulative preferred stock and 3,000 shares of $5 par value common stock have been issued and outstanding for five years. Three years of dividends are in arrears on the preferred stock. Total dividends declared for the current year were $22,500.

Determine the total amounts of dividends received by the common stockholders.

$_____

Calculation:

3. There are 100,000 shares of common stock, which were initially sold at par in 2003, issued and outstanding at December 31, 2013. Ten thousand of these shares were repurchased for $37.50 per share on January 1, 2014. On March 27, 2014, 4,000 of these shares were sold at $39 per share and on June 17, 2014, 6,000 of the shares were sold at $35 per share. No other stock transactions took place between December 31, 2013 and December 31, 2014.

   Prepare the journal entry to record the June 17 transaction.

   Journal entry:

   Calculation:

4. For the year, net income of $1,260,000 and an ending balance in Retained Earnings of $2,880,000 were reported. During the year, a $4.80 cash dividend was declared and paid on 75,000 shares of common stock. After the dividend was paid, 5,000 of the shares were repurchased for the treasury at $28.80 per share.

   Determine the Retained Earnings beginning balance.

   $_____

   Calculation:

5. A company began operations on January 1 by issuing 30,000 shares of common stock and 10,000 shares of 5%, $100 par value preferred stock. On April 1, the company issued 30,000 additional shares of common stock. On August 1, the company purchased 6,000 of the common shares for the treasury. On December 1, the company declared and paid a $90,000 cash dividend on the outstanding common and preferred shares. Net income for the year ended December 31 was $475,600.

   Compute basic earnings per share for the year ended December 31.

   $_____

   Calculation:

Chapter 9

Income Measurement and
Statement of Cash Flows

LEARNING OBJECTIVES

1. Understand the economic implications of the components included in net income and comprehensive income.

2. Interpret amounts reported in the statement of cash flows.

3. Prepare a statement of cash flows from an income statement and comparative balance sheets.

In Chapters 4 through 8 we have examined the "stocks" (i.e., assets, liabilities and equities at a specified date) that make up the balance sheet. Now we take an in-depth look at the "flow" statements (i.e., the videos) that summarize business activities for a period of time as they pertain to *income* and *cash*. **Net income** is the measure that summarizes most of the transactions that impacted the operating performance of the business, as well as certain transactions that are not directly related to operations. **Comprehensive income** starts with net income and adds the impact of four other types of transactions to report a complete measure of the change in net assets *from all non-owner related events*.

In Chapter 8, we described the primary *owner-related* transactions, including issuing common and preferred stock, declaring stock splits and cash dividends and stock dividends, and acquiring and reissuing treasury shares. While owner-related transactions affect the net assets of the business, they have no impact on the wealth of the owners. Comprehensive income, therefore, provides a complete summary of all non-owner related transactions that impact shareholders' wealth.

The statement of cash flows, of course, summarizes the transactions involving the cash inflows and outflows of the business, with the net change accumulated in the cash account. The statement of cash flows provides a useful complement to the income measures. Increases in income should be accompanied by increases in cash flow from operating activities for the business to remain healthy. If the company is not converting its income into cash, financial problems are being encountered.

INCOME MEASUREMENT

Our examination of income thus far has focused on the typical revenues and expenses reported each year in the income statements of most companies. However, the income statement may also include a number of unusual and non-routine gains and losses that we have not discussed in any detail. It is important for analysts and other users of financial statements to understand the economic implications of these other items included in income measurement.

Accrual income is the most important measure of business performance. Analysts and others focus a great deal of effort on predicting future income by carefully studying and understanding income measurement.[1] To predict future earnings analysts must determine which components of the current period's income are expected to continue in future periods. These components are referred to as **persistent components**.

Exhibit 9-1 illustrates a hypothetical income statement in its most complex form. The subtotal, *Operating Income*, summarizes the profits of the company that resulted from the routine, ongoing operations of its primary business activities. Understanding and evaluating operating income is of great importance since it is the central persistent component of income. Analysts often combine operating income with other information (e.g., new product development or expansion into new markets) to predict future income amounts and trends.

Exhibit 9-1 also illustrates several other categories of items that might be included in net income. These additional items belong to one of two categories:

1. **Before tax non-operating items.** These items are included in income from continuing operations (the core business of the company) and are reported <u>before</u> income taxes. They include:

   a. Routine items that are not strictly operating in nature (such as interest); and

   b. Irregular gains and losses that are not a part of routine operating activities (such as restructuring charges).

2. **Items requiring separate reporting.** These items are reported <u>net</u> of their income tax impact below income from continuing operations. These items include:

   a. Discontinued operations (net of taxes); and

   b. Extraordinary items (net of taxes).

---

[1] Future earnings is the single most important number predicted by analysts and others for purposes of determining the value of the firm. Thousands of research studies have been conducted using analysts' earnings forecasts in an effort to better understand the relation between earnings and firm value.

Exhibit 9-1   Income Statement: Complex Example

Total Corporation
Income Statement
For the year ended December 31, 2015
(All dollar amounts in millions)

Revenues:	
Sales of goods	$ 195
Sales of services	144
Total revenues from goods and services	$ 339
Expenses:	
Cost of goods sold	$ 76
Cost of services sold	64
Selling, general and administrative expenses	30
Research and development expenses	24
Depreciation and amortization expenses	36
Operating income	**$ 109**
Other expenses (income):	
Special non-recurring charges	34
Interest and other income	(24)
Interest expense	39
Income from continuing operations before income taxes	$ 60
Provision for income taxes	24
Income from continuing operations	**$ 36**
Loss on discontinued operations (net of $8 tax)	(12)
Extraordinary gain (net of $4 tax)	6
Net income	**$ 30**

Before Tax Non-Operating Items

The items reported after **operating income** and before **provision for income taxes** (the term often used for income tax expense) are sometimes referred to as *above the line items*. The line referred to is the subtotal **income from continuing operations**. These items normally will include:

1.a.   Routine items not considered operating in nature:

- Interest expense and interest revenue; and
- Other gains and losses.

Interest expense, strictly speaking, is not an operating expense because it is the result of the amount of debt the company is using to finance its assets. Interest expense is shown as a separate line item in most all income statements. Similarly, interest revenue is usually shown separately for any business that does not deal in investments as a source of its operations. (Of course, businesses such as insurance companies and banks will consider interest revenue as operating revenue.) Other gains and losses would include gains and losses from the sale or exchange of assets such as buildings and equipment as we saw in Chapter 6.

In addition to these routine non-operating items, companies sometimes report gains or losses that are too large to simply include in other gains and losses. While there is no standard terminology required to describe these irregular items, common examples found in actual financial statements include:

1.b.   Irregular pretax items:

- Restructuring charges;
- Unusual items; and
- Special **non-recurring charges** and/or credits.

Restructuring charges are costs associated with a major reorganization. These costs often involve the closure of a plant and early retirement programs to reduce the workforce (downsizing). "Unusual items" is a common general description, like "other," that might pertain to any number of transactions such as write downs of long-term tangible or intangible assets due to impairment tests.

Items Requiring Separate Reporting

The items in this category are reported on an after-tax basis and are sometimes referred to as *below the line items*. The reporting of these items is governed by specific accounting rules. There are two items that are reported separately below income from continuing operations: discontinued operations and extraordinary items.

Discontinued Operations   Discontinued operations occur when there has been a "major strategic shift" in makeup of a business. This typically means that a major business unit or geographic area of business operations has been eliminated. A plant closure would not qualify.[2] Discontinued operations are reported in the income statement just after the subtotal for *Income from continuing operations*. Details regarding the balance sheet and income statement consequences of the discontinued operations must be provided in the notes to the financial statements.

Extraordinary Items   Extraordinary items are, by definition, rare. A recent FASB decision will result in their elimination as a separate disclosure, net of tax, after 2015. They are defined as gains or losses that are *highly unusual in nature and not expected to recur again in the foreseeable future*. Hurricanes in the Gulf of Mexico and tornados in the Midwest, for example, generally would not qualify as extraordinary items. For example, the parent company of WHOLE FOODS experienced an earthquake in a California operation that resulted in a multi-million dollar loss. The loss was not consider an extraordinary item. In an effort to simplify the income statement these extraordinary items will soon be eliminated. They will be reported in the income statement after operating income and *before* pretax income (no longer net of their separate tax effect), probably identified as something like "other income/loss."

---

[2] In 2014 the FASB narrowed the definition of discontinued operations. Many financial statement users complained that too many companies were calling disposals of bad assets or losing activities "discontinued operations," thus make their "operating incomes" look better.

Comprehensive Income

The measurement of net income in its most complex form could include: (1) both routine and irregular before tax *operating* amounts; (2) discontinued operations; and (3) extraordinary items. Obviously, not all companies will have all of these components included in net income. In addition to these potential complexities in measuring net income, there are several other changes in the net assets of the business from other non-owner related items that impact the wealth of the owners. These other non-owner related transactions are added to net income in the **Statement of Comprehensive Income**.

There are four other components of **comprehensive income** besides net income which must be reported net of their respective income tax consequences (we listed these items in Chapter 8 when we discussed the balance sheet account **Accumulated Other Comprehensive Income**):

1. *Unrealized* **gains and losses** on securities held as investments;
2. Gains and losses on derivative securities not included in net income;
3. *Gains and losses from translation* of the financial statements of foreign subsidiaries into U.S. dollars; and
4. Pension and OPEB (other post-employment benefits) liability adjustments.

While a detailed explanation of these four components goes beyond the scope of this text, the general nature of these gains and losses is not difficult to understand. The first two items are essentially measures of the changes in the fair market value of investment securities and/or contracts controlled by the business. These securities and contracts are reported at their fair market value in the balance sheet (referred to as **fair-value accounting**). The change in their market value from the prior period results in a holding gain or loss. These **holding gains and losses** have not been realized in cash, and they are not included in net income, but they are reported in comprehensive income to offset the change in the value of the securities in the asset section of the balance sheet. **Derivative securities** are securities that derive their value from changes in the value of a related security and include all types of option contracts and other commitments to buy or sell commodities, notes, foreign currencies, etc.

Translation gains and losses from foreign operations result when a company has a foreign subsidiary whose accounting records are kept in a foreign currency. The parent company must translate the subsidiary's financial statements into U.S. dollars at each year-end so the amounts can be included in the consolidated financial statements. For example, THE WALT DISNEY COMPANY is a multinational company with operations all over the world. It has many foreign subsidiaries that are reported as a part of its consolidated financial statements, and each year it has an adjustment in comprehensive income to record the gain or loss on their translation of the foreign financial statements into U.S. dollars. The policy footnote to DISNEY's 2014 annual report describes this process as follows:

Translation Policy

The U.S. dollar is the functional currency for the majority of our international operations. The local currency is the functional currency for the International Theme Parks, international locations of The Disney Stores, our UTV businesses in India, our English language learning centers in China and certain international equity method investments.

For U.S. dollar functional currency locations, foreign currency assets and liabilities are remeasured into U.S. dollars at end-of-period exchange rates, except for non-monetary balance sheet accounts, which are remeasured at historical exchange rates. Revenue and expenses are remeasured at average exchange rates in effect during each period, except for those expenses related to the non-monetary balance sheet amounts, which are remeasured at historical exchange rates. Gains or losses from foreign currency remeasurement are included in income.

For local currency functional locations, assets and liabilities are translated at end-of-period rates while revenues and expenses are translated at average rates in effect during the period. Equity is translated at historical rates and the resulting cumulative translation adjustments are included as a component of AOCI.

DISNEY's Consolidated Statements of Income and Comprehensive Income for 2014, provided in Exhibit 9-2, illustrates the most typical way that companies currently report OCI.

From DISNEY's Consolidated Statements of Comprehensive Income, we see that their foreign currency translation adjustment, net of tax, for 2014 was an $18 loss. This $18 loss was a small part of the total "other comprehensive income/loss" of $817 million for 2014. The most significant part was the comprehensive loss of $925 million from pension and OPEB adjustments. The $925 loss and related increase in the pension and OPEB liabilities indicates that, based on current estimates, not enough expense was recorded in prior years. Although pensions and OPEBs are actually part of employee wages and salaries, current accounting procedures require some portion of their current period amounts (adjustments) to be reported in comprehensive income.

Formats for Reporting Comprehensive Income

Comprehensive income should be reported either as a continuation of the income statement, or as a separate Statement of Comprehensive Income as in the DISNEY example in Exhibit 9-2. Note that this format measures and reports EPS between the Income Statement, and the Statement of Comprehensive Income. As noted, this is the most common format for reporting comprehensive income. The second format allowed by GAAP presents a single statement that includes both net income and comprehensive income. WALGREEN CO.'s 2013 *Consolidated Statements of Comprehensive Income* in Exhibit 9-3 is an example of a combined income and comprehensive income statement. Notice that WALGREENS' comprehensive income is also impacted by its pro-rata share of the comprehensive income for a subsidiary, ALLIANCE BOOTS. Current examples of the single statement format like WALGREENS are not common. In fact, WALGREEN switched to the two statement format in 2014. This is probably due to the fact that the EPS measures *only pertain to net income*, not comprehensive income. Hence, it could be confusing to show these EPS measures after the comprehensive income totals as in Exhibit 9-3.

CONSOLIDATED STATEMENTS OF INCOME
(in millions, except per share data)

	2014	2013	2012
Revenues:			
Services	$ 40,246	$ 37,280	$ 34,625
Products	8,567	7,761	7,653
Total revenues	48,813	45,041	42,278
Costs and expenses:			
Cost of services (exclusive of depreciation and amortization)	(21,356)	(20,090)	(18,625)
Cost of products (exclusive of depreciation and amortization)	(5,064)	(4,944)	(4,843)
Selling, general, administrative and other	(8,565)	(8,365)	(7,960)
Depreciation and amortization	(2,288)	(2,192)	(1,987)
Total costs and expenses	(37,273)	(35,591)	(33,415)
Restructuring and impairment charges	(140)	(214)	(100)
Other income/(expense), net	(31)	(69)	239
Interest income/(expense), net	23	(235)	(369)
Equity in the income of investees	854	688	627
Income before income taxes	12,246	9,620	9,260
Income taxes	(4,242)	(2,984)	(3,087)
Net income	8,004	6,636	6,173
Less: Net income attributable to noncontrolling interests	(503)	(500)	(491)
Net income attributable to The Walt Disney Company (Disney)	$ 7,501	$ 6,136	$ 5,682

CONSOLIDATED STATEMENTS OF COMPREHENSIVE INCOME
(in millions)

	2014	2013	2012
Net Income	$ 8,004	$ 6,636	$ 6,173
Other comprehensive income (loss), net of tax:			
Market value adjustments for investments	5	92	(3)
Market value adjustments for hedges	121	135	2
Pension and postretirement medical plan adjustments	(925)	1,963	(609)
Foreign currency translation and other	(18)	(80)	(41)
Other comprehensive income (loss)	(817)	2,110	(651)
Comprehensive income	7,187	8,746	5,522
Less: Net income attributable to noncontrolling interests	(503)	(500)	(491)
Less: Other comprehensive (income) loss attributable to noncontrolling interests	36	(31)	15
Comprehensive income attributable to Disney	$ 6,720	$ 8,215	$ 5,046

Exhibit 9-3 WALGREEN CO. 2013 Statements of Comprehensive Income

Consolidated Statements of Comprehensive Income

Walgreen Co. and Subsidiaries for the years ended August 31, 2013, 2012 and 2011 *(In millions, except per share amounts)*

	2013	2012	2011
Net sales	$72,217	$71,633	$72,184
Cost of sales	51,098	51,291	51,692
Gross Profit	21,119	20,342	20,492
Selling, general and administrative expenses	17,543	16,878	16,561
Gain on sale of business	20	—	434
Equity earnings in Alliance Boots	344	—	—
Operating Income	3,940	3,464	4,365
Interest expense, net	(165)	(88)	(71)
Other Income	120	—	—
Earnings Before Income Tax Provision	3,895	3,376	4,294
Income tax provision	1,445	1,249	1,580
Net Earnings	$ 2,450	$ 2,127	$ 2,714
Other comprehensive income (loss), net of tax:			
Change in postretirement liability	(5)	52	40
Share of other comprehensive income of Alliance Boots	(59)	—	—
Unrecognized gain on available-for-sale investments	1	—	—
Cumulative translation adjustments	(103)	—	—
Comprehensive Income	$ 2,284	$ 2,179	$ 2,754
Net earnings per common share – basic	$ 2.59	$ 2.43	$ 2.97
Net earnings per common share – diluted	2.56	2.42	2.94
Average shares outstanding	946.0	874.7	915.1
Dilutive effect of stock options	9.2	5.4	9.4
Average diluted shares	955.2	880.1	924.5

The accompanying Notes to Consolidated Financial Statements are integral parts of these statements.

Purpose and Use of Income Measurements

Income measurements provide important information about the performance of the business. One or more measurements developed from income information are used in nearly all economic decisions made by external users related to past or future performance of the entity. However, using various income measurements to make decisions requires a depth of understanding of the most relevant accounting data for the decision at hand as well as the limitations of these data. Further study will be necessary before we can fully understand the relevance and limitations of GAAP-based income measurements and their role in business decision making.

STATEMENT OF CASH FLOWS

The statement of cash flows (SCF), like the income statement, describes the nature of the changes in an important element of the balance sheet during a period of time. Unlike the income statement, which measures the performance of the business (the change in net assets from operating activities), the SCF describes the nature of the inflows and outflows of cash. The SCF is not based on accrual accounting. It can best be described as an analysis of the company's checkbook, with each deposit made or check written classified as an inflow or outflow pertaining to:

- Operating activities;

- Investing activities; or

- Financing activities.

The sum of these cash flows must, of course, explain the change in the cash account that is observed in the comparative balance sheets. Therefore, it is easy to determine the bottom line of the SCF by measuring the change in the cash account from the start of the period to the end of the period.

Current accounting rules under both U.S. GAAP and IFRS require the SCF. However, it is still not required in some emerging economies or in companies that are not publicly-traded. Most external financial statement users find it helpful to have a SCF, and it is an important skill to be able to create a SCF from the comparative balance sheets and the income statement if one is not provided by the entity. Banks, for example, supply much of the capital for small, closely-held companies and lenders rely heavily on the information in the SCF to evaluate the credit worthiness of such borrowers. It is customary for most banks to prepare a SCF from a company's other financial statements if a SCF is not presented by a credit applicant.

Relation of the Statement of Cash Flows to the Other Statements

To illustrate the relationship between the SCF and the accrual financial statements, we prepare a SCF from the comparative balance sheets and income statement of Four Wolves Company. The balance sheets and income statement are shown on the next page (the balance sheet has been annotated to show the location of the amounts pertaining to operating, investing, and financing activities); the completed SCF is shown on page 139 in Exhibit 9-4.

At a basic level, we see that the change in cash for 2014 was a positive $25 million, since the cash balance reported in the balance sheets increased from $50 million at the end of 2013 to $75 million at the end of 2014. One financing cash flow that can be computed from the balance sheets and the income statement is the amount of dividends. Net income was $70 million for 2014, but retained earnings only increased by $50 million (from $300 million to $350 million). The most likely explanation for this difference is that the company declared (and probably paid) a cash dividend of $20 million during the year. In a similar fashion, the company's other financing and investing cash flows can be inferred by analyzing changes in the noncurrent asset, noncurrent liability, and shareholders' equity amounts in the balance sheets. Finally, the details of the company's *operating* cash flows can be determined by converting the accrual measure of net income on the income statement to a measure of *cash* flows from operating activities.

Four Wolves Company
Comparative Balance Sheets
For the Years Ended December 31, 2014 and 2013
(All dollar amounts in millions)

	Assets	2014	2013		Liabilities	2014	2013	
Status of operating activities here	Cash	$ 75	$ 50		Accounts payable	$ 90	$ 80	**Status of operating activities here**
	Accounts receivable	150	125		Wages payable..................	35	50	
	Inventory	250	300		Other liabilities	20	25	
	Current assets	$475	$475		Current liabilities	$145	$155	
					Long-term loans	150	215	**Status of financing activities here**
Status of investing activities here	Plant & equipment	$800	$750		Mortgage payable	55	55	
	Less: Accumulated depreciation	(500)	(420)		Total liabilities	$350	$425	
	Net plant & equipment	$300	$330		**Shareholders' Equity**			
	Investments	24	19		Contributed capital	$100	$100	
	Intangibles (net)	1	1		Retained earnings	350	300	
	Total L-T assets	$325	$350		Total shareholders' equity .	$450	$400	
	Total assets	$800	$825		Total liabilities and shareholders' equity......	$800	$825	

Four Wolves Company
Income Statement
For the Year Ended December 31, 2014
(All dollar amounts in millions)

Revenues

Sales of products.................................	$ 345
Sales of services	144
Total revenues.................................	$ 489

Costs and expenses

Cost of goods sold	$ 132
Cost of services provided	72
Depreciation expense...........................	80
General expenses	41
Advertising expense	33
Total operating expenses	$ 358
Operating income............................	$ 131
Interest expense	15
Net income before taxes	116
Income tax expense	46
Net income.....................................	$ 70

Exhibit 9-4   Statement of Cash Flows – Indirect Method (Most Common)

Four Wolves Company
Statement of Cash Flows
For the Year Ended December 31, 2014
(All dollar amounts in millions)

Cash flows from operating activities:

Net income	$ 70
Depreciation expense	80
Increase in accounts receivable	(25)
Decrease in inventory	50
Increase in accounts payable	10
Decrease in wages payable	(15)
Decrease in other liabilities	(5)
Cash provided by operating activities	$ 165

Cash flows from investing activities:

Purchase investments....................................	$ (5)
Purchase plant & equipment..........................	(50)
Cash used by investing activities..............	$ (55)

Cash flows from financing activities:

Repay long-term loan	$ (65)
Pay dividends	(20)
Cash used by financing activities	$ (85)
Net increase in cash	$ 25

We will illustrate the preparation of the Four Wolves SCF by calculating each amount in the statement, beginning with the numbers in the section reporting the cash flows from operating activities and ending with the numbers in the investing and financing sections.

Operating Activities Section

The **operating cash flows** can be determined by converting the accrual measure of net income to a measure of cash flow from operating activities. This is achieved by deleting all non-cash effects that affected net income, effectively turning the accrual measure of income into a cash-based measure of income. That is, we consider each income statement amount and determine how much cash was provided by revenues and how much cash was used for each expense listed. The conversion from net income to cash from operating activities is made in two steps:

Step 1:   Add back all expenses deducted in computing net income that did not require the payment of cash (e.g., depreciation, amortization, and depletion).

Step 2:   Adjust the accrual measure of net income for changes in the operating accounts (current assets and current liabilities).

Step 1   The first step in preparing the operating activities section is to add back all the expenses that were deducted in computing net income that did not use cash. Depreciation expense from the income statement is added back as shown below:[3]

Cash flows from operating activities:

Net income	$ 70
Depreciation expense....................................	**80**
Increase in accounts receivable	(25)
Decrease in inventory....................................	50
Increase in accounts payable	10
Decrease in wages payable...........................	(15)
Decrease in other liabilities	(5)
Cash provided by operating activities	$ 165

Step 2   The second step in preparing the operating activities section uses the T-account analysis we have illustrated throughout the text. We review this process to underscore the important role T-account analysis plays in the effective use of information from the financial statements.

To prepare the operating activities section, we take the beginning and ending balances of each current asset (other than cash) and current liability and examine the role that operating cash flows likely played in explaining the change in the account. The first current asset other than cash is accounts receivable. For all accounts, we ask: *What makes it increase and what makes it decrease?* For Accounts Receivable, we answer this question as follows:

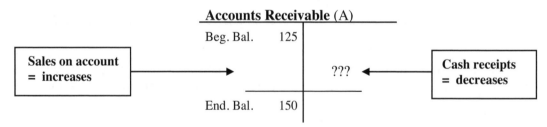

From the income statement we know revenues totaled $489 for the year. Entering this amount in the Accounts Receivable account, we can then compute the amount of cash received from customers as $464, as shown below (all amounts are in millions).

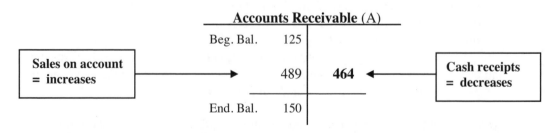

---

[3] In more advanced accounting courses, you will learn about other noncash adjustments (e.g. amortization of bond discounts or premiums) that will be added or subtracted from net income. We use depreciation to demonstrate this concept at the introductory level.

We see that the $25 increase in Accounts Receivable means that the $489 of revenue reported in the income statement is $25 more than the cash inflow from sales of $464. For this reason, the SCF <u>deducts</u> the $25 increase in Accounts Receivable from net income, to convert it to cash from operating activities (i.e., less cash was received than the revenue that was recognized on the income statement):

Cash flows from operating activities:

Net income	$ 70
Depreciation expense..................................	80
Increase in accounts receivable	**(25)**
Decrease in inventory	50
Increase in accounts payable........................	10
Decrease in wages payable	(15)
Decrease in other liabilities.........................	(5)
Cash provided by operating activities	$ 165

The next current asset is Inventory. Recall from our study of Inventory that we can determine the amount of cash paid for inventory by examining the change in Inventory and the change in Accounts Payable at the same time:

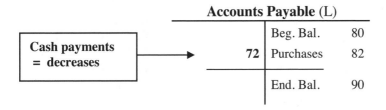

Since cost of goods sold (= $132) <u>reduces</u> inventory and the balance in inventory decreased by $50, the inventory purchases must have been $82. This means cost of goods sold was $50 more than purchases and we <u>add</u> the $50 decrease in Inventory to net income to convert it to cash from operating activities. Further, we see that since Accounts Payable increased by $10 and purchases were $82, cash payments on Accounts Payable must have been $72. We <u>add</u> the $10 increase in Accounts Payable to net income to convert it to cash from operating activities. In summary, cost of goods sold reduced net income by $132, but cash paid to suppliers was only $72. The income statement reflects the cost of inventory of $132; however, Four Wolves purchased $50 less ($82) than that and paid $10 less ($72) than it purchased. The $60 difference ($50 from Inventory and $10 from Accounts Payable) is added to net income to convert net income to cash from operating activities:

Cash flows from operating activities:

Net income		$ 70
Depreciation expense		80
Increase in accounts receivable		(25)
Decrease in inventory		**50**
Increase in accounts payable		**10**
Decrease in wages payable		(15)
Decrease in other liabilities		(5)
Cash provided by operating activities		$ 165

This same analysis can be used to explain how the changes in Wages Payable and Other Liabilities impact cash. To interpret these last two current accounts we make the assumptions that the account Cost of Services Provided (salaries of the employees directly working on the projects), is accrued in the Wages Payable account and that general expenses and advertising expense are accrued in the Other Liabilities account.[4] We can further assume that the interest expense and income tax expense amounts are both cash expenses with no accrual components to them since there are no related liabilities associated with those expenses. Based on these assumptions, the following cash flow implications can be inferred:

Wages Payable (L)				**Other Liabilities** (L)		
	Beg. Bal.	50			Beg. Bal.	25
	Cost of				Gen'l Exp. &	
Cash paid 87	services			**Cash paid** 79	Adv. Exp.	74
	provided	72				
	End. Bal.	35			End. Bal.	20

From this analysis, we can see that cash paid for wages was $15 more than the cost of services provided that was recognized on the income statement, and that cash paid for other liabilities was $5 more than the General and Advertising expenses reported in the income statement. This requires the following two adjustments to convert net income to cash from operating activities:

Cash flows from operating activities:

Net income		$ 70
Depreciation expense		80
Increase in accounts receivable		(25)
Decrease in inventory		50
Increase in accounts payable		10
Decrease in wages payable		**(15)**
Decrease in other liabilities		**(5)**
Cash provided by operating activities		$ 165

---

[4] As we saw in earlier chapters, these assumptions do not affect the analysis, as the change in the accounts would be the same regardless of which income statement accounts affected which balance sheet accounts.

Exhibit 9-5 Common Adjustments to Net Income for the SCF

Item	Action	Reason
Depreciation and amortization	Add to net income	These amounts were deducted in computing net income but they did not require the use of cash.
An increase in accounts receivable	Subtract from net income	This amount is included in revenue but the cash will not be collected until a future period.
A decrease in accounts receivable	Add to net income	This amount is cash received in the current period that was reported as revenue in a prior period.
An increase in inventory	Subtract from net income	These purchases required cash in the current period but were not included in current cost of goods sold.
A decrease in inventory	Add to net income	These purchases are included in cost of goods sold but were paid for in a prior period.
An increase in prepaid expenses	Subtract from net income	These prepayments required cash but are not included as expenses in current net income.
A decrease in prepaid expenses	Add to net income	These are expenses included net income of the current period but were paid for in a prior period.
An increase in current payables	Add to net income	These are expenses included in current net income that will be paid in cash in a future period.
A decrease in current payables	Subtract from net income	These are cash payments for resources that were included in net income in a prior period.
An increase in unearned revenue	Add to net income	This is cash received in the current period that will not be reported as revenue until a future period.
A decrease in unearned revenue	Subtract from net income	This is revenue included in current net income, but the cash was collected in a prior period.

To summarize our discussion to this point, Exhibit 9-5 lists the usual items that appear in a SCF to adjust net income to cash from operating activities.

Investing and Financing Activities Sections

Similar analysis of the long-term asset, long-term liability, and shareholders' equity sections of the balance sheet provide the amounts for **investing cash flows** and for **financing cash flows**. Consider first the long-term asset section, the part that shows the status of investing activities. The first change we see in this section that likely affected cash is the change in the Investments account.

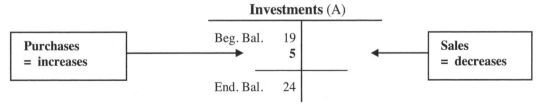

This analysis suggests that $5 of cash was used to acquire additional investments, and the $5 would be shown as a <u>use</u> of cash for investing activities in the SCF.

The second change we see is the increase in Plant & Equipment:

Plant & Equipment (A)

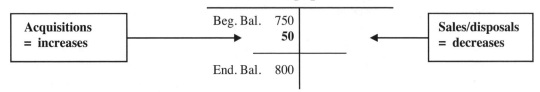

This increase suggests that cash was used to acquire $50 of long-term assets and this amount would be shown as a <u>use</u> of cash for investing activities in the SCF. These two items would be shown in the investing section of the SCF as follows:

Cash flows from investing activities:

Purchase investments	$ (5)
Purchase plant & equipment	(50)
Cash used by investing activities	$ (55)

Analysis of the noncurrent liability and shareholders' equity sections produce the amounts for the financing section of the SCF. Long-term loans decreased from $215 to $150, and this likely required the <u>use</u> of cash to repay a long-term loan.

Long-term Loans (L)

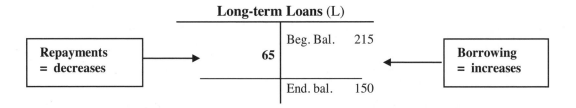

Finally, the change in Retained Earnings indicates the <u>use</u> of $20 of cash to pay dividends ($70 of net income but Retained Earnings only increased $50).

Retained Earnings (SE)

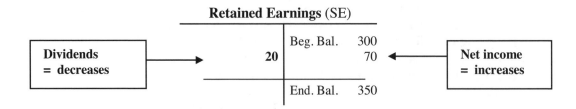

These items would be shown in the financing section of the SCF as follows:

Cash flows from financing activities:

Repay long-term loan	$ (65)
Pay dividends	(20)
Cash used by financing activities	$ (85)

Exhibit 9-6 Summary of the Investing and Financing Items in a SCF

Investing Inflows: Cash received from the sale of long-term assets
Cash received from the sale of long-term securities

Investing Outflows: Cash paid for long-term assets
Cash paid for investments in long-term securities

Financing Inflows: Cash received from long-term borrowings
Cash received from issuing stock

Financing Outflows: Cash paid for principal amounts on long-term borrowings
Cash paid to acquire treasury stock
Cash paid for dividends

To summarize, the investing and financing items that most frequently appear in a SCF are listed in Exhibit 9-6. Each of these should be reported separately in the statement, and related inflows and outflows are not netted against each other.

Alternate Version of the Operating Activities Section

The operating activities section of the SCF that we illustrated is known as the **indirect method**, the most common format found in practice. An alternative presentation, called the **direct method**, is illustrated in Exhibit 9-7.

Exhibit 9-7 Statement of Cash Flows – Direct Method (Uncommon)

Four Wolves Company
Statement of Cash Flows
For the Year Ended December 31, 2014
(All dollar amounts in millions)

Cash flows from operating activities:

Cash collected from customers	$ 464
Cash paid to suppliers	(72)
Cash paid to employees	(87)
Cash paid for G&A, advertising, and promotion	(79)
Cash paid for interest	(15)
Cash paid for income taxes	(46)
Cash provided by operating activities	$ 165

Cash flows from investing activities:

Purchase investments	$ (5)
Purchase plant & equipment	(50)
Cash used by investing activities	$ (55)

Cash flows from financing activities:

Repay long-term loan	$ (65)
Pay dividends	(20)
Cash used by financing activities	$ (85)
Net increase in cash	$ 25

The direct format presents the operating activities section in the form of a cash-based income statement, showing cash collected from customers minus cash paid for resources. Some feel this method is more appealing to financial statement users. The investing and financing sections of the SCF are identical under both methods.

Purpose and Use of Cash Flow Information

The SCF is an important flow statement, providing a detailed summary of how the cash flows of the business help explain the changes in the balance sheet accounts from the beginning to the end of each accounting period. While it does not measure the operating performance of the business like the income statement, it does provide useful information for decision making, particularly for lenders and others who are more interested in the short-run ability of the business to repay loans from its cash flows rather than its long-run performance or the value of its stock.

Of the three sections of the SCF, the one of most interest to users of financial statements is the first subtotal, *cash provided by operating activities*. Cash provided by operating activities will be greater than net income in most cases. Even if there were no changes in any of the current asset or current liability accounts, depreciation and amortization would be significant non-cash expenses that would be added back to net income, making cash provided by operations greater than net income. Operating cash flows are often thought of as the lifeblood of the business and are the focus of much analysis. If operating cash flows are negative for a series of consecutive periods, it is usually considered a sign that the company is encountering financial distress with potentially grave consequences.

A popular measure used by analysts and derived from the SCF is free cash flow. **Free cash flow** is the cash available to shareholders, after investing for the future. It is essentially cash provided by operating activities minus cash paid for capital assets. In our example, free cash flow for 2014 normally would be computed to be *$115 million* ($165 million in cash from operating activities minus $50 million for the investment in plant and equipment from the investing activities section). Like most measures, you may encounter some variations in this definition in practice so be sure to ask what specific definition is being used.

INCOME, CASH FLOW AND DECISION MAKING

Obviously many, if not most, important economic decision made by investors, creditors and other external users employ some measure(s) of income and/or cash flows. Investing decisions focus heavily on income and cash from operations in an effort to help predict future net income. The leading theory-based model for valuing an entity's stock is based on forecasts of EPS (along with book value per share and the cost of equity for the firm). Lenders focus heavily on historical cash flows from operations to make lending decisions. Many other outside parties, including vendors, franchisors, corporate executives, and labor unions enter into contracts with business entities where the future costs or benefits are based on accounting measures of income and/or cash flows. And, of course, the amount of taxes paid and the amount of dividends declared by an entity are directly related to income measurement.

Despite the obvious relation between income, cash flow and business decisions, the actual links between these remain largely unclear! While we know past income impacts future value, it is not clear exactly what subcomponents of any actual set of complex comparative income statements over the past three years are best employed to help predict future performance. As we have seen in this chapter, comprehensive income, which encompasses net income (earnings), potentially includes many components. An in-depth understanding of the various components of comprehensive income might help us decide on a company-by-company basis which components of comprehensive income are most relevant for the decision at hand. However, it is unlikely that any simple decision making formula can be developed to apply across all companies.

Understanding the intricacies of income and cash flow measurement will lead to more economically relevant decision making. It will help us realize flaws and limitations of conventional broad brush approaches for common business decisions and allow you to make better decisions. But expecting this deeper understanding to lead to decision making routines that can be programed by a computer or repeated without in-depth analysis is not realistic given the complexities inherent in corporate financial reporting.

INTERNATIONAL FINANCIAL REPORTING STANDARDS

Revenue Recognition The primary difference between IFRS and U.S. GAAP is in the amount of guidance provided by the two sets of standards for the recognition of revenue. U.S. GAAP includes over 100 pronouncements dealing with a wide variety of detailed revenue recognition issues. However, until 2014 IFRS covered revenue recognition in a single standard, IAS 18. After several years of working together in a joint project task force the IASB and FASB have agreed on a sweeping set of uniform standards that will make revenue recognition very similar under both sets of standards. These new standards are scheduled to take effect after 2018. However, there have been many concerns expressed by companies and auditors who, at a minimum, want more time to prepare for these changes.

Given the importance of revenue recognition to the entire accounting measurement process, it is unsettling to have so much ambiguity regarding when and how to recognize revenue. Much of the detailed guidance, which U.S. GAAP now provides and IFRS is seeking to add to its standards, involves two aspects of revenue recognition:

1. How much uncertainty in the realization of future benefits is acceptable to allow revenue to be recognized; and

2. In bundled sales transactions (e.g., when both goods and services or multiple services or multiple products are sold as a package deal), how is the sales price allocated to the various components and when can each of the component revenues be recognized as having been earned (i.e., recorded).

While other aspects of revenue recognition have also called for the FASB to issue specific standards to guide when and how much to recognize in various situations, much of the uncertainty involves the two aspects identified above. Essentially, standard setters are trying to prevent companies from recognizing revenue too soon, before it is both **realizable** and **earned**. More advanced financial accounting courses will deal with esoteric situations where special revenue recognition standards need to be studied and applied to complex business transactions.

Extraordinary Items U.S. GAAP still allows extraordinary items until 2016. However, IFRS makes no mention of extraordinary items and no special disclosures are ever observed under IFRS. This recent change was made, in part, to converge US GAAP with IFRS. It also is part of a broader movement to simplify income measurement and reporting. We expect that eventually there will be only one continuous statement of comprehensive income with few or no items reported as separate elements net of their own specific tax consequences. This is likely to be organized like the SCF with operating, financing and investing subtotals.

SUMMARY

Net income is the income statement measure that includes normal revenues and expenses, before tax non-operating gains and losses, and discontinued operations and extraordinary items that are reported after tax. Comprehensive income is the final income measure that begins with net income and adds unrealized gains and losses on investment and derivative securities, gains and losses on the translation of foreign financial statements, and pension and OPEB liability adjustments to produce a measure of the total change in net assets from all non-owner transactions.

While net income is accrual accounting's measure of business performance, cash is the lifeblood of a business, and the sources and uses of cash are important to financial statement users. A useful exercise for gaining insight into the numbers in a statement of cash flows that was illustrated in this chapter is to prepare a statement of cash flows from a balance sheet and an income statement. This exercise also has practical appeal for those who must analyze a set of financial statements that does not include a statement of cash flows. Together, net income and cash report the primary economic flows of the business.

KEY TERMS

accumulated other comprehensive income See "other comprehensive income" 133.

before tax non-operating items Items included in the measurement of income from continuing operations that are not strictly operating in nature (e.g., interest). *130-133*

comprehensive income A complete measure of income that includes all changes in net assets from non-owner related events and transactions. Comprehensive income includes net income and adds to it the impact of several other items such as the unrealized gains and losses on securities held as investments and the gains and losses on the translation of the financial statements of foreign subsidiaries into U.S. dollars. *129, 133-134*

derivative securities Securities that derive their value from another instrument or measurable quantity. Derivative securities include stock options and the option to convert preferred stock or bonds to shares of common stock. They also include contracts to purchase goods or services in the future at a specified price, in which case the value of the derivative is based on the future market value of the goods or services contracted for. Derivative securities can give rise to holding gains or losses. *133*

direct method Presentation method for the operating activities section of the statement of cash flows that presents the cash flow information in the form of a cash-based income statement. Compare to the *indirect format*. *145*

discontinued operations The abandonment or sale of a separate line of business. The amounts reported in the income statement for discontinued operations include the income or loss from the discontinued line of business for the period as well as the amount of gain or loss from the disposal of the discontinued line of business. Both the income/loss from the operations and the gain/loss on the sale of the assets are reported net of taxes. *132*

extraordinary items Gains or losses from events considered to be "highly unusual in nature and not expected to reoccur again in the foreseeable future." Separate line item disclosure, net of tax effects, will no longer be permitted after 2015, bringing US GAAP in line with IFRS. *133*

fair-value accounting Required reporting of certain securities and contracts at their fair market value rather than historical cost. *133*

financing cash flows Cash flows related to long-term debt and the stock accounts. *143*

free cash flow Generally defined as cash from operating activities minus cash used for investments in capital expenditures (e.g., new plant assets). This measure is not found in the financial statements but can be computed from amounts in the statement of cash flows. It represents the net cash flow for a period that is freely available to shareholders for the payment of dividends after paying the interest payments on debt and making necessary investments in long-term productive assets. *146*

holding gains and losses Holding gains and losses are the difference between the fair market value of an asset or liability and its recorded value. Some holding gains and losses are recognized in the financial statements, such as those pertaining to marketable securities. This means their financial statement amounts were recorded at fair value at year end and a gain or loss resulted. Other holding gains or losses are not recognized in the financial statements, such as those pertaining to changes in the value of land and buildings; also called *unrealized gains/losses* and *paper gains/losses*. *133*

income from continuing operations The core business of the company as well as routine items that are not strictly operating in nature (such as interest) and irregular gains and losses that are not part of routine operating activities but do occur. *131*

indirect method Presentation method for the operating section of the statement of cash flows that begins with net income and adjusts net income for non-cash items on the income statement (e.g., depreciation) and for the changes in current assets and current liabilities that affected operating cash flows. *145*

investing cash flows Cash flows arising from acquiring and disposing of long-term assets. *143*

items requiring separate reporting   Items on the income statement that are reported below income from continuing operation net of their related income taxes. There are only two types: *discontinued operations* and *extraordinary items*. *130, 132*

net income   Earnings from the continuing operations of the business plus any gains or losses from: (1) discontinued operations and (2) extraordinary items. It does not include the additional items that make up in other comprehensive income. Conceptually, net income is the change in wealth, which under certain (restrictive) assumptions represents the amount that an owner may consume and leave the business as well off at the end of the period as it was as the beginning of the period; also called *earnings*, *net earnings*, and *net profit* (rare). *129-134*

non-recurring charges   Any number of items considered to not be a part of normal operating activities. These can be identified as Special Charges, Restructuring Charges, Other Gains and Losses, In-process R&D, or similar items that are non-operating in nature and not expected to repeat. *132*

operating cash flows   Operating cash flows are cash flows related to the items reported in the income statement. The measure of operating cash flows is typically computed by turning the accrual measure of income into a cash-based measure of income. *139*

operating income   Income statement subtotal measuring the revenues from sales of goods and/or services less the operating costs incurred to achieve these revenues. *131*

other comprehensive income   This term could refer to either the stocks or the flows. The "stocks" for the elements of comprehensive income are reported in the equity section of the balance sheet to show the *accumulated amounts* for these (potentially four) items, and are correctly called *"accumulated other comprehensive income"*. The "flows" (i.e., changes in the stocks) for these items are reported in the statement of comprehensive income. *129, 133-134.*

persistent components   Those components of income measurement that are expected to continue to impact future years earnings measures. *130*

provision for income taxes   Another name for income tax expense. *131*

restructuring charges   Costs associated with a major reorganization; see *non-recurring charges.* *132*

statement of comprehensive income   Separate financial statement detailing the changes in other comprehensive income; information is also included the statement of changes in shareholders' equity; *also called statement of income and comprehensive income when net income and comprehensive income are reported in one statement. 133-136*

translation gains and losses   Unrealized gains and losses from activities that are conducted in another country where the books and records are kept in a foreign currency throughout the year and then translated back into U.S. dollar equivalents at year end. *133*

unrealized gains and losses   See *holding gains and losses. 133*

Review Questions

Test your understanding of the material covered in the chapter by answering the following questions. The correct answers to these questions are shown below.

NOTE: Assume an income tax rate of 40% if necessary.

1. Income from continuing operations before income taxes was $2,634,800. In addition, there was a before tax gain on the sale of discontinued operations of $291,200 and a before tax loss from an extraordinary item of $509,600. What was net income for the year?

    a. $1,449,840
    b. $2,503,760
    c. $1,362,480
    d. $1,566,320

2. Several cars of an automobile rental company were damaged by a hailstorm. Hail frequently damages cars in this area, and the company has decided not to buy insurance but to pay for repairs or sell the cars at a loss instead. Losses from hail have averaged $10,000 for the company in past years. During the current year, damaged cars were repaired at a cost of $12,000. How would the cost of the hail damage be reported in the company's financial statements?

    a. $10,000 would be reported in income from continuing operations.
    b. $6,000 would be reported as an extraordinary item.
    c. $12,000 would be reported in income from continuing operations.
    d. $7,200 would be reported as an extraordinary item.

3. The following items appeared in the accounting records:

Cash received from the sale of treasury stock	$14,000
Cash received from the sale of old equipment	$105,000
Cash paid to acquire land	$53,200

    What amount was reported in the statement of cash flows as cash provided by investing activities?

    a. $119,000
    b. $51,800
    c. $91,000
    d. $65,800

Answers: a., c., b.

PROBLEMS

9-1 Income Statement and Statement of Comprehensive Income

Answer the following questions related to the income statement.

1. Describe items included in income from continuing operations but not operating income. On the income statement, where would you find persistent components?
2. Describe the two categories of items reported separately from income from continuing operations. Why?
3. How does a gain or loss on the sale of discontinued operations' assets differ from a gain or loss on the sale of manufacturing equipment?
4. How does an extraordinary gain/loss differ from an ordinary gain/loss?
5. Describe the other components of the change in net assets that are included in comprehensive income but not net income. Tie those components with the balance sheet account, Accumulated Other Comprehensive Income.
6. Describe how income taxes are treated on the various components of a statement of comprehensive income as shown in Exhibit 9-2 on page 135. What impact does intraperiod tax allocation have on the amount of an item that is reported on an after-tax basis?

9-2 Business Decision Case

Assume you are an economist working for a labor union with over 20,000 members employed in the automobile suppliers industry. You have been taking accounting classes at night and have learned to appreciate the complexities of accounting measurements and financial reports. The union has historically pushed for higher wages and benefits whenever the industry has had a series of years where profits have been reported. The industry members covered by this union are essentially domestic businesses. None of the companies have foreign subsidiaries or operations so all of the labor is U.S. based. Also, the companies' financial statements are not complicated with unusual assets or liabilities. They are mostly about inventory and plant assets and debt. They have no meaningful long-term investments in any assets other than land, plant and equipment. The general feeling of the union membership is that labor should participate fully in profits of these businesses. At the same time, concessions have historically not been made by labor during prolonged periods of loss in the industry.

Required:

1. Based on your newly acquired understanding of accounting, what financial statement measures would you focus on in evaluating the performance of companies in the industry? In other words, what are the key indicators to look at in deciding when to call for improvements in wages and benefits?
2. What might be some of the limitations of the measures you identified above?

3. Assume you have summarized industry data for the past three years and found the following aggregated data for all 25 unionized companies in the industry:

($ in billions)	2014	2013	2012
Income Data:			
Net income	$2.4	$2.3	$2.4
Comprehensive income	$1.8	$2.0	$2.2
Balance Sheet Data:			
Plant assets	$33	$35	$36
Total assets	$47	$49	$50
Other Data:			
D/E ratio (average)	3.0X	2.9X	2.9X

Your current labor contract with the industry does not expire for another year. However, the union leaders have focused on the increasing trend in net income and have decided that it would be a good time to strike if wage and benefit increases are not opened up for negotiations. The outlook for the industry will probably not improve by next year and the bargaining power is thought to be better at this time. Provide any thoughts you have on this "plan of attack."

9-3 Income Statement

The following amounts (in thousands) are available for Urban Enterprises, Inc. at December 31, 2014. The company's income tax rate is 40%.

Cost of goods sold	$ 954.7
Cost of services sold	648.6
Depreciation expense	111.1
General and administrative expenses	189.5
Income tax expense	?
Interest expense	55.4
Loss on sale of obsolete inventory	30.8
Sales commissions	248.2
Sales revenue	1,489.1
Service revenue	992.7

Required:

Using the information provided, prepare an income statement for the year ended December 31, 2014.

9-4   Income Statement

Consider the following items for a delivery company:

a. Loss on the sale of used equipment.
b. Gain that resulted from the insurance settlement on a building that was destroyed by the first earthquake to hit the area in over 100 years.
c. Higher expenses that will result in future years from a large increase in fire insurance on the delivery equipment.
d. Loss due to a two-week strike by the delivery truck drivers.
e. Gain on translating the financial statements of a foreign subsidiary into dollars.

Required:

Indicate in which section of the income statement each of the items a. through e. would be reported. Also describe whether each amount will be shown net of taxes or not.

9-5   Income Statement and Statement of Comprehensive Income

Progressive, Inc. began 2014 operating in two business segments: manufacturing and logistics. During 2014, the company discontinued the logistics operations. The following amounts (in thousands) are available. All amounts are before income taxes and the company's income tax rate is 40%.

Cost of goods sold	$219,900
Extraordinary loss	3,900
Foreign currency translation loss	600
Gain on sale of assets from logistics operations	1,800
Income tax expense	?
Loss on logistics operations	300
Sales revenue	279,300
Selling, general and administrative expenses	38,700

Required:

Prepare the combined income statement and statement of comprehensive income for the year ended December 31, 2014.

9-6 Income Statement and Statement of Comprehensive Income

Smart Electronics, Inc. had the following accounts and amounts at December 31, 2014. All amounts are in thousands. The amounts shown for all items that are to be reported net of income tax effects are already net of tax.

Operating loss on discontinued operations	$ 120
Gain on sale of used equipment	30
Sales revenue	5,890
Service revenue	3,490
Cost of goods sold	3,000
Cost of services	1,290
Foreign currency translation loss	160
Unrealized loss on securities held as investment	340
Income tax expense	428
Gain on sale of assets of discontinued operations ...	430
Marketing and distribution expenses	1,550
General and administrative expenses	2,100
Other income	50
Restructuring charges	260
Extraordinary loss	250
Interest expense	160

Required:

1. Prepare a complete combined income statement and statement of comprehensive income for the year ended December 31, 2014.
2. Assume the tax rate is 40%. Compute the gross amount for the operating loss on discontinued operations, the gain on sale of assets of discontinued operations, and the extraordinary loss.

9-7 Discontinued Operations

The operations of a segment were discontinued during the year. Total revenue for the year was $3,360,000, of which $2,270,000 was related to continuing operations and the rest was related to the discontinued operations. Total expenses for the year were $3,185,000, of which $1,890,000 was related to continuing operations and the rest was related to the discontinued operations. The discontinued segment's assets had a book value of $12,980,000 and were sold for $13,200,000. The income tax rate is 40%.

Required:

1. Compute the amount that will be reported on the income statement as operating income or loss from discontinued operations.
2. Compute the amount that will be reported on the income statement as gain or loss on the disposal of discontinued operations.
3. Explain the benefit to the firm and investors from separating discontinued operations from continuing.

9-8 Comparative Income Statements

Advanced Equipment reported the following results for **2013** (in thousands) for its combined manufacturing and retail segments:

Sales	$7,550.0
Expenses:	
Cost of goods sold	3,888.0
Selling expenses	822.0
Administrative expenses............	1,997.0
Interest expense	212.0
Income before tax	$ 631.0
Income tax expense (40%)	252.4
Net income	$ 378.6

During 2014, the company discontinued the operations of the retail segment. The following amounts relate to the **continuing** manufacturing operations in **2014** (in thousands):

Sales	$7,993.0
Expenses:	
Cost of goods sold	4,203.0
Selling expenses	901.0
Administrative expenses..........	2,023.0
Interest expense	215.0
Income before tax	$ 651.0

The discontinued retail operations had the following **separate** results in 2013 and 2014 (in thousands):

	2014	**2013**
Sales	$ 265.0	$ 305.0
Expenses:		
Cost of goods sold	200.0	210.0
Selling expenses	45.0	44.0
Administrative expenses	155.0	106.0
Pre-tax loss	$(135.0)	$ (55.0)
Income tax credit (40%)	54.0	22.0
Net loss	$ (81.0)	$ (33.0)

The sale of the discontinued assets resulted in a pre-tax gain of $68,000 in 2014.

Required:

1. Prepare the income statement for 2014 through net income, using the amounts that relate to the continuing manufacturing operations and the separate amounts for the retail operations that were discontinued.
2. Recast the 2013 income statement that was reported for the combined operations by subtracting out the amounts for the discontinued retail operations in order to show those discontinued operations separately. This must be done so the 2013 income statement can be shown in comparative form with the 2014 income statement. Assume an income tax rate of 40% throughout both years.

9-9   Statement of Cash Flows

Answer the following questions related to the statement of cash flows.

1. How are the amounts in the statement of cash flows different from the amounts in the balance sheet and income statement?
2. How do operating, investing, and financing activities differ from one another?
3. Why are dividends on contributed capital treated as a financing activity but interest on borrowed capital is treated as an operating activity?
4. Which section of the statement of cash flows is of primary interest to the majority of financial statement readers?
5. Could operating cash flows be negative at the same time that net income is positive? Why or why not?
6. Could operating cash flows be positive at the same time that net income is negative (net loss)? Why or why not?
7. Is positive cash flow from investing or financing activities good? Why or why not?

9-10   Statement of Cash Flows

The following information is available from the financial statements (in thousands):

	December 31	January 1
Balance Sheet accounts:		
Cash and cash equivalents ...	$1,698.5	$1,632.4
Accounts receivable..............	1,266.3	1,125.6
Inventories	2,244.5	2,493.4
Accounts payable	1,570.4	1,374.1
Unearned revenue................	345.6	682.0

Net income for the year was $1,772.8 thousand, depreciation expense was $316.6 thousand, and amortization of finite-life intangibles was $201.6 thousand.

Required:

1. Compute cash provided or used by operating activities for the year.
2. Explain why net income is adjusted for each item.

9-11 Statement of Cash Flows

Consider the following items:

a. The issuance of bonds payable
b. The purchase of a building for cash
c. The payment of interest on a long-term note payable
d. The sale of obsolete equipment at its book value
e. The payment of a dividend on the company's common and preferred stock

Required:

Indicate in which section of the statement of cash flows each of the items a. through e. would be reported.

9-12 Statement of Cash Flows (Partial)

The following information is available from the financial statements reported for the year ending December 31, 2014 *(all dollars in millions)*:

	December 31	January 1
Balance Sheet accounts:		
Cash and cash equivalents...................	$6,598	$7,324
Accounts receivable	2,709	3,914
Inventories...	4,314	3,126
Prepaid amounts.................................	936	2,230
Accounts payable	2,256	2,249
Accrued salaries	1,644	2,110
Income taxes payable	1,797	1,960
Other current operating liabilities	2,800	2,915
Income Statement accounts:	**2014**	**2013**
Net revenue	$35,382	$38,826
Cost of sales	17,164	15,777
Net income	5,044	8,664
Depreciation and amortization	4,912	4,595

Required:

Prepare the operating activities section of a statement of cash flows (indirect method) for the year ending December 31, 2014 from the balance sheet and income statement amounts provided.

9-13 Statement of Cash Flows

The comparative balance sheets, income statement, and notes for Medical Imaging, Inc. are shown below (all amounts are in thousands):

Medical Imaging, Inc.
Balance Sheets
December 31,

Assets	2014	2013
Cash	$ 54.0	$ 60.5
Accounts receivable	67.0	91.6
Prepaid rent	61.7	59.5
Plant and equipment (net)	137.2	205.1
Total assets	$319.9	$416.7

Liabilities and Shareholders' Equity		
Accounts payable	$ 36.8	$ 39.7
Income taxes payable	4.5	2.5
Bonds payable	101.8	190.0
Total liabilities	$143.1	$232.2
Common stock	$ 98.0	$ 98.0
Capital in excess of par	20.0	20.0
Retained earnings	58.8	66.5
Total shareholders' equity	$176.8	$184.5
Total liabilities and shareholders' equity	$319.9	$416.7

Medical Imaging, Inc.
Income Statement
For the Year Ended December 31, 2014

Sales	$271.6
Cost of goods sold	213.4
Depreciation expense	18.0
Other operating expenses	17.5
Income tax expense	8.9
Net income	$ 13.8

Additional information:

- Dividends were declared and paid during the year.
- No plant and equipment was acquired and there was no gain or loss on the plant and equipment sold.

Required:

Prepare a statement of cash flows (indirect method) for the year ended December 31, 2014 from these balance sheet and income statement amounts.

9-14   Statement of Cash Flows

The comparative balance sheets, income statement, and notes for Continental Freight, Inc. are shown below (all amounts are in thousands):

Continental Freight, Inc.
Balance Sheets
December 31,

Assets	2014	2013
Cash	$ 53.9	$ 79.1
Accounts receivable	130.9	102.2
Inventory	88.2	105.0
Plant and equipment (net)	357.0	168.0
Total assets	$630.0	$454.3

Liabilities and Shareholders' Equity		
Accounts payable	$ 56.7	$ 46.2
Salaries payable	2.1	4.9
Bonds payable	280.0	140.0
Total liabilities	$338.8	$191.1
Common stock	$172.0	$140.0
Capital in excess of par	32.4	28.0
Retained earnings	86.8	95.2
Total shareholders' equity	$291.2	$263.2
Total liabilities and shareholders' equity	$630.0	$454.3

Continental Freight, Inc.
Income Statement
For the Year Ended December 31, 2014

Sales	$385.0
Cost of goods sold	305.2
Depreciation expense	28.0
Other operating expenses	23.8
Income tax expense	8.4
Net income	$ 19.6

Additional information:

- Dividends were declared and paid during the year.
- No plant and equipment was sold.

Required:

Prepare a statement of cash flows (indirect method) for the year ended December 31, 2014 from these balance sheet and income statement amounts.

9-15 Cash Flow Analysis

Assume for this problem that you are a bank loan officer. The owners of a company have approached you to borrow money. The owners hired an accounting firm to prepare a balance sheet and income statement for the company, but not a statement of cash flows. One of the owners has taken the balance sheet and income statement accounts and prepared the following cash flow analysis for the most recent year:

Net income per the income statement	$ 200,000
Cash invested by a venture capital firm for shares of stock	800,000
Loan from the bank	200,000
Dividends to the owners	(160,000)
Additional investments in long-term assets	(980,000)
Net change in cash for the year	$ 60,000

The owners have come to you for help because they know that their change in cash is more than $60,000 and they do not understand what they may have missed in their computations. Upon looking over their financial statements you have discovered the following additional facts:

a. Depreciation taken in the past year was $216,000.
b. Accounts receivable increased by $48,000 during the past year.
c. Inventory decreased by $16,000 during the year.
d. Accounts payable increased by $12,000 during the year.

Required:

1. Explain to the owners the essential flaw in their analysis and tell them how each of the additional facts would impact their analysis.
2. Recast the analysis into the format of a statement of cash flows based on normal assumptions about the information provided.

9-16 Changes in Estimates (Comprehensive)

Several years ago, GENERAL MOTORS CORPORATION (GM) reported a positive trend in earnings on its common stock. In a three-year period, EPS was:

	Year 3	**Year 2**	**Year 1**
EPS on $1-2/3 par value Common Stock	$7.17	$5.03	$4.11

The following footnote is from the GM Year 3 annual report in the section of the policies footnote that concerns the depreciation and amortization of assets.

Depreciation and Amortization

Depreciation is provided based on estimated useful lives of groups of property generally using accelerated methods, which accumulate depreciation of approximately two-thirds of the depreciable cost during the first half of the estimated useful lives.

Expenditures for special tools are amortized over their estimated useful lives. Amortization is applied directly to the asset account. Replacement of special tools for reasons other than changes in products is charged directly to cost of sales.

GMAC (GENERAL MOTORS ACCEPTANCE CORPORATION) provides for depreciation of automobiles and equipment on operating leases or in company use on a straight-line basis. In the first quarter of Year 2, GMAC revised the rates of depreciation for automobiles on operating leases to retail customers to give effect to current experience with respect to the residual values of leased vehicles. These revisions had the effect of increasing GMAC's Year 2 net income by $254.7 million, or $0.41 per share of common stock (post-split).

In the third quarter of Year 2, the Corporation revised the estimated service lives of its plants and equipment and special tools retroactive to January 1, Year 2. These revisions, which were based on Year 2 studies of actual lives and periods of use, recognized current estimates of service lives of the assets and had the effect of reducing Year 2 depreciation and amortization charges by $1,236.6 million or $1.28 per share of $1-2/3 par value common stock.

Required:

1. Assume that GM made the changes in estimates for assets under *operating leases to retail customers* and *plant and equipment and special tools* for both book and tax (IRS) reporting purposes. Further assume the effective tax rate for GM was 30% in each year. Show the impact on both depreciation expense and net income for each change in estimate separately in the schedule below.

	Year 2	
	From change in estimate for:	
Provide answers in millions of $	**Operating leases**	**Plant & Equipment and Special Tools**
Impact on Depreciation Expense (+ or −)	$	$
Impact on Net Income (+ or −)	$	$

2. Compute the amount of EPS on ($1-2/3 par) common stock that would have been reported in Year 2 if these two changes in estimates had not occurred.
3. GM says it "Revised the estimated service lives of its plants and equipment and special tools retroactive to January 1, Year 2." This retroactive change was made even though it was not decided to change the estimated lives of these assets until the third quarter. Did GM correctly account for this change?

9-17 Changes in Estimates (Comprehensive)

FOUR WINNS CORPORATION, located in Cadillac Michigan, produces fiberglass hulled watercraft. One of the more popular product lines is its series of 18-foot boats, which are equipped with a variety of interior configurations and power plants to provide 6 different boats on the same 18-foot fiberglass hull. Assume that on July 31, 2014, FOUR WINNS decided to revise the estimated useful life of its machinery and equipment used to produce the 18-foot hull. The machinery and equipment for this production line had originally been acquired on December 1, 2008, at a cost of $887,500. It was expected to have a nine-year life at the time of acquisition. The company has a March 31 year end. The most recent year-end report provided the following information on the machinery and equipment at March 31, 2014.

Machinery and equipment (18' fiberglass hull)………….	$ 887,500
Accumulated depreciation…………………………………..	522,500
Machinery and equipment, net book value………………	$ 365,000

FOUR WINNS has always used straight-line depreciation on all depreciable assets. Furthermore, their policy calls for all depreciable assets to have one-half a year depreciation taken in the year of acquisition, regardless of when the assets were actually acquired. At July 31, 2014, the company believes the equipment will be useful for nine (9) years beyond the most recent year-end (March 31, 2014). Moreover, they believe the salvage value will only be 50% of the originally estimated salvage value after nine additional years (from March 31, 2014) of use.

One of the things that has given the company confidence in their change in estimates is that no new technology has been introduced in this manufacturing process since the equipment was originally purchased. Also, in considering an additional line of this machinery and equipment for expansion purposes, the company looked into some used machinery and equipment that was 6 years old and had a market value of $800,000. This equipment was very similar to their existing machinery and equipment, but was not exactly the same age. They decided instead to acquire new machinery and equipment to facilitate the expansion of their production capacity at a cost of $1.4 million, exactly doubling their ability to produce 18-foot hulls. They plan to increase their penetration into markets on the West Coast with this new capacity.

Required:

1. Compute the previous rate of depreciation per year before the change in estimate was made on July 31, 2014.
2. Compute the old salvage value. Compute the new salvage value.
3. Compute the depreciation expense for the years ended March 31, 2015 and March 31, 2016.
4. What is your estimate of the real (economically relevant) depreciation on the old equipment for the year ended March 31, 2015, based on the data provided in the case?

9-18   Reading Financial Statements – WALMART

Locate the excerpts 2014 annual report of WALMART STORES, INC. Refer to WALMART's *consolidated statements of income* and *consolidated statements of comprehensive income* on page 17 of the file (labeled page 36 of the annual report).

Required:

1. Take a few minutes and scan the first 16 pages of the file (annual report cover page and the first 15 pages of the annual report). Briefly describe something that you learned about WALMART (its business, where it operates, something unique that you learned from these pages). How do you see these pages differing from the financial statement information that begins on page 17 of the file (labeled page 26 of the annual report)?
2. Identify the amounts reported for *Income from continuing operations* for 2014, 2013 and 2012 as well as the amount for discontinued operations for each of the three years. What would you say about WALMART's continuing operations? Refer to footnote 13 on page (labeled page 57 of the annual report). To what do the discontinued operations relate? Be as detailed as possible in your answer.
3. Identify the amounts reported for *Currency translation and* other and *Minimum pension liability* as a part of comprehensive income for 2014.
4. Who are WALMART's independent auditors?

9-19   Financial Statement Analysis – STARBUCKS

Locate the excerpts from the 2014 10-K of STARBUCKS CORPORATION. Refer to STARBUCKS' *consolidated statements of cash flows* on page 13 of the file (labeled page 48 of the file).

Required:

1. Take a few minutes and scan pages 3 through 11 of the file (labeled pages 2 through 9 of the 10-K). Briefly describe something that you learned about STARBUCKS CORPORATION (its business, where it operates, something unique that you learned from the 10-K, etc.).
2. Identify the format used for reporting cash provided by operating activities in the statement of cash flows. Why did STARBUCKS add the $140.8 million related to Deferred revenue liability to net earnings? Be sure to explain your answer.
3. How much more or less was the investment in Property, Plant, and Equipment compared to the amount of Depreciation and Amortization in this statement? Is STARBUCKS growing the business or shrinking it? Explain your answer.
4. Identify the largest cash inflow item from either investing or financing activities. Comment on the information and how it relates to any other item on the *consolidated statements of cash flows*.
5. In previous years STARBUCKS has very little long-term debt on the balance sheet ($549.6 million at September 30, 2012), and yet they had been spending a large amount of cash on new property, plant, and equipment. Identify how STARBUCKS was financing those acquisitions in previous years. Now, review the year ending September 28, 2014, does it appear there is a change in STARBUCKS' philosophy. Review STARBUCKS' statement of cash flows investing and financing sections as well as its total cash from operating activities and its balance sheet (cash and long-term debt).

Chapter 9 Study Quiz

For each of the five questions, show your calculations and place your answer in the spaces provided.

NOTE: Assume an income tax rate of 40% if necessary.

1. A segment was discontinued during the current year. Total revenue was $98,000, of which $31,300 was related to the discontinued segment and total operating expenses (not including income taxes) were $92,800, of which $42,800 related to the discontinued segment.

    Compute the reported operating income (loss) from the discontinued operations.

    $_____

    Calculation:

2. In the income statement, $257,400 of net income was reported. Operating expenses not including income taxes were $643,500.

    Compute revenues for the year. $_____

    Calculation:

3. In its December 31, 2013 balance sheet, a company reported a balance of $35,100 in long-term notes payable, and in its December 31, 2014 balance sheet, the company reported a balance of $42,000 in long-term notes payable. During 2014, $11,400 of long-term notes were issued for cash and $4,500 of long-term notes payable were repaid.

   Describe how the changes in long-term notes payable will reported on the statement of cash flows.

4. On its statement of cash flows a company reported *cash provided by operating activities* of $147,000. The following information also is available: depreciation expense was $105,000, there was a decrease in wages payable of $42,000, there was an increase in accounts receivable of $52,500, and there was an increase in accounts payable of $21,000.

   Compute net income (loss) for the year. $_____

   Calculation:

5. The following items were included in the accounts for the year:

Proceeds from the sale of land	$180,000
Proceeds from the issuance of $600,000 of bonds	540,000
Dividends paid	114,000
Treasury stock purchased	222,000

   Compute cash provided (used) by financing activities $_____

   Calculation:

Chapter 10

Evaluating Financial Statements:
A Framework for Analysis

LEARNING OBJECTIVES

1. Understand the framework for evaluating the strengths and weaknesses of accounting information.
2. Understand the common set of ratios used to evaluate accounting information.
3. Apply our understanding of accounting to conduct analysis of financial statements.

This text was designed to help you become familiar with the nature and purpose of the financial statements provided to external users. While reading and understanding GAAP-based accounting information is essential for making business decisions, there are no simple formulas showing exactly how to employ accounting in any given decision context. It is reasonable to ask why there are not well-traveled paths for using accounting information to make business decisions. After all, many important business decisions are made over and over again, such as developing executive compensation contracts, negotiating lending agreements, and acquiring another business. So why aren't there known algorithms for using accounting information that would lead to a "correct" or "optimal" decision?

Arriving at a good understanding of the current position and performance of a business is not as simple as looking at the balance sheet, income statement and statement of cash flows. And beyond the complexities of understanding the financial statements, we have shown there are numerous additional steps, or links, to applying that understanding in actual decision making situations.

TIME TO SUMMARIZE AND APPLY

From the first nine chapters observed at a very summary level, we can conclude that making good business decisions typically will require: (1) an in-depth understanding of general and specific accounting data which are then (2) digested using a set of common analysis tools (i.e., ratios) to provide the insights and support for business decisions. While this two-stage process is generally accepted by decisions makers, the actual application of the process is far from routine, as noted above. The real key to good business decisions is in the first stage of the process: *gaining an in-depth understanding of general and specific accounting data.*

We know that accounting information is not perfect, and throughout the text we have been frank in discussing both the strengths and weaknesses of accounting data. As a result of this evaluation process, we can now make the following list of three important attributes of accounting information which represent the key limitations of "raw" accounting data as reported in GAAP (or IFRS) based financial statements.

1. Accounting rules permit *alternative accounting methods* to be used to account for many assets and/or liabilities. Inventory methods and depreciation methods are two such choices that allow the exact same set of economic circumstances to produce different accounting results, distorting comparison and analysis of accounting data.

2. Accounting rules require *management estimation* of numerous aspects of accounting which also impact the reported results. Examples include the useful life of a depreciable or amortizable asset, the amount of receivables that will not be collected, the timing for revenue recognition, and the estimated amount for warranty obligations, among others. Again, this permits a given set of economic circumstances to be reported in several ways.

3. Accounting rules present *measurement problems* in the data. GAAP require measurements of certain assets and liabilities that are not always appropriate for all business decisions. For example, as discussed in Chapter 6, the use of depreciated historical cost for PP&E or the use of amortized historical cost for intangibles produce reported amounts that are not economically relevant measurements for most, if not all, business decisions related to these assets.

To effectively use accounting information requires that, at a minimum, we recognize the existence of these limitations.[1] Once we understand and accept the fact that audited financial statements of publicly-owned companies around the world have certain inherent limitations in their decision usefulness, we can begin to find ways to better use and modify these reported data to improve their economic relevance. This process needs to take place before stage two of decision making. If we do not have an understanding of the strengths and weaknesses of the accounting data, and possibly the ability to adjust these data to improve their relevance, there is no point in conducting any stage-two analysis. Gaining an in-depth understanding of financial accounting and its strengths and limitations is the key to effective business decisions. Hence, the goal of this text has been to help you build this understanding.

In this final chapter we introduce you to a framework designed to help you evaluate the strengths and weaknesses of accounting information. This framework is *timeless*. This framework should provide significant benefits to structure your current and *future* thinking about accounting as changes in GAAP and changes in your level of understanding from future accounting studies or future actual business experiences occur. This framework was developed by the authors to guide your present and future understanding of accounting information. Again, it is not dependent on any particular

---

[1] Further study of GAAP and/or IFRS rules for financial accounting will reveal even more examples of these same three limitations.

set of accounting rules or standards and should prove useful even as the detailed rules making up current GAAP[2] change over time.

WHAT IS THE IDEAL INFORMATION NEEDED FOR DECISION MAKING?

In order to evaluate the strengths and weaknesses of any individual or group of accounting measurements we need to identify an "anchor" measurement that can serve as a benchmark, or as the ideal or "perfect" measure. A key attribute of such an anchor measure is that it must be economically relevant. At a highly summarized level, this ideal anchor might be thought of as the "true value" of the entity (versus the accounting measure of the book value of the entity—net assets), with changes in "true value" providing the "perfect" benchmark for flow-based accounting data (e.g., net income or cash flow).

True value has a great deal of appeal as an anchor measurement. However, if we actually knew what truth was, we would simply report it. The framework provided here assumes that the closest we can get to an observable true value of the firm is the **market value of the firm** at any point in time. The market value of the entity (also known as **market capitalization**), measured as the stock price times the number of shares outstanding, is an *unbiased* and readily observable measure for all publicly-owned companies. It is a measure of the market's estimate of the net worth of the entity; all of its assets less all of its liabilities at any point in time.[3] Understand that market value of the firm, while unbiased, can only reflect the impact of all publicly-available information. In a strict sense, market value does not represent the true value of the firm, even for those who believe that capital markets are (strong form) efficient.[4] However, despite any limitations, we find that the market value of the entity is the best benchmark to allow us to evaluate the limitations with GAAP-based financial statements.

What's Wrong with Accounting-Based Book Value?

As previously noted, our framework for analysis suggests that there are three limitations which prohibit accounting-based book value from representing the true value of the entity. The first two limitations (multiple *methods* and management

---

[2] While we tend to refer to rule-based financial statements as GAAP, it is generally the case that we could substitute IFRS-based financial statements as well. The differences between IFRS and U.S. GAAP do not have an impact on the process of evaluating financial accounting and performing financial statement analysis as discussed in this chapter.

[3] Another way to view the market value is that it is the market's estimate of the present value of all future cash flows generated by the entity discounted at the appropriate interest rate (i.e., the cost of equity capital). These two views of market value are theoretically equivalent to one another.

[4] Management and other "insiders" who have economically relevant information about the firm unknown to the public provides at least one reason why the market price may not be "truth." And some, like the authors, feel that the complexity of information processing also leads to a degree of market inefficiency.

estimates) are the result of the underlying ambiguity permitted within GAAP (or IFRS) concerning the measurement of the assets and the liabilities that make up accounting-based book value.[5] Hence, the reported net assets of the entity is a "fuzzy" number that is subject to the influence of the same people (managers) who are responsible for reporting the financial statements to external users. For example, as discussed in Chapter 4, the measurement of accounts receivable is a managerial *estimate* that assumes some portion of the receivables will not be collected. There is no way to know if these receivables are measured at their "true" value even though the outside auditor has examined those estimates for reasonableness. More obvious still, in Chapter 5 we saw that many companies use the LIFO inventory *method*, which is known to produce measures of the asset inventory that are understated relative to their true value. And in Chapter 6, we pointed out that the accounting measurements of depreciable assets like buildings, machinery and equipment along with measurements of the amortizable intangible assets all depend on managerial *estimates* of the useful life and salvage value (if any) as well as the appropriate depreciation or amortization *method* that depicts their expected usefulness in each future period. All of these and other estimates or method choices result in the reported GAAP-based measurements of book value and income being only one of many possible "generally accepted" measurements for the exact same set of transactions and events. As a result, no single accounting-based measure of the book value of the equity can represent the "true" value of the entity.

The third limitation of GAAP *(measurement problems)* is more challenging to identify and evaluate than the first two discussed. It involves the following two aspects that further explain the differences between accounting-based book value and the market value of the entity:

1. GAAP measures of assets and liabilities that overstate or understate the *real economic value* of the assets and/or liabilities; and

2. Economically relevant "assets" and/or "liabilities" that are not reported at all in the financial statements.

These two aspects of the third limitation can be used to explain all other differences between the market value and book value of the entity at any specific point in time.[6] Due to the limitations of GAAP, we may find some assets or liabilities to be over- or under-stated from an economic viewpoint. For example, in Chapter 6 we pointed out that the reporting of net property, plant and equipment (PP&E) in the balance sheet at its depreciated historical cost will nearly always *understate* the real economic value (i.e., market value or replacement cost) of PP&E. We may also find that the shortcomings of GAAP result in some things we would consider to be assets and/or liabilities completely missing from the financial statements. For example, in Chapter 6 we noted that research and development activities might have significant economic value despite the fact that GAAP requires all R&D to be expensed as incurred.

---

[5] While we might seem to be ignoring revenues, expenses and income, keep in mind that these and all other "flow" statement components are simply the result of changes in the balance sheet elements.

[6] Once again, our focus on the balance sheet for this third limitation implicitly considers income as well. Income is simply a flow describing the changes in comparative balance sheets. Any limitation that impacts book value will, over time, impact income measurement as well.

Exhibit 10-1 offer a "stocks" (balance sheet) based depiction of all three limitations of GAAP-based measures of book value. This depiction is one that should prove useful as a framework for evaluating and using accounting information.

In studying the framework in Exhibit 10-1, we note that the assumption is that the market value of the entity will be greater (higher) than the book value of the entity. While it is true that there are some situations when book value has been higher than market value, this is obviously the exception to the norm. When book value exceeds market value, it implies that there are significant missing or understated liabilities. Such cases appear most often prior to business failure. Because of impairment rules and other safeguards written into GAAP, we will normally find *net undervalued assets* and *net missing assets* from the application of our framework to actual corporate financial statements. It is for these two reasons that the market value of the entity is typically much greater than its book value.

Understanding these limitations of GAAP involves understanding why, at any point in time, all of the GAAP measurements of assets less all of the GAAP measurements of liabilities (= shareholders' equity, or "book value") does not equal the true (market) value of the entity. This framework implies that, for virtually all decision contexts, we are most interested in knowing the "true" value of the entity. All GAAP limitations may be evaluated using the framework depicted in Exhibit 10-1. Once we have identified the limitations of GAAP, we can begin to learn about the various ways that expert users have attempted to compensate for these limitations in making business decisions. Future coursework in financial accounting will be necessary for you to increase the depth and breadth of your understanding of account-

Exhibit 10-1   Framework for Evaluating Limitations of GAAP

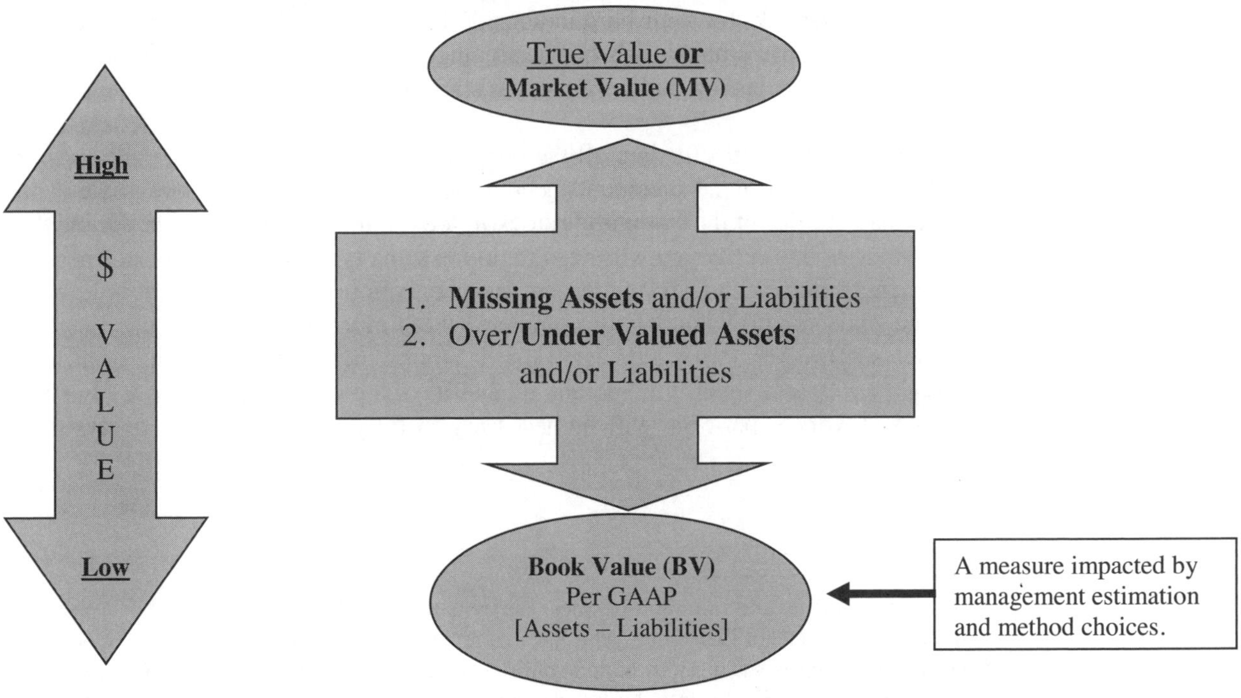

Chapter 10 *Evaluating Financial Statements: A Framework for Analysis*   171

ing, and your ability to critically evaluate its strengths and weaknesses. However, in many cases, you will find that *simply recognizing these limitations of GAAP* data will improve your decision-making abilities.

Using the Framework for Specific Decisions

This framework for analysis of accounting information should prove to be useful in nearly any decision situation employing accounting information. However, its use as a tool for evaluation can vary considerably depending on the decision situation at hand. It is not necessarily the case that every decision situation will require that you consider the entire set of financial statement data for weaknesses or limitations and correct for them before you use accounting information. However, virtually all *investment decisions* call for information regarding the value of the firm, which requires a complete and comprehensive set of adjustments to the financial statements for all three weaknesses.[7] Clearly investment decisions are among the most complex and difficult decisions to make. But there are far more decision situations related to the contractual relationships between the entity, its managers, its union employees, its lenders and the thousands of other constituents it interacts with that also employ accounting information. In many of these decision making cases, simply understanding the nature of the limitations of accounting and using the framework provided here can lead to improved business decisions.

To illustrate these points, consider the following two decision situations:

1. A large corporation is considering acquiring another company and asks your help in valuing a closely-held business that has provided them with audited financial statements, but has no publicly-owned debt or equity.

2. A lender asks for your help in considering a loan application from a closely-held company that already has borrowings exceeding the amount of their long-term assets in their audited financial statements.

In the first decision situation, all the possible issues involved in the limitations of the GAAP-based financial statements need to be considered. Furthermore, there is no current market price of the company's stock to look to for guidance. To determine the "true" value of this entity you will need to do the same type of analyses performed by investment bankers who assist in mergers and acquisitions. The framework in Exhibit 10-1 can guide you in evaluating the complete set of limitations impacting the financial statements. However, this is a decision that is among the most challenging of all and we might easily lose sight of the potential benefits of the analysis framework. Further studies and work experience will be necessary to fully understand how analysts go

---

[7] The state-of-the art for valuing a business entity is the "residual income model." Applying this theoretical model of firm value, which is mathematically derived from the discounted cash flow model, requires an in depth understanding of accounting information. More advanced accounting courses will illustrate how the residual income model is used to estimate the true value of the entity.

about adjusting the GAAP data to improve its relevance and to permit them to estimate a "true" value of the target entity to recommend to the acquiring investor.[8]

The second decision situation should be a bit more encouraging in illustrating the usefulness of the framework for analysis, even after one course in accounting. Based on our studies we can see that there may be good reason to lend the company an amount that exceeds the book value of their long-term assets. As noted in the limitations and in our discussion of tangible and intangible assets in Chapter 6, most productive long-term assets as measured and reported within GAAP are significantly undervalued.[9] If you can obtain sufficiently reliable information that the fair value of these productive assets significantly exceeds their recorded value, and other aspects of the company's business appear reasonably profitable, you might readily recommend the additional borrowing. For example, it is common practice for corporations to buy insurance policies covering the damage or loss of certain long-term assets like buildings, vehicles or machinery. Professional appraisers who work for insurance companies will usually provide the appraisals of the current replacement cost of such assets and suggest that the insurance coverage be for this amount, typically well above the book value of these assets.

There are many other ways that the framework can be used to improve business decisions. Consider the common example of compensation contracts for operating management (e.g., factory managers) which usually reward managers based on an accounting measure of operating income. Our framework and our understanding of how certain assets are accounted for within GAAP should allow us to see that certain limitations will result in overstating operating income. For example, based on the information in Chapter 6 we know that the current replacement value of depreciable assets is usually significantly greater than their reported amount. As a result of understating the economic value of the depreciable assets, GAAP depreciation expense will also be understated. Understating depreciation expense for a plant with relatively old assets will overstate operating income when compared to a new plant producing the same products with newer assets Hence, a bonus scheme based on accounting measures of operating income will usually offer unfair rewards to the managers of aging plants! This is another example of how simply understanding the framework can help us make better business decisions, and/or avoid making decisions based on flawed information. Again, future study of accounting will lead to the understanding needed to make economically relevant adjustments to GAAP data (such as operating income) to improve business decisions.

---

[8] In reality, most investment bankers who advise on mergers and acquisitions use several different approaches to estimating the "true" value of the target company and they normally will present a range of recommended offer prices to the acquiring firm's managers.

[9] Remember, the impairment tests required by GAAP should prevent the long-term assets from being overvalued. Hence, accounting conservatism for long-term assets normally leaves them undervalued.

RATIOS: TOOLS FOR ANALYSIS OF FINANCIAL STATEMENTS

Financial statement analysis is challenging under the best of circumstances. Even after we feel we have corrected or adjusted for all of the limitations of GAAP accounting reports, we are still left with the challenge of how to do comparative analysis. Throughout this text we have introduced ratios as an important tool for making comparisons within a company over time and between companies. So far we have introduced the following financial ratios (with the chapter identified in parentheses):

1. Accounting performance ratios
   a. Return on equity – ROE (Chapter 3)

2. Accounting measures of risk (financial leverage)
   a. Debt-to-equity ratio – D/E (Chapter 3)
   b. Debt-to-assets ratio – D/A (Chapter 3)

3. Accounting efficiency ratios
   a. Accounts receivable turnover ratio (Chapter 4)
   b. Inventory turnover ratio (Chapter 5)
   c. Total asset turnover ratio (Chapter 6)

4. Other ratios
   a. Current ratio (Chapter 1)
   b. Acid-test ratio (Chapter 4)
   c. Return on sales ratio – ROS (Chapter 2)
   d. Dividend payout ratio (Chapter 1)
   e. Earnings per share – EPS (Chapter 8)

Here we introduce three additional ratios which are among the most popular measures used in evaluating financial accounting information. The first of these three ratios is **return on assets (ROA)** which, along with ROE, provides a ratio describing firm performance. The second two ratios (discussed later in the chapter) are what we refer to as "market multiples." They combine accounting information with the market price of the firm or its shares of stock. These are known as the price-to-earnings ratio (P/E ratio) and the price-to-book ratio (P/B ratio).

Return on Assets

The return on assets ratio (ROA) is *the most important measure* of the relative performance of a company. ROA tells an analyst how much profit is being obtained from the investment that has been made in the assets of the business. Assets represent the investment in the company's resources, and these resources should have been acquired to earn profits. ROA is a measure of how much profit is earned relative to the investment. It is defined as:

$$\textbf{ROA} \quad = \quad \frac{\textbf{Operating income before interest expense after taxes [or Net Operating Profit After Tax (NOPAT)]}}{\textbf{Average total assets}}$$

Note that the numerator is an amount that nearly always *needs to be computed* rather than simply found in the income statement. NOPAT is a common term used in finance to describe the numerator for ROA, which is an operating income measure that excludes interest expense (and potentially other non-operating items) but is net of income tax expense. This numerator for ROA must be measured in a way that makes it comparable from one company to another and from one time period to another. Therefore, the numerator *should not be influenced by the way the assets of the business are financed*. So the numerator must be an amount that is (1) **before** interest expense is deducted; but (2) **after** income tax expense is deducted. Since *this amount is seldom provided for you in the income statement*, you will usually need to calculate the numerator. This step is challenging but necessary to permit ROA to be a meaningful ratio for comparison across companies with different amounts of debt.

To illustrate, assume two companies have the exact same amount of assets that generate the exact same amount of operating profit. However, one company's assets are financed almost entirely with debt and the other company's assets are financed almost entirely with equity. In this situation, although the operating profits are the same, the net income numbers will be different. This is because the company with nearly all debt financing will incur interest expense that will reduce its pretax income (as well as reducing its income tax expense) while the company with nearly all equity financing will have no interest expense and hence a higher pretax income (and higher income tax expense) than the all-debt company. If ROA were based on net income (instead of NOPAT), the performance of the all-equity firm would appear to be superior when, in fact, the two companies have earned the same operating profit on the same asset amounts.

To show this effect, consider the information on Debt Company and Equity Company in Exhibit 10-2.

Exhibit 10-2 Debt Company and Equity Company – Case 1

Balance Sheet Profiles:	Debt Company	Equity Company	
Average total assets (exactly the same)	$ 210,000	$ 210,000	
Average total debt (8% interest)	200,000	–	
Average total equity	10,000	210,000	

Income Statement Profiles:

			Difference
Revenues (exactly the same)	$ 300,000	$ 300,000	
Operating expenses (exactly the same)	250,000	250,000	
Operating profits (exactly the same)	$ 50,000	$ 50,000	
Interest expense	16,000	–	$ (16,000)
Pretax income	$ 34,000	$ 50,000	
Income tax expense (40%)	13,600	20,000	6,400
Net income	**$ 20,400**	**$ 30,000**	**$ (9,600)**

Debt Company has lower net income because of how the company is financed. To obtain a measure of operating income that would produce the same ROA ratio when the performance of the companies is actually the same, we must take the net income number and add back the *after-tax cost of interest expense*. In the income statement, we see that the before tax cost of interest expense is $16,000. But we also see that the interest expense allows Debt Company to pay $6,400 less in income taxes ($13,600 versus $20,000 for Equity Company). Therefore, the after-tax cost of interest expense is only $9,600 ($16,000 minus the tax advantage of $6,400). The ideal numerator for ROA, operating income before interest expense but after taxes (NOPAT), provides a measure of the profits achieved from the *use* of the company's assets that is *not* dependent on how the company decided to finance those assets. As a result, using NOPAT as the numerator improves the relevance of the ROA comparison among companies that have made different choices about how to finance their assets. In essence, this measure of ROA permits a meaningful comparison of how profitable a company has been with the assets entrusted to it, irrespective of how the assets were acquired.[10]

Since there are no unusual non-operating items, the numerator of the ROA measure for Equity Company is simply net income in this case ($30,000),. For Debt Company, the numerator is net income plus the after-tax cost of interest expense (the net impact of the interest cost on net income). The ROA ratio may be computed for each company as follows:

$$\text{Equity Company ROA} = \$30{,}000 \div \$210{,}000$$
$$= 14.3\%$$

$$\text{Debt Company ROA} = (\$20{,}400 + \$9{,}600) \div \$210{,}000$$
$$= 14.3\%$$

The ROA ratios are the same because both companies earned the same amount of operating profit from identical amounts of assets. The difference in the net income measures is strictly the result of the fact that the two companies employed different methods of financing. If we had used net income as the numerator instead of operating income before interest expense after taxes, the ROA ratios would have been 14.3% for Equity Company ($30,000 ÷ $210,000 = 14.3%) and 9.7% for Debt Company ($20,400 net income ÷ $210,000 = 9.7%). This would have made Equity Company look like it was using its assets more efficiently than Debt Company when, in fact, the difference has nothing to do with operating performance but is an artifact of how the company is financed.[11]

---

[10] Using a numerator like NOPAT also enhances the comparison of the ROA within a company over several time periods when the financing decision during these periods is changing.

[11] ROA is sometimes referred to as return on capital or return on investment capital. Also, there are numerous variations on ROA with many of them used for internal analysis of divisions, segments, plants or product lines within the company. For example, return on net operating assets (RONA) is like ROA except the total assets are reduced by the "free" liabilities (e.g., taxes payable, accounts payable, and other non-interest bearing liabilities). RONA is used extensively by GENERAL MOTORS for internal analysis purposes.

ROA, ROE and Financing the Business

In the example above, we see that both companies earned an ROA of 14.3%. However, the net income to shareholders is greater for Equity Company. At the same time, the amount of shareholders' equity is also much greater for Equity Company. In fact, the return on equity (ROE) is much lower for Equity Company than it is for Debt Company. Recall from Chapter 3 that ROE is defined as net income to common shareholders divided by average common shareholders' equity (defined as total shareholders' equity minus the book value of preferred stock). For the two companies illustrated above, we can compute ROE as follows:

$$\text{Equity Company ROA} = \$30,000 \div \$210,000$$
$$= 14.3\%$$

$$\text{Debt Company ROE} = \$20,400 \div \$10,000$$
$$= 204\%$$

The ROE ratio shows that, for the assumed facts in the case described above, the return to shareholders is much greater for Debt Company. Why is the return so much better? Understand that Debt Company elected to finance its assets with mostly debt capital and very little equity capital. As we learned in Chapter 3, this resulted in Debt Company having a relatively high debt-to-equity (D/E) ratio, suggesting a relatively high risk. Still, the superior results for Debt Company beg the question of why all companies do not finance their assets with relatively large proportion of debt capital? Let's review the example above and see if we can better understand why the Debt Company's results were so good.

Recall that companies with relatively high Debt-to-Equity (D/E) ratios are considered to be relatively riskier than low D/E ratio companies. Now, we note that in the example above, both companies had an ROA of 14.3%, which is a relatively high ROA ratio signaling strong financial performance. What we can now prove mathematically is that, *as long as ROA is higher than the after-tax cost of borrowing, companies with more debt financing will have higher ROEs than companies with less debt financing.* The interest rate for Debt Company was 8%. Since interest expense is tax deductible, the after-tax cost of debt is less than 8%. To be exact, the after-tax cost of borrowing is the interest rate times one (1) minus the tax rate. Assuming a 40% tax rate, the after tax cost of interest for the debt of Debt Company is 8% times 60% [.08 x .6 = .048 = 4.8%], or 4.8%.

In the case illustrated here, since both companies are earning the exact same ROA of 14.3% by using the exact same set of assets with equal efficiency, and since 14.3% is well above the 4.8% after tax cost of borrowing, the company with the most debt (i.e., DEBT Company) will earn the highest ROE for its shareholders. However, if future ROA measures fall below 4.8%, then the company with the least amount of debt will earn the highest ROE for its shareholders. By considering a situation where the ROA ratio falls below the after-tax cost of debt we can see the additional risk of companies who finance a high percentage of their assets with debt.

To illustrate this, let's consider Case 2, a situation where both the ROA of Debt Company and Equity Company are the same. However, while revenues remained at $300,000, costs increased from $250,000 to $293,000 resulting in an ROA of only 2% for both companies, which is less than the after tax cost of debt (4.8%). Consider

Exhibit 10-3   Debt Company and Equity Company – Case 2

Balance Sheet Profiles	Debt Company	Equity Company	
Average total assets (exactly the same)	$ 210,000	$ 210,000	
Average total debt (8% interest)	200,000	–	
Average total equity	10,000	210,000	

Income Statement Profiles:

	Debt Company	Equity Company	Difference
Revenues (exactly the same)	$ 300,000	$ 300,000	
Operating expenses (exactly the same)	293,000	293,000	
Operating profits (exactly the same)	$ 7,000	$ 7,000	
Interest expense	16,000	–	$ (16,000)
Pretax income	$ (9,000)	$ 7,000	
Income tax expense (Credit) (40%)	(3,600)	2,800	6,400
Net income	**$ (5,400)**	**$ 4,200**	**$ (9,600)**

the information in Exhibit 10-3. We can see from this second example that the interest expense Debt Company is required to cover each year may exceed the amount of profit before interest expense, resulting in a net loss for the period even though the ROA is still a positive 2%.

As we saw in Case 1, the shareholders of Debt Company enjoyed a very high ROE when ROA was above the after-tax cost of debt. However, as Case 2 shows, the shareholders of Debt Company can also experience large negative returns (–54%) when the ROA falls below the after-tax cost of debt. This effect that debt capital has on ROE (positive or negative) is known as **financial leverage**.

The ROA and ROE calculations for these companies are:

	Debt Company	Equity Company
ROA:	$(5,400) + ($16,000 x .60) ÷ $210,000 = $4,200 ÷ $210,000 = 2.0%	$4,200 ÷ $210,000 = 2.0%
ROE:	$(5,400) ÷ $10,000 = – 54%	$4,200 ÷ $210,000 = 2.0%

Risk and Return to Shareholders

Another important issue in deciding how to finance the assets of the business is the fact that the more debt you use, the higher the risk to both the shareholders and the lenders, and, therefore, the higher the interest rate on the debt the market will require. We expect that the interest rate required by a lender will increase as the amount of debt increases. In the examples above, Debt Company had an assumed interest rate of 8%. If Equity Company decided to borrow $20,000 and use the money to buy back and retire its own stock, we would expect the interest rate for the first $20,000 to be less than the 8% charged to Debt Company.

The three key ratios to consider for any company, then, are ROA, ROE, and D/E. The ROA ratio is the most important of the three. Once ROA has been computed in a meaningful way (by removing the after-tax interest costs), we can predict what we should find for ROE, given the way the assets have been financed, as measured by the D/E ratio. The general relationship that we see between these three ratios helps us understand the risk-return tradeoff from an accounting viewpoint. This is summarized in Exhibit 10-4.

The decision of how to finance the assets of the company is an important one that will have an impact on the return to shareholders (ROE). The managers of the entity must understand the risk (D/E) versus return (ROE) tradeoff, for its shareholders. However, understanding the risk-return tradeoff cannot and will not lead management to the "optimal" amount of debt (i.e., risk) to employ. When it comes to risk there is no right or wrong, Risk is simply a matter of "taste" or preference. Some investors or managers might seek more risk than others, and some investments or financing schemes offer more risk than others. As we can see from the examples above, the Debt Company owners took more risk than the Equity Company owners, and since ROA in the first case was 14.3% the risk paid off with high ROE for the owners. This did not make the decisions of Equity Company wrong. Their low risk strategy paid off in Case 2 above, where ROA fell below the after-tax cost of borrowing and Debt Company shareholders were the biggest losers. The lesson is that we must understand the risk-return tradeoff, but we cannot judge what is the correct amount of risk in an given situation.

Based on the examples above, we can appreciate that it is also not possible to determine whether a given ROE is good or poor, without also knowing the amount of

Exhibit 10-4   Relationships between ROA, ROE, and D/E Ratios

| Situation →

Action ↓	When ROA is less than the weighted average after-tax interest rate from all interest-bearing obligations:	When ROA is greater than the weighted average after-tax interest rate from all interest-bearing obligations is:
Increasing the D/E ratio will	• Reduce ROE • Increase Risk	• Increase ROE • Increase Risk
Decreasing the D/E ratio will	• Increase ROE • Reduce Risk	• Decrease ROE • Reduce Risk

Note: D/E is the ratio of all interest-bearing debt to common shareholders' equity.

risk that was taken by the company (D/E). However, this is not the case with ROA, and, as a result, ROA is a superior measure of performance for comparison purposes, all else being equal.

Components of ROA and Strategic Analysis

ROA is also an interesting ratio to consider from a strategic point of view. We often see the ROA ratio broken into two parts: one measuring profitability and the other measuring efficiency. The profitability component is a variation on the return on sales ratio from Chapter 2, and the efficiency component is simply the total asset turnover ratio introduced in Chapter 6. The two parts are:

Profitability	x	**Efficiency**	=	**Return on Assets**
$\dfrac{\text{Operating income before interest after taxes (NOPAT)}}{\text{Total revenues}}$	x	$\dfrac{\text{Total revenues}}{\text{Average total assets}}$	=	$\dfrac{\text{NOPAT}}{\text{Average total assets}}$

The breakdown of ROA into these two components shows that a business can improve the efficiency with which it uses its assets in two ways. One way is to increase the amount of profit in each dollar of sales (profitability); and this can be achieved by cutting costs without reducing sales, by increasing the selling price without losing units of sales, or decreasing the selling price with a compensating increase in sales volume. The second approach to improving ROA is to increase the efficiency of the business. Efficiency improvements can be achieved by reducing the amount of assets needed to generate the same amount of sales revenues (e.g., renting out excess floor space to another company or improving inventory systems to reduce the amount of inventory required). Efficiency can also be improved by finding ways to increase the amount of sales revenues without an increase in the amount of assets (e.g., keeping the business open longer or adding a second shift to the plant). We can appreciate how important it might be for a business to have the correct amount of productive capacity for the given level of sales. If we build a plant that can produce 8 million units of product a year but we can sell only 5 million units a year, we have excess capacity that will show up as a total asset turnover ratio (sales divided by average total assets) that is relatively low. This will also, through higher depreciation charges, result in a negative impact on profitability.

Understanding the impact of business decisions on both profitability and efficiency will help us to evaluate the performance of the business as measured by the ROA ratio. ROA is perhaps the most relevant overall performance measure for conducting financial statement analysis.

Market Multiples: Price-to-Earnings and Price-to-Book Ratios

Two popular ratios that combine both accounting information and the market price of a company's shares are the **price-to-earnings ratio (P/E ratio)** and the **price-to-book ratio (P/B ratio).** These two ratios may be computed using per-share measures in both numerator and denominator, or financial statement totals in both the numerator and denominator. The P/E ratios are most often based on per-share measures of earnings and stock price. The earnings per share measure (EPS) discussed in Chapter 8 is usually the denominator of the price-to-earnings (P/E) **ratio**. This ratio looks at the current market price of the company's stock as a multiple of its current EPS. The ratio is computed by taking the stock price and dividing it by the EPS number.[12] The P/E ratio is so common that it is a part of the daily stock information provided by the stock market listings found in the popular business press.

Price-to-Earnings Ratio   Although the P/E ratio is quite popular, the meaning of its numerical amount is unclear. Many analysts feel that a relatively high P/E ratio means that the market is bidding the stock price up to a high multiple of current earnings *on the belief* that future earnings will be higher (thereby reducing the ratio in future periods). In other words, some feel a high P/E is assigned to stocks that have good prospects for high growth in future earnings. However, there is no substantive evidence to support this belief. There are at least two fundamental problems with using the P/E to make any meaningful judgments about the attractiveness of a particular stock. First, it is not at all clear that the income number used to compute EPS is a relevant measure. As we discussed in Chapter 9, net income can include items that are not relevant to either the real current economic performance of the entity or its future performance. Second, (any) current earnings measures used to compute EPS may have been influenced by economic factors that are not expected to be representative of future earnings. Research on P/E ratios across companies has shown that the variation in P/E ratios has more to do with how net income is measured and what it does or does not include than on the future growth opportunities of the company. We do not recommend using the P/E ratio for making investment decisions.

Price-to-Book Ratio   The price-to-book (P/B) ratio plays an important and economically significant role in helping analysts understand the value of the business. The denominator, is total common shareholders' equity, typically called **book value**. This is a measure of the *net assets* of the business. Technically, the **book value of the business** is the total shareholders' equity less any amounts related to *non-voting* stocks, such as preferred stock or possibly non-voting common stock. The concept of book value is to measure the net assets that belong to the voting ownership interests. The numerator, "price," is the total market value of the company (e.g., "market capitalization") and is measured as the current stock price times the number of shares of common (voting) stock outstanding. This ratio, commonly called the **price-to-book (P/B) ratio**, tells shareholders the relation between the market price of their stock and its accounting value as determined by GAAP. Book value (B) is often reported on a per-share basis, so that it may be easily compared to the current market price (P) for any publicly-traded stocks.

Notice that the P/B ratio is essentially a ratio of the two measures central to our analysis framework illustrated in Exhibit 10-1. Based on our framework, we can understand that a company with a P/B ratio close to 1.0 will probably have relatively few measurement issues indicating undervalued or missing net assets. Alternatively,

---

[12] For companies with complex capital structures, most sources will compute this ratio using fully-diluted EPS, and you can assume this is used unless it is otherwise noted.

companies with relatively high P/B multiples are likely to have numerous measurement issues indicating either undervalued net assets, missing net assets, or both. The P/B ratio is an important measure of the differences between GAAP-based accounting measures of the net value of the company and the capital market's estimate of the fair value of the company. Understanding this ratio as an investment and decision-making tool requires an understanding of the nature of GAAP and its limitations in measuring fair value—something we have tried to communicate throughout this text.

A Word of Caution about Ratios

Financial ratios are excellent tools to help us see through the effects of size in making comparisons and in evaluating dimensions of performance, efficiency, risk and other important attributes about the entity. Attempting to compare the financial results of two or more companies without the aid of financial ratios is ill advised, and may easily lead to faulty analysis. We have provided a relatively extensive and commonly used set of ratios to aid you in performing financial statement analysis. However, you must always keep in mind that the ratios can only be as useful as the underlying data used in computing the ratios. If the information inputs have weaknesses or limitations, putting them into ratios will not improve them.[13] The relevance and usefulness of the ratios are completely dependent on the relevance and usefulness of the underlying data.

SUMMARY

In this last chapter we have added the tools for financial statement analysis to your understanding of the fundamentals of accounting and financial reporting. The first three chapters of the text provided you with an understanding of how the economic activities of the business entity are measured and recorded and then reported in a set of three or more financial statements. The next six chapters provided you with a somewhat more detailed understanding of the most common components of financial statements for publicly-traded entities. We illustrated and evaluated the information that is typically provided to external decision makers in both GAAP- and IFRS-based financial statements, pointing out the salient features of these assets and liabilities as they might impact their usefulness for business decision. In this final chapter, we offer a framework designed to help external users evaluate the strengths and weaknesses of the reported financial accounting information. Early applications of the framework should prove useful by focusing our understanding on the identification of the weaknesses inherent in GAAP data. Once the weaknesses are identified we can begin to learn how expert users attempt to compensate for these weaknesses in order to improve business decision making.

As your understanding of accounting and financial reporting continues to develop, you should not let your failures or lack of in-depth understanding dampen your enthusiasm for learning. Understand that using accounting information to make decisions will never become simple. If using accounting were easy, we would not continue to observe things like the failure of businesses or entire economies (e.g.,

---

[13] This caution is often expressed as "garbage-in, garbage-out" (GIGO).

Greece), failures of huge numbers of mortgage loans issued by "sophisticated" money center banks who then need to be propped up with government funds, experienced pension fund managers getting fired for poor performance of their portfolios, CEOs getting replaced due to underperformance, and many other easily observable events that suggest decision-making failures.

Finally, this last chapter provided a recap of the financial ratios introduced earlier in the text, and added three more ratios as tools to be used in evaluating the financial statements. The return on assets (ROA) ratio introduced here is probably the single most useful ratio to compare and evaluate the performance of the entity, its segments, and its competitors. The two ratios that combine accounting data with market data, P/E and P/B, were also introduced in this chapter. While ratios are extremely helpful for the analysis and comparison of financial accounting data, two cautions are noted. First, the ratios are only as good as the data inputs. And second, due to the wide variety of definitions employed in practice for many of the ratios defined and considered here, you should always make sure you understand how the ratios from any specific source are defined before attempting to use them for analysis purposes.

KEY TERMS

book value   The value of a financial statement item in the accounting records. See *book value of the business*. *171, 181*

book value of the firm/business   Common shareholders' equity (total shareholders' equity minus any preferred stock accounts). In a company with only common stock, book value is simply net assets (total assets minus total liabilities). *171, 181*

financial leverage   The effect that debt capital has on ROE (positive or negative). *178*

market capitalization   See *market value of the firm*. *169*

market value of the firm   The total capitalized value of the business, measured as the current stock price multiplied times the number of common (voting) shares of stock outstanding. *169*

price-to-earnings ratio (P/E ratio)   Stock price (generally on a per share basis) divided by current earnings (generally on a per share basis. Measures the relationship between the year-end stock price and EPS for the year. Sometimes measured as the relationship between the average stock price for the year and EPS for the year. *180-181*

price-to-book ratio (P/B ratio)   Market capitalization divided by the book value of the business. *180-182*

return on assets (ROA)   Operating income before interest expense after taxes (NOPAT) divided by average total assets. The most important measure of the relative performance of a company telling an analyst how much profit is being obtained from the investment that has been made in the assets of the business. *174-175*

PROBLEMS

10-1   Evaluating Financial Statements: A Framework for Analysis

1. Describe the three characteristics of GAAP-based financial statements that should be viewed as key limitations when analyzing a company's financial statements. Provide examples of each from what you have learned this semester in financial accounting.
2. Differentiate book value of the firm from market value of the firm.
3. Explain the Framework for Evaluating Limitations of GAAP as given in Exhibit 10-1. How is this framework helpful for decision making?
4. Describe the ROA ratio. What information does it provide users?
5. Describe the D/E ratio. What information does it provide users?
6. How does the concept of financial leverage relate to a firm's capital structure?
7. Describe the ROE ratio. What information does it provide users? How can the amount of debt a firm carries relative to the owners' interests impact ROE?
8. Describe the two market multiple ratios given in the chapter. What information does each provide and how might you use that information in decision making?

10-2   Business Decision Case

Throughout the text we have provided some decision-making focus in each chapter. Most important business decisions are based in part or in total on the analysis of accounting related information. When non-accounting information is employed, it is often as an attempt to compensate or mitigate the weaknesses or limitations of the accounting information. Here we ask you to consider a set of routine but important business decisions, and to identify possible concerns you might have about the decision if GAAP-based accounting data are "blindly" employed as a basis for making that decision.

For each of the decisions and related information given below, provide one or more issues regarding the _limitations of the accounting data_ identified with the decision. Note that, while there may be other issues about the decision not related to accounting information, we ask you to simply focus on the accounting limitations of which you are aware.

1. A decision to specify interest rates on loans your large, money center bank is about to make to a group of 20 publicly-traded companies is to be based primarily on their existing debt-to-equity (D/E) ratio measured as total liabilities over total shareholders' equity as reported in their most recent audited financial statements. The companies with the highest D/E ratio will be charged the highest interest rate.

2. You are working for a private pension trust portfolio manager to identify securities to be included in the trust's portfolio. The manager is a strong believer in P/E ratios, and has quizzed you on your understanding of how EPS is calculated before hiring you to help her. She wants to focus on long-term

growth in the portfolio, and believes that companies with the highest P/E ratios will provide the greatest opportunities for future growth. She thinks that the past trend in P/E of a firm is not important and that only the current P/E is relevant. She asks you to comment on the investment strategy of adding only investments with very high P/E ratios to the portfolio.

3. You are working as an intern for the CFO of a holding company which owns the controlling (i.e., between a 55% and a 75% ownership) interest in a dozen separate businesses. Each of the business units reports to the holding company with GAAP financial statements since they have other shareholders too. Each year the CFO receives requests from these twelve companies for additional capital resources which stem from the earnings and any additional borrowing by the holding company. The CFO explains to you that he has historically made these resource allocation decisions based on the return on assets (ROA) of each unit as measured using the audited financial statements. Businesses with the highest ROA have received the greatest amount of additional resources in each of the three years the CFO has been in the job. He asks you for your thoughts on this decision making process.

10-3   The Impact of Leverage on ROE

Assume the following facts about a hypothetical company:

- Total assets = $8,000,000
- Income tax rate is 40%
- Operating income before interest expense and income taxes = $800,000

The objective of this assignment is that you understand the impact of leverage on the shareholders of an entity. To illustrate this effect, you are to consider the following alternative financing schemes for the company described above:

      A. Shareholders' Equity = $2 million
           Interest-bearing debt = $6 million at 8% interest

      B. Shareholders' Equity = $4 million
           Interest-bearing debt = $4 million at 8% interest

      C. Shareholders' Equity = $6 million
           Interest-bearing debt = $2 million at 8% interest

Required:
1. Compute ROE for each of the three cases above, assuming that the only items in the income statement not included in the $800,000 operating income figure are interest and income taxes.
2. Repeat your analyses of ROE above, but this time assume that the interest rate has increased to 12%.
3. Determine ROA for the example described.
4. What is the after tax cost of borrowing in requirement 1 above?
5. What happens when ROA is above/below the after tax cost of borrowing? Why?

10-4   The Impact of Leverage on ROE

Assume the following facts about a hypothetical company:

- Total assets = $12,000,000
- Income tax rate is 40%
- Operating income before interest expense and income taxes = $1,100,000

The objective of this assignment is that you understand the impact of leverage on the shareholders of an entity. To illustrate this effect, you are to consider the following alternative financing schemes for the company described above:

A. Shareholders' Equity = $3 million
Interest-bearing debt = $9 million at 10% interest

B. Shareholders' Equity = $6 million
Interest-bearing debt = $6 million at 10% interest

C. Shareholders' Equity = $9 million
Interest-bearing debt = $3 million at 10% interest

Required:

1. For each alternative financing scheme, compute net operating income. Follow the format used in the chapter's Exhibits 10-2 and 10-3 (operating income before interest expense and income taxes is the same thing as operating profits).
2. Compute ROE for each of the three cases above, assuming that the only items in the income statement not included in the $1,100,000 operating income figure are interest and income taxes.
3. Repeat the first two requirements, but this time assume that the interest rate has decreased to 7%.
4. What is the after tax cost of borrowing in requirement 1 above?
5. Determine ROA for the example described; calculate ROA under each alternative financing scheme.
6. Contrast the use of ROA and ROE for each scenario—when the cost of borrowing is 10% and when it is 7%. Why does this occur?
7. What happens when ROA is above/below the after tax cost of borrowing? Explain why?

10-5   Comparing Financing Methods (Comprehensive)

The board of directors is considering three alternatives to improve the return on shareholders' equity (ROE), defined in Chapter 3 as net income divided by average shareholders' equity. The current balance sheet and income statement profile data for the company is as follows:

Balance Sheet Data for 2014   (in thousands)

Total assets	$358,000
Total interest-bearing liabilities	$200,000
Total other liabilities	$ 98,000
Shareholders' equity	$ 60,000

Income Statement Data for 2014

Revenues	$400,000
Operating expenses	380,320
Income before interest and taxes	$ 19,680
Interest expense	12,000
Profit before taxes	$ 7,680
Income taxes (35%)	2,688
Net income	$ 4,992

ROE is currently 8.3% [$4,992 ÷ $60,000 = .0832]. The average cost of interest-bearing liabilities is currently 6% [$12,000 of interest expense ÷ $200,000 of interest-bearing debt = .06]. The directors are considering the following alternatives to improve ROE:

Alternative 1	Alternative 2	Alternative 3
Borrow $50 million at 7% interest and invest it in new assets expected to earn income before interest and taxes of $3 million per year	Issue $50 million in stock and buy new assets expected to earn income before interest and taxes of $3 million per year	Borrow $20 million at 7% and use it to purchase treasury stock. This alternative will not impact net income before interest and taxes.
Impact: Assets and liabilities both increase by $50 million; income before interest and taxes increases to $22.68 million; interest expense increases by $3.5 million.	*Impact:* Assets and shareholders' equity increase by $50 million; income before interest and taxes increases to $22.68 million	*Impact:* Liabilities increase and shareholders' equity decreases by $20 million; interest expense increases by $1.4 million

Required:

Determine the impact each option would have had on 2014 ROE by recalculating ROE with each alternative. Assume that the impact noted in the above is the only change in the financial statements, and that the action would have been taken on January 1, 2014. Also assume that all earnings are paid out in dividends so that shareholders' equity is impacted only by the stock transactions.

10-6   Alternate Financing Decisions

The City Art Company (a family-owned business) makes themed art out of plastic figures, which are sold to various cities around the world. Chicago, for example, has purchased a number of plaster cows that are about three feet high by three feet long, each with different spots and a different facial expression and stance. Boyne City, Michigan, purchased a dozen plaster fish, each colored depending on the type of fish (bass, trout, etc.), mounted on a pole stand to appear as though they were swimming or jumping out of water, etc.

Business has been booming and the company is thinking of expanding to meet the increased demand. The following is a profile of its recent comparative balance sheets:

As of September 30,	2014	2013
Assets		
Current assets	$ 85,000	$ 78,000
Long term productive assets (net)	295,000	235,000
Other assets	15,000	18,000
Total assets	*$395,000*	*$331,000*
Liabilities and Owners Equity		
Non-interest-bearing liabilities	$ 66,000	$ 71,000
Interest-bearing liabilities	260,000	196,000
Total liabilities	$326,000	$267,000
Owners' equity	$ 69,000	$ 64,000
Total liabilities and owners' equity	*$395,000*	*$331,000*

The income statement for the year ending September 30, 2014, reported the following information:

Operating income before interest expense and taxes	$ 36,000
Interest expense	16,000
Income before income taxes	$ 20,000
Income taxes (40%)	8,000
Net income	$ 12,000

It is expected that with an investment of $125,000 the company could increase operating income *before interest and taxes* by between 15% and 30%. The family currently own 100% of the company and they prefer not to share their ownership of the business with outsiders. They are currently paying an average of 7% interest on their debt and the bank has indicated they would lend the $125,000 to them at 8% interest per year with certain covenants concerning profits to protect them.

The family has asked for your advice on how they should finance the growth of their business. The four options they would like your advice on are:

1. Sell a $125,000 stake to a venture capital company in exchange for a 50% voting stock interest in the company.

2. Contribute more of the family money to finance the entire $125,000 expansion.

3. Borrow another $125,000 from the bank at 8% interest.

4. Finance the expansion with rented assets by signing a long term lease agreement calling for annual rent payments of $9,000 per year for the next 30 years, after which time the assets would revert to the Lessor.

Required:

Your assignment is to prepare a comparison of these alternatives. You should assume that income taxes will continue to be 40% per year, and that the best borrowing rate is 8% per year. Your analysis should begin with the current ROA, ROE, and D/E ratios (let D = interest bearing debt only) of the company as of the end of fiscal 2014. Then present separate forecasted 2015 balance sheet and income statement information for each of the alternatives, based on the information provided (do not make other assumptions). Separate forecasts should be made for the 15% and 30% increases in "Operating Income before interest and taxes." (Hint: *be sure to deduct the rent expense from alternative 4 from the forecasted operating income before interest and taxes number.*) Finally, once you have prepared the high and low forecasted balance sheet and income statement data, you should compute the forecasted ROA, ROE, and D/E ratios that would be associated with each alternative. To prepare your forecasts you should make the following important additional assumptions.

    a. The amount of total assets for alternatives 1-3 will increase by $125,000 at **October 1, 2014,** and will be offset by an increase of $125,000 to interest-bearing debt (alternative 3) or owners' equity (alternatives 1-2) on that date.

    b. Assume there are **no changes** in the amount of total assets or interest-bearing liabilities from October 1, 2014 to September 30, 2015 once the changes from assumption a. above have been made on October 1, 2014.

    c. Assume no dividends are paid out of 2014 income.

    d. Add the amount of the *forecasted Net Income for 2015* to Owners' Equity as of September 30, 2015. (In order to make the balance sheets balance with these assumptions, you should deduct the *forecasted Net Income for 2015* from non-interest-bearing liabilities.)

10-7   Ratios: SIEMENS AG

Locate the PDF file containing the SIEMENS 2014 annual report. (Note that the file begins with page 252.) Notice this annual report is prepared under IFRS rather than GAAP.

1. Take a few minutes to review and briefly describe something unique that you learned from SIEMENS' 2014 annual report.
2. Compute the return-on-assets (ROA) and the two separate components (margin and turnover) of ROA for SIEMENS for the year 2014. To measure the ROA you will need to consider the *Consolidated Statements of Income* on page 254 of its 2014 annual report and also note 8 on pages 279-280 of the report. Use the German statutory income tax rate of 39% when considering the interest expense. The denominator is average total assets, as always.
3. Compute the debt-to-equity ratio (D/E) for SIEMENS as of the end of fiscal 2014. Consider the *Consolidated Statements of Financial Position* on page 256 and use only interest bearing debt in the numerator. (Hint: pension plans are interest bearing debt.)
4. Compute the return on equity (ROE) ratio for 2014.

10-8   MICROSOFT Financial Ratios

Locate the PDF file with the 2014 annual report for MICROSOFT and answer the following:

1. What percentage of MICROSOFT's total assets were current assets at the end of fiscal 2014?
2. Assume "equity and other investments" in MICROSOFT's balance sheet at the end of 2014 is made up of stocks, bonds, and notes of other companies. What percentage of total assets at the end of fiscal 2014 was invested in cash, short and long term investments?
3. Compute the two separate components of the return-on-assets ratio (ROA) for MICROSOFT for fiscal 2014 and the ROA. If you need to use a tax rate, use 25% which is the approximate rate in the 2014 income statement.
4. Compute the debt-to-equity (D/E) ratio for MICROSOFT at the end of fiscal 2014. Use only long-term interest bearing debt in the numerator.
5. Compute return on equity (ROE) for MICROSOFT for fiscal 2014.
6. The stock price for MICROSOFT was $33.55 per share at the close on June 28, 2014. Compute the price-to-earnings (P/E) ratio for MICROSOFT at the end of fiscal 2014.
7. Compute the following additional ratios for MICROSOFT's year ended June 30, 2014:
    a. Quick ratio
    b. Current ratio
    c. Accounts receivable turnover ratio
    d. Inventory turnover ratio
    e. Price-to-book (P/B) ratio

10-9   AMGEN Corporation Financial Ratios

Locate the PDF file with the 2014 AMGEN annual report. AMGEN is a major biotech company that was one of the first of this new generation of biotechnology firms to become independent of the large old line drug companies. AMGEN was selling at $112.88 per share at December 31, 2014.

Required:

1. Take a few minutes to review and briefly describe something unique that you learned from AMGEN's 2014 annual report.
2. Compute the following ratios for AMGEN for 2014:

    a. Total asset turnover   g. Quick ratio
    b. Return on assets (ROA)   h. Current ratio
    c. Debt-to-equity (D/E)   i. Accounts receivable turnover ratio
    d. Return on equity (ROE)   j. Price-to-earnings ratio (P/E)
    e. Price-to-book (P/B)   k. Return on sales ratio
    f. Inventory turnover

10-10 Comparison of MICROSOFT and AMGEN Financial Statements

Locate the 2014 PDF files for AMGEN and MICROSOFT. Consider only their formal financial statements in answering the following questions which are designed to compare these two technology-based companies at the end of fiscal 2014. If you have already worked 10-8 and/or 10-9, you can use those calculations.

Required:

1. Compute the following ratios:
   a. ROA for each company for fiscal 2014. Use a 25% tax rate for MICROSOFT and a 13% tax rate for AMGEN if necessary to compute ROA.
   b. Return on equity (ROE) for each company at the end of fiscal 2014.
   c. Percentage of total revenues spent on R&D for each company.
   d. Price-to-earnings (P/E) multiple for each company. At fiscal year-end, Microsoft's common stock was selling for $33.55 per share and Amgen's common stock was selling for $112.88 per share.
   e. Price-to-book (P/B) ratio for each company.
2. What ratio do you feel is the best single ratio to compare the performance of the two companies? Why?
3. What ratio is the least appropriate to compare? Why?
4. What questions, if any, do the comparative data suggest? Describe and explain at least two.

Notes

Index

Note: The first number for each reference is a *1* or *2* designating the volume number, with the page number reference following the volume number. So, for example, for the entry "entity concept *1.9*," the reference is to volume 1 page 9.

Corporation Index

Note: The first number for each reference is a *1* or *2* designating the volume number, with the page number reference following the volume number. So, for example, the entry, "ALCOA, INC. *2.37*" the reference is to volume 2 page 37.

Notes